HIPPOCRENE BEGINNER'S SERIES

BEGINNER'S CHINESE

WITH *AUDIO CDs*

Yong Ho

Hippocrene Books
New York

Acknowledgements

The *pinyin* portion of this book was prepared using Pintone Plu 6, an easy-to-use software program developed by Professor Teng Shou Hsin of National Taiwan Normal University. I would like to thank him for his unfailing support and assistance with my use of the program. It is true, as one of my colleagues commented, that we as teachers of Chinese all depend on his utility to survive.

I owe a special debt to Mr. Jorge A. Estrella, whose readiness to help and masterly troubleshooting computer skills have made easier my PC life in general and the preparation of this manuscript in particular. Whenever I run into problems, I can always count on him for help.

Thanks are also due to my daughter Adele, who helped type portions of the manuscript and set the *pinyin* marks. Just as I benefited from her valuable service, she found it an educational and rewarding experience.

Text copyright © 1997 by Yong Ho
Audio copyright © 2005 by Yong Ho
Cover photograph © Jiaxuan Zhang

1st paperback-with-audio edition, 2005.
3rd printing, 2006.

ISBN 0-7818-1095-7
ISBN of previous edition: 0-7818-0299-7

Jacket design by K & P Publishing Services

For information, address:
HIPPOCRENE BOOKS, INC.
171 Madison Avenue
New York, NY 10016
www.hippocrenebooks.com

Cataloging-in-Publication data available from the Library of Congress

Printed in the United States of America

Contents

Possible Sound Combinations in Mandarin Chinese

(c)	a	ai	ao	an	ang	o	ong	ou	e	ei	en	eng	er	i	ia	iao	ie	iu	ian	iang	in	ing	iong	u	ua	uo	ui	uai	uan	un	uang	ueng	ü	üe	üan	ün
b	ba	bai	bao	ban	bang	bo				bei	ben	beng		bi		biao	bie		bian		bin	bing		bu												
p	pa	pai	pao	pan	pang	po		pou		pei	pen	peng		pi		piao	pie		pian		pin	ping		pu												
m	ma	mai	mao	man	mang	mo		mou		mei	men	meng		mi		miao	mie	miu	mian		min	ming		mu												
f	fa			fan	fang	fo		fou		fei	fen	feng												fu												
d	da	dai	dao	dan	dang		dong	dou	de	dei		deng		di		diao	die	diu	dian			ding		du		duo	dui		duan	dun						
t	ta	tai	tao	tan	tang		tong	tou	te			teng		ti		tiao	tie		tian			ting		tu		tuo	tui		tuan	tun						
n	na	nai	nao	nan	nang		nong	nou	ne	nei	nen	neng		ni		niao	nie	niu	nian	niang	nin	ning		nu		nuo			nuan				nü	nüe		
l	la	lai	lao	lan	lang	lo	long	lou	le	lei		leng		li	lia	liao	lie	liu	lian	liang	lin	ling		lu		luo			luan	lun			lü	lüe		
z	za	zai	zao	zan	zang		zong	zou	ze	zei	zen	zeng		zi										zu		zuo	zui		zuan	zun						
c	ca	cai	cao	can	cang		cong	cou	ce		cen	ceng		ci										cu		cuo	cui		cuan	cun						
s	sa	sai	sao	san	sang		song	sou	se		sen	seng		si										su		suo	sui		suan	sun						
zh	zha	zhai	zhao	zhan	zhang		zhong	zhou	zhe	zhei	zhen	zheng		zhi										zhu	zhua	zhuo	zhui	zhuai	zhuan	zhun	zhuang					
ch	cha	chai	chao	chan	chang		chong	chou	che		chen	cheng		chi										chu	chua	chuo	chui	chuai	chuan	chun	chuang					
sh	sha	shai	shao	shan	shang			shou	she	shei	shen	sheng		shi										shu	shua	shuo	shui	shuai	shuan	shun	shuang					
r			rao	ran	rang		rong	rou	re		ren	reng		ri										ru	rua	ruo	rui		ruan	run						
j														ji	jia	jiao	jie	jiu	jian	jiang	jin	jing	jiong										ju	jue	juan	jun
q														qi	qia	qiao	qie	qiu	qian	qiang	qin	qing	qiong										qu	que	quan	qun
x														xi	xia	xiao	xie	xiu	xian	xiang	xin	xing	xiong										xu	xue	xuan	xun
g	ga	gai	gao	gan	gang		gong	gou	ge	gei	gen	geng												gu	gua	guo	gui	guai	guan	gun	guang					
k	ka	kai	kao	kan	kang		kong	kou	ke	kei	ken	keng												ku	kua	kuo	kui	kuai	kuan	kun	kuang					
h	ha	hai	hao	han	hang		hong	hou	he	hei	hen	heng												hu	hua	huo	hui	huai	huan	hun	huang					

If the 19th century belonged to Britain, and the 20th century to the United States, then the 21st century will surely belong to China. My advice: Make sure your kids learn Chinese.

- Jim Rogers, *Worth Magazine*

Introduction

Congratulations on the two right choices you have made. You decided to study Chinese and you picked the right book.

The decision to study Chinese is a good one because it is a language of twenty-first century as Jim Rogers observed above. Believe it or not, there are more people in the world speaking Chinese than English or any other language. Chinese is one of the six official languages for the United Nations. Above all, the ability to speak and write Chinese goes a long way to the understanding of 5,000 years of Chinese civilization, the exchanging of ideas with its people, and the conducting of business in or with China.

The selection of this book for your study of Chinese is a good one because it is unique and it fills a void. This book has been written for the adult learner who has no background in Chinese, and for travelers who want to take a quick course on Chinese. The majority of courses offered to these students in the United States (variously called elementary, beginning or level 1 Chinese) consists of ten to twelve sessions, yet most textbooks used for such courses contain thirty to forty lessons. It would take at least three or four levels or semesters to finish such a book. Obviously by the time the students reach the end of the book, they are no longer beginners. For beginning students of Chinese, such textbooks are unwieldy and intimidating. *Beginner's Chinese* consists of ten lessons. Each lesson is comprised of the following components: basic sentence patterns, a series of conversations that illustrate the communicative use of these patterns, words and expressions, supplementary words and expressions, language points, exercises, and cultural insights about the topic of the lesson. The book has been written in such a way that it is teachable and learnable during one academic semester for adult students. By the time students finish this book, they will have learned about ninety basic sentence patterns, three hundred characters, basic grammar, and basic communicative skills.

This book is based on the premise that less is more. When presented with only the basic and most crucial words and patterns, students will be able to start talking and communicating immediately without being concerned about the intricacies of grammar and vocabulary. For this reason, *Beginner's Chinese* is truly a beginner's guide.

Chinese Language: Its Prominent Features

Students come to my Chinese classes for different reasons. Some are looking for a tool to gain an in-depth understanding of Chinese culture and society. Others, primarily those of Chinese descent, try to connect with their roots and cultural heritage. Still others want to learn the language to communicate with their Chinese friends, parents of their spouses, and business partners. These are all valid reasons. Interestingly, there are also students who come to study Chinese just for the thrill of taking up an academic challenge by learning a language drastically different from English.

If learning a drastically different language is the sole purpose, the choice of Chinese is definitely a right one. Although similarities do exist between the two languages, Chinese differs from English significantly in sounds, grammar, and writing. I should hasten to add that these differences are not insurmountable hurdles. With enough practice and exposure, they will ultimately prove to be aids in gaining access to the perceptions and conceptions of the people whose language they are learning. Didn't some philosopher once say that to know a second language is to gain a second soul?

Chinese is the language spoken by more people in the world than any other language, yet in the West it is often categorized as a less commonly taught language. Poor knowledge and misinformation have produced an abundance of myths and misconceptions about the language. Hopefully, the following discussion will help dispel some of the mysteries that shroud Chinese.

You are about to study the Chinese language and you should know the word for Chinese language in Chinese. Instead of one, there are two terms: *Hanyu* and *Zhongwen*. The term *Hanyu*, which is widely used in China to refer to the Chinese language and is adopted as the title for most Chinese language textbooks, literally means "the language of the *Han*." If you have some familiarity with Chinese history, you will know that *Han* was the second imperial dynasty of China (the first imperial dynasty was *Qin*, formerly *Chin* from which *China* derives). Due to its importance in history, the name *Han* came to be used to refer to ethnic Chinese. It is not difficult to see that *Hanyu* is not a politically correct term to use, because Chinese is also spoken by most of the minority groups in China as the second language and some of them as the first language. For this reason, *Zhongwen,* meaning the language of the Chinese people, would be a better term.

As one of the seven major dialect groups in China, Mandarin is spoken by over 900 million or 70% of the Chinese people in northern and parts of southern China and is understood by 94% of the population. Mandarin is not a language, but is a vocal representation of Chinese. The dialect, which is referred to in China as *beifanghua* (northern speech), has its own subvarieties of northern Mandarin, northwest Mandarin, southern Mandarin and southwest Mandarin. The standard Mandarin, called *guoyu* or *putonghua*, is based on, but not equivalent to, the Beijing dialect. The term *guoyu*, which means "national language," is used in Taiwan, Hong Kong, and overseas Chinese communities; the term *putonghua*, which means "common speech," is used in mainland China. This standard form has become an administrative and official medium. It is used on television, in radio broadcasts, and in movies. More importantly, it has been promoted to the language of instruction in primary and secondary schools. *Guoyu/putonghua* has been chosen as the standard dialect because of the sheer number of speakers. With a multitude of mutually unintelligible dialects, there is a need for a lingua franca through which speakers of various dialects can communicate. If you speak Mandarin, chances are you may not understand people who speak a different dialect, but they may understand you. Besides those in China, Mandarin is also spoken by more than one million people in Singapore, Malaysia, Indonesia, Brunei, Mongolia, Thailand, and Philippines.

People outside China are often under the impression that there are two languages in China: Mandarin and Cantonese, but this is not the case. Cantonese or *Guangdonghua*, which is spoken by only 5% of the population in China, is popular in the United States and elsewhere primarily due to the fact that early immigrants to the United States were mostly from Canton, a coastal province where residents have easy access to the sea. However since then, more people from the Mandarin-speaking areas in China have been finding new homes in this and other countries.

Chinese belongs to the family of Sino-Tibetan languages. As the world's second largest language family (next only to the Indo-European family), the Sino-Tibetan family is comprised of more than 300 languages that are spoken over a vast geographic area extending from Northeastern India to Southeast, South, and East Asia. Other members of the family include Tibetan, Burmese, and a number of lesser known languages. These languages share a number of common features including, among others, monosyllabism, tonality, and the use of classifiers. Let us now take a look at monosyllabism and the use of classifiers. (Tonality will be discussed in the next chapter on Chinese phonetics.)

Monosyllabism refers to a language phenomenon where each morpheme is represented by a syllable. While the syllable may be easy to understand, the morpheme may not be. The morpheme has been traditionally regarded as the smallest unit of meaning, although contemporary linguists have distinguished finer units. In languages like English, a morpheme can consist of one or more syllables such as *kind* (one syllable, one morpheme) and *monosyllable* (five syllables and two morpheme -*mono* and *syllable*) and can even be realized by a consonant, such as -*s* in *cats*. Morphemes in English are often bound, meaning that individual morphemes cannot stand alone but have to be strung together to form a word. In a monosyllabic language, syllables are coterminous with morphemes. In other words, a syllable is a morpheme. In this sense, Chinese is truly monosyllabic, because each morpheme is indeed represented by a syllable and most morphemes in the language are free rather than bound (they can stand alone as independent words). However, it would be wrong to assume the reverse: a word always consists of a morpheme and thus a syllable. The majority of words used in contemporary Chinese are disyllabic or polysyllabic, consisting of two or more morphemes/syllables. What is noteworthy in this regard is that most of these disyllabic and polysyllabic words are formed by freestanding rather than bound morphemes. Juxtaposing two freestanding morphemes/words doesn't mean that the meaning of the new word is the sum total of the meanings of the component words. They can be very different.

The use of classifiers is another feature that characterizes Chinese and most other Sino-Tibetan and Southeast Asian languages. Basically, a classifier is a word that comes between a number or a demonstrative pronoun (e.g., *this, that*) and a noun. Classifiers are also referred to as measure words. They are occasionally used in English *(a piece of paper, a school of fish, two heads of cauliflower)*, but in Chinese the use of classifiers is the rule rather than the exception. Classifiers help disambiguate homophones and supply additional semantic rather than quantitative information about the nouns they are used with. For this reason, it is inappropriate to refer to them as measure words. Refer to Lesson Four for a detailed discussion of classifiers.

Although Chinese shares these characteristics with other Sino-Tibetan languages, there are other features that are unique to Chinese. These include morphological simplicity, syntactic economy, meaning taking precedence over the form, and the topic-comment sentence structure.

Morphological simplicity. As compared with English and other Indo-European languages, Chinese grammar is very simple. It is considered by some people to be so simple that they say Chinese does not have grammar. These people would be right if grammar were equated with inflection, but unfortunately it is not. Grammar is a system of rules which govern the use of language, so every language has grammar. Chinese is for the most part not inflectional—words are invariable, unaltered and allow no internal changes; affixes signaling lexical or grammatical meaning do not figure very large; syntactic and lexical meanings are not indicated through the manipulation of word forms, but through word order, specific particles and vocabulary items.

Syntactic economy. Many syntactic distinctions made in English are not made in Chinese. These include the distinctions between singular and plural *(book* vs. *books)*, nominative case and objective case *(I* vs. *me)*, first/second person and third person *(I speak* vs. *he speaks)*, active voice and passive voice *(call* vs. *be called)*, the positive degree and comparative degree *(pretty* vs. *prettier)*, past time and present time *(I was a teacher* vs. *I am a teacher)*. Tense is another example. For nonnative speakers, verbs are usually the most difficult part of an inflectional language. The concept of tense has two components: *time* and *aspect.* Since time is conceived of differently in different languages, let's confine ourselves to English, where time can be divided into past, present, future and future in the past (e.g., when you reflect on a comment about a future event that you made on a past occasion). Aspect refers to the manner in which an action takes place. The distinction of aspects made in English are indefinite, continuous/ progressive, perfect, and perfect continuous/progressive. These four times and four aspects form a matrix which generates a total of sixteen different verb forms: *I write a letter, I wrote a letter, I will write a letter, (I said) I would write a letter, I am writing a letter, I was writing a letter, I will be writing a letter, (I said) I would be writing a letter, I have written a letter, (I thought) I had written a letter, I will have written a letter, (I said) I would have written a letter, I have been writing a letter, (I thought) I had been writing a letter, I will have been writing a letter, (I said) I would have been writing a letter.* Notwithstanding the controversies that abound as to whether some of these structures are really tenses, the number and complexity of these verb forms seems daunting. Fortunately for students of Chinese, verbs do not present a major problem because time is expressed lexically and aspect markers are few and far between. There are only two aspects distinguished in Chinese: complete and continuous. The gender distinction of nouns is also absent. *Fuwuyuan* can be both waiter and waitress, and *yanyuan* can be both actor and actress. (Many of the problems that beset English and other languages in relation to gender simply do not exist in Chinese. I once gave a talk on the relationship between language and thought. The original title was *Linguistic Shaping of Thought: Man at the Mercy of His Language*. You may quickly notice, as I did at the time, that this is not a politically correct title . It didn't seem to sound right either if I changed it to *Linguistic Shaping of Thought: Person/People at the Mercy of His/Her/Their Language*. Fortunately, my Chinese came to the quick rescue. The final title became *Language and Thought: Ren at the Mercy of Tade Language*. *Ren* (person or people) and *tade* (his or her) did their job and no one was offended.)

Syntactic economy is prominently manifested in what I would call a single-signal system. Chinese allows only one signal for one meaning. In the English sentence *I have two books*, the plural meaning of the word *book* is indicated by two signals: *two* and the suffix *-s*. In Chinese people would simply say (equivalent to English) *I have two book*. The negative of the sentence *wo baba qu le Zhongguo* (my father has gone to China) is *wo baba meiyou qu Zhongguo*, where the aspect marker *le* has to be dropped because the negative word *meiyou* already signals a completed action. *-Men* is one of the few suffixes used in Chinese. It is used after personal pronouns and human nouns to indicate plurality such as *xueshengmen dou hen hao* (the students are all good). However, when there is another signal present in the sentence indicating plurality, *-men* is dropped. We cannot say *wo you san ge Zhongwen laoshimen* (I have three Chinese teachers), we instead say *wo you san ge Zhongwen laoshi*, since *san ge* (three) already signals plurality. Similarly we cannot say *tamen shi laoshimen* (they are teachers), because *tamen* (they) already makes the number clear. *Yes/no* questions are another case in point. They are formed in Chinese by either using the sentence final particle *ma* or by repeating the verb using its negative form such as *ni shi Zhongguoren ma* (are you a Chinese) or *ni shi bu shi Zhongguoren*. In the second form *ma* is not used because the verb plus its negative form is only used in Chinese to indicate a *yes/no* question.

Meaning takes precedence over form. Since morphological changes are nonextant and conjunctions are sparingly used, word order becomes paramountly important in indicating meaning. In stringing sentence constituents together, Chinese is characterized by parataxis whereby grammatical elements such as phrases or clauses are coordinated without the use of conjunctions. This is different from English, which relies on hypotaxis whereby grammatical elements are joined with connectives. Sentences in paratactic languages such as Chinese are necessarily simpler and less embedded than those in hypotactic languages such as English. The most noticeable feature of word order in Chinese is the natural iconicity between syntactic structure and temporal sequence or chronological succession of events—what happens earlier in time and what exists earlier in concept comes earlier in the sentence. Expressions of time and place precede the verb in Chinese because they provide the scene and setting for the action. Modifiers, adjectives, adverbs, phrases or clauses, always come before modified, nouns or verbs. Lacking an article system, Chinese resorts to word order to indicate definiteness or indefiniteness. Generally, nouns with definite or specific reference are placed at the beginning of the sentence, whereas those with indefinite or unspecified reference are placed towards the end of the sentence. Renowned linguist Yuen Ren Chao once said that all Chinese grammar is syntax, all Chinese syntax is word order, and therefore all Chinese grammar is word order.

Topic-comment sentence. About 50% of sentences in Chinese contain a binary division of two parts between *topic* and *comment*. The topic is what the speaker takes as his/her point of departure and the comment is a statement on that topic. This structure is considered by some as a substandard way of expression, but in languages such as Chinese, it is quite normal and standard. Examples of topic-comment sentences (topic and comment are separate by |) include: *wo | duzi e le* (I'm hungry, literally *I stomach hungry*), *ta mama | shenti hen hao* (her mother enjoys good health, literally *her mother health good*), *Yingyu | wo hui nüli* (I will work hard on my English, literally, *English I will work hard on*).

A particular linguistic structure reflects a particular cognitive process. The Chinese topic-comment structure characterizes a type of thinking wherein the speaker, in communicating an idea, would first decide upon a topic without considering the syntactic representation of the assertion. This is made possible by the freedom from abiding by the subject-verb agreement. If you are interested in the corollary of this two-step cognitive organization, refer to my other book, *Aspects of Discourse Structure in Mandarin Chinese*.

As a final note, Chinese is not a phonetic language and the characters do not bear any resemblance to actual pronunciation, therefore a system of transcribing Chinese phonetics was needed to assist people learning to read words in Chinese. There are two systems currently in use. One is the Wade-Giles system and the other is the *pinyin* system. The Wade-Giles system was developed by Sir Thomas Francis Wade in the mid-nineteenth century and modified by the Cambridge professor Herbert Allen Giles at the beginning of this century. This system makes it easier, particularly for English speakers, to pronounce Chinese sounds, but is not an accurate representation of the sounds. For example, the Wade-Giles system often uses one symbol to represent different sounds and different symbols to represent the same sound. In mainland China, the Wade-Giles system has been replaced by the *pinyin* (which literally means *putting sounds together*) system which was developed in 1958 with the purpose of introducing standard pronunciation of Mandarin to school children. This system has been adopted worldwide since the late 1970s and is used in this book. A cross-reference between the Wade-Giles system and the *pinyin* system is given in the back of the book.

Chinese Phonetics

There are six vowels and twenty-one consonants in Mandarin Chinese. As we discussed in the previous chapter, the majority of Chinese morphemes are monosyllabic. The syllabic structure in Chinese is such that a syllable always consists of a vowel (V) or a consonant with a vowel (CV), such as ba, fo, ne. Consonant clusters—two or more consonants used in succession—are not permitted in Chinese. Syllabic combinations common in English such as VC (up, at), CVC (big, pat, map), CCVC (bred, dread, stone), CVCC (mask, best, sand), CCV (fly, blue, grow), CCCV (screw, spray, stray), VCC (old, and, ink), VCCC (Olds, ants, amps), CCVCC (brand, trains, swings), CVCCC (tests, tenths, lunged), CVCCCC (thirsts, texts, worlds), CCVCCC (slurps, prints, flirts), CCCVC (street, squat, strut), CCCVCC (struts, squats, sprained), and CCCVCCC (scrimps, sprints, squelched) are not possible in Chinese. CVC, on the other hand, is possible in Chinese, but the final C can only be the nasal sounds -n and -ng and the retroflex -r, such as *jing, nan, yong* and *er*. Consonants are often called initials because they invariably appear initially in a word with the exception of the final -*n*, -*ng* or *r*, which can appear finally. Vowels are also called finals because they appear medially or finally in a word. Vowels can stand by themselves when no initial consonant is present.

The 6 vowels are: *a, o, e, i, u, ü*, which should be learned in this sequence for two important reasons. First, this sequence shows a pattern or regularity of articulation. When you pronounce *a*, the mouth is open the widest, and the tongue is the lowest. As you move down the list, the mouth gradually closes and the tongue gradually rises. By the time you pronounce *ü*, the mouth is almost closed and the tongue reaches the highest point. Second, the tone mark used in *pinyin* always falls on the vowel, but two or three vowels can be combined to form a compound vowel, such as: *ao, ai, ou, ei, ia, iao, ie, iu, ua, uo, ue, ui, uai*. When this happens, the tone mark will fall on the vowel that comes earlier in the sequence (with the exception of *iu* and *ui*, where the tone mark always falls on the second sound):

āo, āi, ōu, ēi, iā, iāo, iē, iū, uā, uō, uē, uī, uāi

The 21 consonants are: *b, p, m, f, d, t, n, l, g, k, h, j, q, x, z, c, s, zh, ch, sh, r*

A question that I like to ask students in my introductory class is: what kind of problem can you envision for a language that has only 6 vowels, 21 consonants and is of the CV (with limited CVC possibilities) syllabic structure? It doesn't take them very long to come up with the answer: the lack of sound combinations to express all the meanings and ideas. Simple math will tell us that there are only about 400 possible sound combinations in Chinese. By introducing four tones, the total number of possible sound combinations increases to about 1600. In contrast, according to the Danish grammarian Jespersen, there are 158,000 possible sound combinations in English.

Although the severely restricted number of possible sound combinations poses a hindrance to effective communication, the student of Chinese don't have to learn too many sound combinations. To help you practice Chinese phonetics, a list of all possible sound combinations in Mandarin is provided in the back of the book with the four tones indicated.

Tones

As mentioned above, tones are an effective means of reducing homophones (and consequently ambiguity). Tones are variations of pitch contours. Such variations also occur in English, but are only phonetic, not phonemic in that they may change the pragmatic meaning of a word, but they do not change its lexical meaning. For example, there may be a variety of ways to say the word *yes* in English, but *yes* will never become *desk* or *horse*. In Mandarin however pitch change is not only phonetic, but also phonemic in that tones distinguish meaning. By varying the pitch of a sound combination, you get a totally different word. Here are some examples:

mā (mother), má (hemp), mǎ (horse), mà (scold)
yī (one), yí (move), yǐ (chair), yì (hundred million)
wū (house), wú (none), wǔ (five), wù (fog)

In Mandarin Chinese, there are four tones, which are referred to as the first tone, the second tone, the third tone and the fourth tone and are indicated by the tone graphs respectively as -, ´, ˇ, ˋ . The workings of these four tones are demonstrated by the following chart:

The first tone is called high level tone. As the name suggests, it should be high, almost at the upper limit of your pitch range, and level, without any fluctuation. A common mistake observed among the students is that it is not high enough. The key to getting this tone right is that if you feel there is still room at the top of your pitch range, you should go for it.

The second tone is called rising tone. It starts from the middle of your pitch range and rises. This is usually not a difficult tone.

The third tone is called falling-rising tone. As such, it has two parts: first falling, then rising. Although this tone is represented by the graph v, the two sides of the v are not of equal size. A better representation would be a check mark √. It moves down from the lower half of the pitch range and moves up to a point near the top. A common mistake is that students often start too high. It is only too natural that if you start too high, it would be very difficult to maneuver the bend at the bottom of the valley when you need to rise. What you should do is to try to start low. In fact, it doesn't matter very much how low you start. Start as low as you can. If you still have trouble, try to lower your chin as you produce the tone (but try not to get into an irreversible habit).

The fourth tone is called falling tone. It falls precipitously from the top of the pitch level. It is interesting to observe that although we use this tone from time to time in English, particularly when we put our foot down by saying *Yes!* or *No!*, when it comes to pronouncing the fourth tone in Mandarin, a lot of students suddenly become indecisive and ineffectual. The key to getting this tone right is to be resolute.

In addition to these four tones, Mandarin Chinese has a "fifth" tone, which is actually a toneless tone. As such it is usually called neutral tone. Its pronunciation is soft and quick. The neutral tone is not diacritically marked. It occurs either on grammatical particles or the second character of some words that do not receive stress. For example:

Grammatical Particles:

Nǐ hǎo ma? (How are you?)
Nǐ ne? (How about you?)
Wǒde shū (my book)
Tā qù le xuéxiào (He has gone to the school.)

Second character of some words:

xièxie (thank you), māma (mother), bàba (father), lǎoshī (teacher)

Tone Change

The juxtaposition of two tones may sometimes result in a tone change known as *tone sandhi*. This happens when

1. A third tone becomes a second tone when immediately followed by another third tone, e.g.:

   Nǐ hǎo → Ní hǎo (Hello)!
   Wǒ hěn hǎo → Wó hén hǎo (I'm fine).

2. When a third tone is followed by the first tone, the second tone, the fourth tone and the most neutral tones, it becomes a half third tone. A half third tone is a modified third tone that falls but not rise, e.g.:

   wǒ māma (my mother), Nǐ máng ma? (Are you busy?)

It is clear from the above that the third is seldom used in full in Chinese unless it falls on a word in isolation or is followed by a long pause. Although the third tone undergoes changes in connection with other tones, by convention it is still given the original tone mark in print.

There are a number of other conventions and rules that should be noted:

1. i is written as y when it occurs at the beginning of a syllable, e.g., ie → ye, ian → yan. i is written as yi when it forms a syllable by itself, e.g., i → yi.

2. u is written as w when it occurs at the beginning of a syllable, e.g., uo → wo, uan → wan. u is written as wu when it forms a syllable by itself, e.g., u → wu.

3. ü is written as yu when it occurs at the beginning of a syllable or forms a syllable by itself, e.g., üe → yüe, üan → yüan, ü → yu.

4. i does not have any phonetic value when it follows z, c, s, zh, ch, sh and r. It is placed there to fulfill the syllabic requirement. That is, there must be a vowel in every syllable.

5. When preceded by a consonant, uei and uen become ui and un.

6. ü is written as u after j, q, x and y.

7. When a syllable beginning with a, o, and e is juxtaposed with another syllable, the mark (') is often used to demarcate the boundary between two syllables, e.g., nǚ'er (daughter) and pèi'é (quota).

8. In Mandarin, an extra syllable is often attached to another syllable to make it retroflexed. This extra syllable is phonetically transcribed as "r" instead of "er", e.g., yìdiǎnr (a little bit), xiǎoháir (child), and should not be pronounced separately.

Written Chinese

Of all the major writing systems in the world, Chinese is the only one that did not develop a phonetic alphabet. Its writing system is neither alphabetic or phonetic, because it does not use romanization and its form does not bear any resemblance to the actual sound. The Chinese writing system uses a logographic script in the form of characters.

Mention was made in a previous chapter that most of the major dialect groups in China are not mutually intelligible, but the written form is the same. People in China who cannot communicate through speech can communicate through the written language. A commonly heard expression in China is "Qǐng xiě xià lái (please write it down)." This linkage can even facilitate to some extent communication between Chinese, Japanese, and Koreans, who use Chinese characters extensively. It may be reasonable to assume that this unified writing system has helped preclude China from disintegration through the last two millennia. If anything, the writing system is definitely a link for the Chinese to connect to their literary tradition and cultural past. There have been debates about whether Chinese should abandon its characters and adopt romanization as its writing system. These discussions are fruitless and serve no purpose. If you followed our discussion in the previous chapter on Chinese phonetics, you would have noticed the limited number of possible sound combinations and the abundance of homophones in Chinese. Although the use of tones and classifiers, and dissyllabizing words can help alleviate the situation to some extent, characters are the ultimate and the only way to distinguish words. Ten words may be pronounced exactly the same, but they will all be written differently. There is simply no way that characters can give way to romanization in Chinese.

Chinese characters are often thought of as pictures representing objects and concepts. This may be true of the earliest Chinese writing traceable to the fourteenth century BC when it was largely pictographic in nature, but pictograms were soon found inadequate to represent everything, especially abstract ideas. Ideograms were then introduced as graphic representations of abstract and symbolic ideas. For those pictographic characters, centuries of refining and stylizing resulted in the almost total loss of images and graphic quality.

Seventy-five percent of Chinese characters are composed of two parts, a left part and a right part or a top part and a bottom part. In either formation, one part, called the radical, usually appears on the left or the top. Radicals are category labels or specifiers that provide clues to the semantic classification of the word such as person, food, metal, plant, animal, water, gender, feeling, and language. If you know the radical of a character, but do not know the character itself, you can get a general idea of its meaning. For example, all of the following characters share the "water" radical, because all of them have to do with water:

洋	海	河	湖	洗	汗	池	浸
yáng	hǎi	hé	hú	xǐ	hàn	chí	jīn
ocean	*sea*	*river*	*lake*	*wash*	*sweat*	*pond*	*soak*

There are 214 such radicals in Chinese, which are also used in Chinese dictionaries to index words. The other component of the character, usually appearing on the right or the bottom, provides phonetic clues. For example:

羊	样	洋	佯	氧	痒	烊
yáng	yàng	yáng	yáng	yǎng	yǎng	yáng
sheep	*shape*	*ocean*	*feign*	*oxygen*	*itch*	*melt*

The phonetic clue is only a rough one and becomes useful only when you already know a substantial number of characters to make a prediction. In addition, tones may be very different.

Students of Chinese often wonder how many characters they need to learn in order to have a reading knowledge of Chinese materials other than classical literature. Various estimates have been given, ranging from 3,000 to 5,000. Statistics shows that the majority of the 50,000-60,000 existing characters are not in common use. Those that appear with 99.15% frequency amount to about 3,000, which is the vocabulary of the average high school student in China. That is to say, the endeavor to learn the additional 50,000 or so characters can only increase your inventory of commonly used characters by less than 1%. For this reason, knowledge of 2,000 to 2,500 characters is adequate to tackle reading contingencies that are nonacademic and nontechnical. This would probably be equivalent to the vocabulary of the average junior high school graduate in China. Remember that the majority of words used in contemporary Chinese are disyllabic or polysyllabic. The actual number of words you learn from these 2,000 to 2,500 characters is enormous.

Since characters are not phonetic and the emphasis of this or any other beginning course for adult learners is on speaking or communicating, character learning and writing are not given priority. To spend too much time on character writing at this stage would consume too much time that should be spent building a solid foundation in pronunciation and the basic sentence patterns used for various communicative functions. It is advisable that serious study of characters for adult students should follow a comfortable command of pronunciation, basic vocabulary, and basic sentence patterns. In spite of all this, you may find it very hard to resist learning some characters when you study the language. Feel free to pursue if you have the urge as long as you do not lose sight of the main goal at this stage.

In writing a character, it is not only important to get the end product right, but also to follow the proper stroke order. Failure to follow proper sequence is the first sign of illiteracy. That is why teachers and parents in China keep a very close look at how children write and take pains to correct them when they make a wrong move. To that end, I would strongly suggest that students take advantage of the multitude of software programs that teach the writing of characters. You will find a list of character tutoring programs in the resource section of this book. Most of these programs will take you by the hand, animating the basic strokes and stroke order.

In addition, they usually come with quizzes, on-screen flashcards, and a bi-directional dictionary. Some of the programs even have the ability to display *pinyin* for any character by clicking on it.

Characters are also referred to as square characters, because each one is shaped like a square. Irrespective of the complexity of strokes and structures, each character occupies the same amount of space as the next one. To help with balancing and orienting strokes, it is a good idea that you practice writing characters using an exercise book with grid pages.

Complex characters are formed by components. These components are either independent characters when used alone or blocks that recur in many other characters. Try to memorize these components rather than individual strokes. It is easier to build a house using prefabricated materials than individual bricks and loose sands.

A cursory look at any older Chinese dictionary will reveal that many of the characters are very complex in structure, consisting of up to twenty strokes. They are complicated to write and difficult to remember. This also explains why illiteracy had been widespread in China up to the mid-twentieth century. In response to the pressing need to simplify the writing system, the Chinese government has introduced a total of 2,515 simplified characters since 1956. The most common form of simplification is the reduction of strokes in certain characters and assignment of a component to replace the whole. Contrary to the thinking of many people outside China that the simplification was imposed by the Chinese government on its people, the government standardized the simplified forms that had already been in wide use for hundreds of years. Simplification is a boon for millions of people, particularly for those who are struggling to shake off illiteracy. This process has gone a long way towards helping alleviate illiteracy. Studies have found that the literacy rate in China has risen from 20-30% in the early 1950s to 80-90% in the 1990s. Although favorably received, simplification of characters also created new problems. Since the decision to simplify characters was unilaterally made by the Chinese government, people in Taiwan, Hong Kong, and overseas Chinese communities are experiencing tremendous difficulty reading materials from mainland China and children in mainland are also having trouble reading classical materials. But with the reunification of Hong Kong with China, it won't be very far before simplification find its way there.

Beginning students often struggle with the decision whether to study the simplified characters or traditional characters. Unfortunately, there is no easy solution as there is no consensus among teachers of Chinese about which form to teach. Although I've used simplified characters in this book, I suggest making the decision based on your purpose. Study simplified characters if you need to read literature from mainland China, and study traditional characters if you plan to read materials from Taiwan, Hong Kong, and overseas Chinese communities. There are teachers of Chinese who suggest that students learn to read both forms, but write in the simplified form only. The above-mentioned software programs and all the Chinese word-processing programs listed in the resource section of the book can be great aids in cross-referencing between traditional and simplified characters. With a click of a button, most of these programs will convert the simplified characters to traditional characters or vice versa.

Grammatical Terms Explained

Adverbial

A word, phrase or clause that functions to modify a verb, an adjective or another adverb, providing such information as time, place, manner, reason, and condition.

Aspect

The manner in which an action takes place. English distinguishes four aspects: indefinite, continuous, perfect and perfect continuous, whereas Chinese distinguishes only two: continuous and perfect.

Classifier

A word used between a numeral and a noun to show the sub-class to which the noun belongs.

Object

A noun, pronoun, phrase, or clause that is used after, and affected in some way by, a transitive verb. If it is affected in a direct way, it is called the direct object. If it is affected in an indirect way, it is called the indirect object. In the sentence *he gave me a book, a book* is the direct object and *me* is the indirect object.

Particle

A word that has only grammatical meaning, but no lexical meaning, such as *ma, ne* and *ba* in Chinese.

Predicate

The part of a sentence that states or asserts something about the subject. This role is only assumed by the verb in English, but can also be assumed by the adjective in Chinese.

Predicative adjective

An adjective used after the verb *to be* in English as in *the book is interesting*, which is opposed to an attributive adjective used before a noun as in *this is an interesting book.* Predicative adjectives in Chinese are used without the verb *to be.*

Subject

Something about which a statement or assertion is made in the sentence.

Transitive and intransitive verbs

A transitive verb is one that needs to take an object such as *we study Chinese.* An intransitive verb is one that does not take an object such as *walk, run,* and *go.*

LESSON

1

GREETINGS

SENTENCE PATTERNS

你 好!
Nǐ hǎo!

Hello!

你 好 吗?
Nǐ hǎo ma?

How are you?

你 呢?
Nǐ ne?

How about you?

这 是 王 先生.
Zhè shì Wáng Xiānsheng.

This is Mr. Wang.

你 怎么样?
Nǐ zěnmeyàng?

How is everything with you?

我 也 很 好.
Wǒ yě hěn hǎo.

I'm fine, too.

认识 你, 我 很 高兴.
Rènshi nǐ, wǒ hěn gāoxìng.

It's a pleasure to know you.

1

CONVERSATIONS

A: 你好!
 Nǐ hǎo!
B: 你好!
 Nǐ hǎo!

Hello!

Hello!

A: 你好吗?
 Nǐ hǎo ma?
B: 我很好。你呢?
 Wǒ hěn hǎo. Nǐ ne?
A: 我也很好。
 Wǒ yě hěn hǎo.

How are you?

I'm fine. And you?

I'm fine, too.

A: 你爸爸好吗?
 Nǐ bàba hǎo ma?
B: 他很好。
 Tā hěn hǎo.
A: 你妈妈呢?
 Nǐ māma ne?
B: 她也很好。
 Tā yě hěn hao.

How is your father?

He is fine.

And your mother?

She is also fine.

A: 王先生, 你好吗?
 Wáng Xiānsheng, nǐ hǎo ma?
B: 马马虎虎。你呢, 张小姐?
 Mǎmahūhu. Nǐ ne, Zhāng Xiǎojie?
A: 我也马马虎虎。
 Wǒ yě mǎmahūhu.

How are you, Mr. Wang.

So-so. How about you, Miss Zhang?

I'm so-so, too.

A: 你怎么样?
 Nǐ zěnmeyàng?
B: 不错。你呢?
 Bú cuò. Nǐ ne?
A: 我也不错。
 Wǒ yě bú cuò.

How's everything with you?

Not bad. And you?

Not bad, either.

A: 这是张小姐。这是王先生。
 Zhè shì Zhāng Xiǎojie. Zhè shì Wáng Xiānsheng.
B: 认识你我很高兴。
 Rènshi nǐ, wǒ hěn gāoxìng.

This is Miss Zhang. This is Mr. Wang.

It's a pleasure to know you.

2

A: 认识 你, 我 也 很 高兴。   It's a pleasure to know you too.
   Rènshi nǐ, wǒ yě hěn gāoxìng.

WORDS AND EXPRESSIONS

Pronouns

我	wǒ	I
你	nǐ	you
他	tā	he
她	tā	she
这	zhè	this

Nouns

爸爸	bàba	father
妈妈	māma	mother
先生	xiānsheng	Mr., husband
小姐	xiǎojie	Miss

Verbs

是	shì	be
认识	rènshi	know

Adjectives

好	hǎo	good
错	cuò	wrong, bad
马马虎虎	mǎmahūhu	so-so
高兴	gāoxìng	happy

Adverbs

很	hěn	very
也	yě	also
不	bù	not

Grammatical particles

吗	ma	
呢	ne	

Expressions

怎么样	zěnmeyàng	how is ...?

SUPPLEMENTARY WORDS AND EXPRESSIONS

<u>Nouns</u>

老师	lǎoshī	teacher
学生	xuésheng	student
哥哥	gēge	older brother
弟弟	dìdi	younger brother
姐姐	jiějie	older sister
妹妹	mèimei	younger sister
医生	yīshēng	doctor
律师	lǜshī	lawyer
中国	Zhōngguó	China
美国	Měiguó	United States
日本	Rìběn	Japan

<u>Pronouns</u>

它	tā	it

<u>Verbs</u>

来	lái	come
去	qù	go
喜欢	xǐhuan	like

<u>Adjectives</u>

累	lèi	tired
忙	máng	busy

LANGUAGE POINTS

1. 你好 (nǐ hǎo)

你好 (nǐ hǎo) is the most common form of greeting in Chinese. It can be used at any time during the day and on any occasion. 你好 (nǐ hǎo), equivalent to *Hello* or *Hi* in English, does not require any specific answer except 你好 (nǐ hǎo) in return.

2. 是 (shì)

Although Chinese has a verb *to be* in the form of 是 (shì), it is not used the same way as verb *to be* in English. 是 (shì) is used only when the subject and predicative have the same referent or refer to the same person or object such as:

我 是 老师。   I am a teacher.
Wǒ shì lǎoshī.

他 是 学生。   He is a student.
Tā shì xuésheng.

On the other hand, when the predicative is an adjective or prepositional phrase, 是 (shì) is not used at all in Chinese. Adjectives and prepositional phrases thus used are conditions, locations or descriptions of the subject. For example, sentences such as *I am happy, the book is on the table* and *she is there* and *they are home* would be rendered into Chinese without 是 (shì) . It is evident that a Chinese sentence can consist of a subject and an adjective or prepositional phrase only. In such a case, adjectives function as quasi-verbs.

3. 你好吗 (nǐ hǎo ma)?

你好吗 (nǐ hǎo ma) is used when you really want to know how things are with the other person. The expression literally means *are you good?* and requires either a positive or negative answer. Responses to this greeting usually include 我 很 好 (wǒ hěn hǎo), 我 不 错 (wǒ bú cuò), and 马 马 虎 虎 (mǎma hūhu). While 我 很 好 (wǒ hěn hǎo) is probably the most frequently heard, keep in mind that 很 (hěn) in the expression is indispensable because it fulfills a prosodic or rhythmic requirement. People simply do not respond by saying 我 好 (wǒ hǎo).

4. The pronunciation of 不 (bù)

The dictionary form of 不 is the fourth tone (bù), but it becomes the second tone when it precedes a fourth tone word. Compare:

不 来	not come	不 去	not go
bù lái		bú qù	
不 好	not good	不 认 识	not know
bù hǎo		bú rènshi	

5. Yes/no questions

Yes/no questions are questions that require either a yes answer or a no answer. As such, they are also called polar questions. Yes/no questions are formed in English by either reversing the subject and the verb in the case of verb *to be* or one of those modal verbs like *can* and *may*, or by using a dummy word such as *do* before the subject in the case of a regular verb. In Chinese however, we do not switch around sentence constituents to form a yes/no question. Such a question is rather indicated by adding the sentence final particle 吗 (ma) to an affirmative sentence. For example:

你好 吗?   How are you?
Nǐ hǎo ma?

你爸爸忙 吗?   Is your father busy?
Nǐ bàba máng ma?

你 妈妈 来 吗？　　　　　　　　Is your mother coming?
Nǐ māma lái ma?

It may come as a surprise to you that in Chinese there is no equivalent to *yes* or *no* in English. In other words, there is not a single specific word that we can use all the time to respond to various yes/no questions. Equivalents to *yes* and *no* are actually the verbs or predicative adjectives in the questions. For this reason, they vary from sentence to sentence. To give positive and negative answers to the following questions in English:

1. Do you speak Chinese?
2. Do you like Japanese food?
3. Are you a doctor?
4. Can you cook?

All you need to do is to answer by using the verb or the verb-like adjective. Positive and negative answers to the above questions would be:

1. Speak/not speak.
2. Like/not like.
3. Am/am not.
4. Can/not can.

Now, let's look at some real Chinese yes/no questions and answers:

你来吗？　　　　　　　　　　Are you coming?
Nǐ lái ma?
来。　　　　　　　　　　　　　Yes, I am.
Lái.
不来。　　　　　　　　　　　　No, I am not.
Bù lái.

你是老师吗？　　　　　　　　Are you a teacher?
Nǐ shì lǎoshī ma?
是。　　　　　　　　　　　　　Yes, I am.
Shì.
不是。　　　　　　　　　　　　No, I am not.
Bú shì.

你爸爸忙 吗？　　　　　　　　Is your father busy?
Nǐ bàba máng ma?
很 忙。　　　　　　　　　　　Yes, he is.
Hěn máng.
不 忙。　　　　　　　　　　　No, he is not.
Bù máng.

You may have already noticed that in answering a yes/no question in Chinese, you can practically drop everything in the sentence including the subject except the verb or the verb-like adjective.

6. 呢 (ne)

As a sentence final particle, 呢 (ne) is used to avoid repeating a question previously asked. It basically means *what about* ...? or *how about* ...? For example:

你哥哥是学生 吗?	Is your older brother a student?
Nǐ gēge shì xuésheng ma?	
是。	Yes, he is.
Shè.	
你姐姐呢?	What about your older sister?
Nǐ jiějie ne?	
不 是。	No, she is not.
Bú shì.	

Without using this short-hand device, you would have to repeat the whole question. In this instance, you would have to say "你姐姐是学生吗" (Nǐ jiějie shì xuésheng ma)?

7. 怎么样 (zěnmeyàng)

怎么样 (zěnmeyàng) is a colloquial expression of greeting, meaning *how is it going* or *how are things*. It is used between people who know each other very well. It requires the same answers as 你好吗 (nǐ hǎo ma).

8. Sibling terms

There are a number of principles people in different cultures use to call their siblings and relatives. These principles include linearity (direct line of descent or collateral extension), collaterality (father's side or mother's side), generation, sex and seniority. Distinctions made in one culture are very often not made in another culture. Kinship terms often provide clues to how relatives are perceived and treated in various cultures. Cultures that make more distinctions have more terms for their kin than those that make fewer distinctions. Since Chinese is one of those languages that recognize all the above distinctions, it is to be expected that the system of kinship terminology in the language is very complicated. There are two major differences between English and Chinese in this regard. First, the English system does not distinguish relatives on the father's side and relatives on the mother's side, while the Chinese system does. Second, English does not recognize seniority among siblings, while the distinction is important in Chinese. Thus older brother and younger brothers are called by different terms and so are older sisters and younger sisters. There is no way in Chinese to ask, "Do you have a brother/sister?" You must specify whether he or she is an older one or a younger one.

9. Address forms

先生 (Xiānsheng *Mr.*), 太太 (Tàitai *Mrs.*) and 小姐 (Xiǎojiě *Miss*) had been used in China as polite forms of address prior to 1949 when they were replaced by 同志 (Tóngzhì *Comrade*), which was considered revolutionary. However, with the opening of the country to the outside world that began in the late 70s, 先生 (Xiānsheng), 太太 (Tàitai) and 小姐 (Xiǎojie) have reemerged as the popular address forms. Keep in mind when using these address forms together with the family name, the rule is: the name precedes the title, instead of following it as in English. Examples are 王先生 (Wáng Xiānsheng) and 李小姐 (Lǐ Xiǎojie). 太太 (Tàitai) is not used very often to address people simply because it is difficult to determine if the addressee is married or not and even if the addressee is married, she may still prefer to be addressed as 小姐 (Xiǎojie). Another reason that 太太 (Tàitai) is not often used as an address form is that women in contemporary China do not take their husbands' family name after their marriage. To use 太太 (Tàitai) after a woman's own name is therefore not appropriate.

10. 也 (yě)

English uses two different adverbs, *too* and *either*, to indicate that one situation also applies to another. *Too* is used in the affirmative sentence, while *either* is used in the negative sentence. Chinese, however, uses only one word 也 (yě) in both affirmative sentences and negative sentences. This is very similar to *also* in English. As an adverb, 也 (yě) is always placed before the verb or the quasi-verb (adjective).

EXERCISES

I. Respond to the following:

1. 你好!
   Nǐ hǎo!
2. 你好 吗?
   Nǐ hǎo ma?
3. 你怎么样?
   Nǐ zěnmeyàng?
4. 你爸爸好 吗?
   Nǐ bàba hǎo ma?
5. 你妈妈 呢?
   Nǐ māma ne?
6. 你是学生 吗?
   Nǐ shì xuésheng ma?
7. 你爸爸是老师吗?
   Nǐ bàba shì lǎoshī ma?
8. 你妈妈是医生 吗?
   Nǐ māma shì yīshēng ma?
9. 认识你,我很 高兴.
   Rènshi nǐ, wǒ hěn gāoxìng.
10. 你认识我 妈妈吗?
    Nǐ rènshi wǒ māma ma?

II. Translate the following dialogs into Chinese:

1.
A: Hi, Mr. Zhao!
B: Hi, Miss Huang!
A: Are you busy?
B: I'm not. How about you?
A: I am very busy.

2.
A: Is your father going to China?
B: Yes, he is.
A: What about your mother?
B: She is going, too.

3.
A: Is your older brother a teacher?
B: Yes, he is.
A: Is your younger sister also a teacher?
B: No, she is not. She is a student.

4.
A: This is Mr. Hua. This is Miss Wang.
B: It's a pleasure to know you.
C: It's a pleasure to know you, too.

III. Translate the following into Chinese:

1. Are you tired?
2. Mr. Hu is not a doctor. He is a lawyer.
3. My father is very busy, but my mother is not (you do not need to translate "but" in Chinese).
4. I don't know her.
5. His younger brother is very happy.
6. This is my father.
7. My mother is not going to China. She is going to Japan.
8. Mr. Li is a lawyer. Mrs. Li is also a lawyer.
9. Her father and mother are coming to the United States.
10. Does your older brother like my younger sister?

IV. Change the following into yes/no questions and give both affirmative and negative answers:

1. 我 妹妹 来美国.
  Wǒ mèimei lái Měiguó.

2. 沈　小姐 是 老师.
   Shěn Xiǎojie shì lǎoshī.
3. 他 认 识 我 爸 爸.
   Tā rènshi wǒ bàba.
4. 我　妈妈也是医生.
   Wǒ māma yě shì yīshēng.
5. 他 哥 哥 很 喜 欢 中 国.
   Tā gēge hěn xǐhuan Zhōngguó.
6. 他 是 王　　先 生.
   Tā shì Wáng Xiānsheng.
7. 张　　小 姐 很　高 兴.
   Zhāng Xiǎojie hěn gāoxìng.
8. 她 姐 姐 是 学 生.
   Tā jiějie shì xuésheng.
9. 我　爸 爸 妈 妈 很　忙.
   Wǒ bàba māma hěn máng.
10. 你 很　累.
   Nǐ hěn lèi.

CULTURAL INSIGHTS

To many Westerners, the Chinese present a perennial enigma. Their puzzlement and frustration are often heightened when they are involved in a speech situation with the Chinese, who seem to employ a totally different speech style. This unique style is described by various observers as possessing the following characteristics: 1) lack of a clearly-stated topical statement, which is often buried in a mass of information, 2) approach by indirectness and implicitness whereby ideas are developed in a widening circle without dealing with the subject directly and the definition of things in terms of what they are not, rather than in terms of what they are, and 3) fondness of concrete, nonabstractive and nongeneralizing particulars. Many travelers to China have reported the experience that when asked a question, the Chinese tend to give them item-by-item justifications and rationales with a lot of minute details thrown in before giving the most important information being sought. In evolving a particular idea, they often link a single example to multiple examples and take into account facts that are at variance with or contradict it. Such an evasive speech style has given rise to the use of the word "inscrutable" to describe Chinese verbal behavior.

Speech styles are necessarily the result of particular thought patterns, which in turn are often governed or conditioned by the language structure of a given culture. Although there may have been a philosophical source emphasizing indirectness and rectitude that has helped shape the mode of thought of the Chinese, language structure plays a no less important role. One of the major correlations between language structure and thinking pattern/speech style that distinguishes English from Chinese concerns the relative positions of modifiers and modified in the sentence. In

English, modifiers above the word level, namely adjective phrases, adverbial phrases, prepositional phrases and various kinds of subordinate clauses, are generally postposed, i.e. placed after the words (nouns or verbs) that they modify. In Chinese on the other hand, all the modifiers, be they words, phrases or clauses, are as a rule preposed, i.e. appearing before the words that they modify. Thus, the equivalent of the English relative clause, the least moveable sentence element, occurs before nouns. The English sentence *this is the book I bought yesterday* is expressed in Chinese in such order as 这 是 我 昨 天 买 的 书, literally *this is I yesterday buy book*. Notice that the adverbial of time (*yesterday*) is placed before the verb (*buy*) that it modifies.

The relative positioning of modified and modifier presupposes the pattern of thinking to a large extent. Take for example a complex sentence, one that consists of a principal clause and one subordinate clause. In English, the most important information (action, result, effect, etc.) is contained in the principal clause, which is placed generally before the subordinate clause, where less important information (time, place, manner, reason, condition, concession, etc.) is contained. In Chinese, however, the principal clause invariably appears for the most part after the subordinate clause. This feature of ordering leaves the Chinese with no choice but to present the setting and justifications before dwelling on the main point.

It is interesting, however, to note that there are opposite trends in English and Chinese. In English, there has been a tendency of front-shifting, that is, modifiers that are generally postposed, usually those of the attributive function, are shifted to the front of the element they modify such as the following examples: *he has been living a <u>deadline-driven</u> life, UPS strike jolts I-want-it-now temperament.* Conversely in Chinese, it is found that modifiers, usually those of the adverbial function follow the words they modify. But these are too casual to be representative and they are all used in more or less marked cases. In English, heavy front-shifting are restricted only in journalism or for jocular purposes and in Chinese the postposed modifiers are restricted in sophisticated literary writings or as an after-thought in spontaneous speech. Contrary to Chinese grammatical usage, this practice is often thought of as Westernism or Europeanized sentence making.

11

LESSON

2

NAMES

您 贵 姓?
Nín guì xìng?

What is your family name?

我 姓 王.
Wǒ xìng Wáng.

My family name is Wang.

你 姓 什么?
Nǐ xìng shénme?

What is your family name?

你 叫 什么 名字?
Nǐ jiào shénme míngzi?

What is your name?

我 叫 汤姆.
Wǒ jiào Tāngmǔ.

My name is Tom.

你 有 男 朋友 吗?
Nǐ yǒu nán péngyou ma?

Do you have a boyfriend?

没有.
Méiyǒu.

No, I don't.

CONVERSATIONS

A: 您 贵 姓?
   Nín guì xìng?

What is your family name?

B: 我 姓 王。 你 呢?
   Wǒ xìng Wáng. Nǐ ne?

My family name is Wang. And yours?

A: 我 姓 张。
   Wǒ xìng Zhāng.

My family name is Zhang.

A: 你 姓 什么?
   Nǐ xìng shénme?

What is your family name?

B: 我 姓 李。 你 呢?
   Wǒ xìng Lǐ. Nǐ ne?

My family name is Li. And yours?

A: 我 姓 黄。
   Wǒ xìng Huáng.

My family name is Huang.

A: 你 叫 什么 名字?
   Nǐ jiào shénme míngzi?

What is your name?

B: 我 叫 汤姆。 你 呢?
   Wǒ jiào Tāngmǔ. Nǐ ne?

My name is Tom. And yours?

A: 我 叫 莉萨。
   Wǒ jiào Lìsā.

My name is Lisa.

B: 认识 你 很 高兴。
   Rènshi nǐ hěn gāoxìng.

It's a pleasure to know you.

A: 认识 你 我 也 很 高兴。
   Rènshi nǐ wǒ yě hěn gāoxìng.

It's a pleasure to know you, too.

A: 你 有 男 朋友 吗?
   Nǐ yǒu nán péngyou ma?

Do you have a boyfriend?

B: 没有。 你 有 女 朋友 吗?
   Méiyǒu. Nǐ yǒu nǚ péngyou ma?

No, do you have a girlfriend?

A: 我 有。
   Wǒ yǒu.

Yes, I do.

B: 她 叫 什么 名字?
   Tā jiào shénme míngzi?

What is her name?

A: 她 叫 安娜。
   Tā jiào Ānnà.

Her name is Anna.

A: 你 知道 她的 名字 吗?
   Nǐ zhīdao tāde míngzi ma?

Do you know her name?

B: 不 知 道。你 呢？ No, I don't. And you?
  Bù zhīdao. Nǐ ne?

A: 我 也 不 知 道。 I don't, either.
  Wǒ yě bù zhīdao.

A: 你 是 学生 吗？ Are you a student?
  Nǐ shì xuésheng ma?

B: 不 是, 我 是 工人。 No, I'm a worker.
  Bú shì, wǒ shì gōngrén.

A: 你们的 公司 叫 什么 名字？ What is the name of your company?
  Nǐmende gōngsī jiào shénme míngzi?

B: 我们的 公司 叫 宏 光。 Our company is called Hong Guang.
  Wǒmende gōngsī jiào Hóng Guāng.

A: 谢谢。 Thank you.
  Xièxie.

B: 不 客气。 You are welcome.
  Bú kèqi.

A: 再 见。 Good-bye.
  Zàijiàn.

B: 再 见。 Good-bye.
  Zàijiàn.

WORDS AND EXPRESSIONS

Nouns

姓	xìng	family name
名字	míngzi	name
朋友	péngyou	friend
工人	gōngrén	factory worker
公司	gōngsī	company

Verbs

叫	jiào	call
有	yǒu	have
谢谢	xièxie	thank (you)
再见	zàijiàn	good-bye
客气	kèqi	polite, formal
知道	zhīdao	know

Pronouns

您	nín	you (polite form)

Adjectives

贵	guì	distinguished, expensive
男	nán	male
女	nǚ	female

Adverbs

没	méi	not

Interrogatives

什么	shénme	what

Particles

们	men	plural suffix
的	de	possesive marker

Conjunctions

但是	dànshì	but

SUPPLEMENTARY WORDS AND EXPRESSIONS

Nouns

银行	yínháng	bank
学校	xuéxiào	school
餐馆	cānguǎn	restaurant
人	rén	person, people
同事	tóngshì	colleague
老板	lǎobǎn	boss
市长	shìzhǎng	mayor
校长	xiàozhǎng	principal, president (of a school)
经理	jīnglǐ	manager
儿子	érzi	son
女儿	nǚ'ér	daughter
问题	wèntí	question
中文	Zhōngwén	Chinese language
书	shū	book
面条	miàntiáo	noodle

Verbs

看	kàn	read, see
吃	chī	eat

Adverbs

| 都 | dōu | both, all |

LANGUAGE POINTS

1. 您 (nín)

您 (nín) is a polite form of 你 (nǐ), similar to *vous* in French and *usted* in Spanish. It is used primarily in the northern part of China by a younger person to an older person or between strangers irrespective of age. If the use of 您 (nín) turns out to be too complicated resulting from the consideration of age, rank and status of the person spoken to, you may just stick to 你 (nǐ) on all the occasions. People won't get offended being addressed 你 (nǐ) instead of 您 (nín) by foreigners. Although you may not want to use 您 (nín) to address people, you yourself may hear people address you as 您 (nín).

2. 您贵姓 (nín guì xìng), 你姓什么 (nǐ xìng shénme) and 你叫什么名字 (nǐ jiào shénme míngzi)

您贵姓 (nín guì xìng) is a formula question about someone's family name. It is usually the first question asked when people inquire about each other's names. In this polite and formal expression, 贵 (guì) is an honorific, meaning *honorable* or *respectable*. The whole question literally means *what is your respectable family name*? Sometimes, the subject 您 (nín) can be left out. Refer to the *Cultural Insights* at the end of this lesson for more information on this subject.

你姓什么 (nǐ xìng shénme), literally meaning *you are last-named what*, is an informal question about someone's family name, where 姓 (xìng) is a verb. This expression is used between people who don't want to stand on ceremony or by an adult to a child.

In 你叫什么名字 (nǐ jiào shénme míngzi), the exact meaning of 名字 (míngzi) depends on the context or listener's interpretation or preference. 名字 (míngzi) can be the full name or the given name alone, similar to *name* in *what's your name* in English. This question form is most useful because it can be used not only to ask people's names, but also to ask the names of places and things. It is advisable therefore for foreign students to stick to this expression whenever they want to ask people's names.

3. Wh-question forms

The term *wh-question* is borrowed from English grammar to refer to those questions that require specific, rather than yes/no answers. Wh-questions include *who, whose, what, which, when, where, why* and *how*. Contrary to English where these interrogative words are placed at the beginning of the questions, Chinese keeps them where they belong grammatically and logically in the sentence, thus *what is this* in English would be *this is what* in Chinese, and *what do you like to eat* in English would be *you like to eat what* in Chinese. The status of the sentence as a question is indicated not by placing the question word at the beginning of the sentence, but simply by the presence of this interrogative word. This syntactic feature actually makes it easier for nonnative speakers of Chinese. When asked a wh-question, you just need to address the question word, while keeping everything else intact. There is no need to move sentence constituents around:

你 看 <u>什么</u>?　　　　　　What are you reading?
Nǐ kàn shénme?
我 看 书.　　　　　　　　I'm reading a book.
Wǒ kàn shū.

你喜欢 吃 <u>什么</u>?　　　　What do you like to eat?
Nǐ xǐhuan chī shénme?
我 喜 欢 吃 面条.　　　　　I like to eat noodles.
Wǒ xǐhuan chī miàntiáo.

4. 有 (yǒu)

In many languages, the verb *to have* is peculiar in some way. There is usually a separate chapter in English grammar books on *to have*, because conventional rules do not apply. This is also true of 有 (yǒu) in Chinese, although to a much lesser extent. In Chinese 有 (yǒu) is not negated by 不 (bù), but rather by 没 (méi), which is only used with 有 (yǒu). In other words, 不 (bù) is used with all the verbs and adjectives except one. The one exception is 有 (yǒu). Compare:

我 没有 女朋友.　　　　　I don't have a girlfriend.
Wǒ méiyǒu nǚ péngyou.

她不是我的女朋友.　　　　She is not my girlfriend.
Tā bú shì wǒde nǚ péngyou.

5. 知道 (zhīdao) and 认识 (rènshi)

知道 (zhīdao) and 认识 (rènshi), which both appear in this lesson, are both translated as *to know* in English, but they are used quite differently in Chinese. Generally 知道 (zhīdao) is followed by things, while 认识 (rènshi) is followed by people. Examples are:

我 不认识 他.　　　　　　I don't know him.
Wǒ bú rènshi tā.

我 不 知道 他的 名字.　　　I don't know his name.
Wǒ bù zhīdao tāde míngzi.

Sometimes however, 知道 (zhīdao) can be followed by people and 认识 (rènshi) can be followed by things. When this happens, 知道 (zhīdao) means *to know of* or *be aware of*, and 认识 (rènshi) means *to recognize* or *to acquire the knowledge through learning*, e.g.

我 知道 他, 但是 我 不 认识 他.
Wǒ zhīdao ta, dànshi wǒ bú rènshi tā.

I know of him, but I don't know him.

他 不 认识 路.
Tā bú rènshi lù.

He does not know the way.

你 认识 这 个 字吗?
Nǐ rènshi zhè ge zì ma?

Do you know this character?

6. 谢谢 (xièxie)

谢谢 (xièxie) is not used as much or as excessively in Chinese as *thank you* in English. It is unimaginable to a Chinese that husband and wife, and parents and children say thank you to each other. To the Chinese, to say thank you between husband and wife, between parents and children and between close friends is to treat them as strangers. The use of 谢谢 (xièxie) is often taken as being polite and formal. Thus the response to 谢谢 (xièxie) in Chinese is usually 不客气 (bú kèqi) or 不谢 (bú xiè). 不客气 (bú kèqi) means *don't stand on ceremony*, and 不谢 (bú xiè) is simply *do not have to say thank you*.

7. 们 (men)

们 (men) is a suffix used after personal pronouns and human nouns to form plurals. For example: 我 们 (wǒmen *we*), 你 们 (nǐmen *you*), 他 们 (tāmen *they*), 老 师 们 (lǎoshīmen *teachers*), 学 生 们 (xuéshengmen *students*). In keeping with the single-signal feature of Chinese (refer to the chapter on the Chinese language), 们 (men) cannot be used when there is a number preceding the noun or when the subject is already plural such as:

三 个 老师   not   三 个 老师们
sān ge lǎoshī   sān ge lǎoshīmen

他 们 是 学生.   not   他 们 是 学 生 们.
Tāmen shì xuésheng.   Tāmen shì xuéshengmen.

8. 的 (de)

So far you might have been under the impression that the personal pronouns also double as possessive pronouns in Chinese, as seen in 我 爸 爸 (wǒ bàba *my father*), 你 妈 妈 (nǐ māma *your mother*) and 她 姐 姐 (tā jiějie *her older sister*), but it is not the case. Chinese does have possessive pronouns formed by personal pronouns with the possessive marker 的 (de). For example:

我 的(wǒde *my*), 你 的 (nǐde *your*), 他 的 (tāde *his*), 她 的 (tāde *her*), 我 们 的 (wǒmende *our*), 你 们 的 (nǐmende *your*), and 他 们 的 (tāmende *their*)

It is interesting to note that when talking about family members, we generally drop 的 (de), as in 我 爸 爸 (wǒ bàba *my father*) and 你 妈 妈 (nǐ māma *your mother*). By dropping 的 (de), we make the family relationship even closer. This is an illustration of isomorphism between language and real life. It is not grammatically wrong nevertheless to include 的 (de) with family members, but the use of 的 (de) would imply a contrast or strong sense of possession. Thus, if you want to sound possessive (the pun is intended), you could say 她 是 我 的 太 太 (tā shì wǒde tàitai *she is MY wife*), which implies a contrast: *she is not YOUR wife*.

With relationships outside the family, 的 (de) is optional, depending on the closeness of the relationship. 的 (de) is used when the relationship is distant or aloof and is dropped when the relationship is close.

When what is possessed is a place, 的 (de) is optional, but its presence or absence has an implied meaning. The absence of 的 (de) implies that the subject is either a member of, or is identified with the place, whereas the presence of 的 (de) simply indicates a possessive relationship. For example, 这 是 我 们 中 文 系 (zhè shì wǒmen Zhōngwén xì) not only means that *this is our Chinese Department*, it also suggests that the speaker is a member of the department. 这 是 我 们 的 中 文 系 (zhè shì wǒmende Zhōngwén xì) does not have the suggestion that the previous sentence does. The sentence could be said by anyone at the university to a visitor. This also explains why we never use 的 (de) when we say *my home* or *your home*: 我 家 (wǒ jiā) and 你 家 (nǐ jiā) unless we want to emphasize the possessive relationship or show contrast.

With objects, the use of 的 (de) is usually obligatory such as 我 的 书 (wǒde shū *my book*), 他 们 的 汽 车 (tāmende qìchē *their car*).

Apart from being used with personal pronouns to form possessive pronouns, 的 (de) is also used as a possessive similar to apostrophe *s* in English. While English has two possessive forms: apostrophe *s* and the *of* genitive, Chinese has only one form. 的 (de) is used after both animate nouns and inanimate nouns to show possessive relationships. For example:

学 校 的 老 师 xuéxiào de lǎoshī	school's teacher(s)
老 师 的 书 lǎoshī de shū	teacher(s)'s book(s)
公 司 的 名 字 gōngsī de míngzi	name of the company

EXERCISES

I. Answer the following questions:

1. 你 姓 什么?
   Nǐ xìng shénme?
2. 你 叫 什么 名字?
   Nǐ jiào shénme míngzi?

3. 你们的　中文　　老师　叫　什么　名字?
   Nǐmende Zhōngwén lǎoshī jiào shénme míngzi?
4. 你认识 你们　中文　　老师　的 太太 吗? 她 叫 什么　　名字?
   Nǐ rènshi nǐmen Zhōngwén lǎoshī de tàitai ma? Tā jiào shénme míngzi?
5. 你的 学校/　公司　叫　什么　　名字?
   Nǐde xuéxiào/gōngsī jiào shénme míngzi?
6. 你 有　姐 姐 吗? 她 叫　什么　名字?
   Nǐ yǒu jiějie ma? Tā jiào shénme míngzi?
7. 你 有　中 国　　朋 友　吗? 他/她/他 们 叫 什 么 名字?
   Nǐ yǒu Zhōngguó péngyou ma? Tā/tā/tāmen jiào shénme míngzi?
8. 你的 中文　　书 叫 什 么 名字?
   Nǐde Zhōngwén shū jiào shénme míngzi?
9. 你 的 中文　　老师 忙　　吗?
   Nǐde Zhōngwén lǎoshī máng ma?
10. 你的 银行　叫 什么　名字?
    Nǐde yínháng jiào shénme míngzi?

II. Translate the following conversations into Chinese:

1. Do you know his girlfriend's name?
   No. I don't.
2. Do you know my Chinese teacher?
   Yes, I do.
3. Is your family name Wang?
   No. My family name is Zhang.
4. Do you know him?
   I heard of him, but I don't know him.
5. Are you Mr. Zhao's wife?
   Yes, I am.
   It's a pleasure to know you.
   It's a pleasure to know you, too.

III. Translate the following sentences into Chinese:

1. What is this?
2. She is my older brother's girlfriend.
3. I know of her, but I don't know her.
4. My wife's name is Lily.
5. His daughter doesn't have any Chinese friends.

IV. Change the following into negative sentences:

1. 她 有　男　朋 友.
   Tā yǒu nán péngyou.

2. 我 叫 大卫.
   Wǒ jiào Dàwèi.
3. 我们的 中文 老师 姓 王.
   Wǒmende Zhōngwén lǎoshī xìng Wáng.
4. 我 妈妈很 高兴.
   Wǒ māma hěn gāoxìng.
5. 她有 儿子.
   Tā yǒu érzi.
6. 他太太有 哥哥.
   Tā tàitai yǒu gēge.
7. 我 认识她先生.
   Wǒ rènshi tā xiānsheng.
8. 他们 有 美国 朋友.
   Tāmen yǒu Měiguó péngyou.
9. 我 爸爸很 忙.
   Wǒ bàba hěn máng.
10. 我们 去中国.
    Wǒmen qù Zhōngguó.

V. Translate the following into English:

1. 我 有 哥哥, 也 有 姐姐. 哥哥 叫 小 华, 姐姐 叫 小 君.
   Wǒ yǒu gēge, yě yǒu jiějie. Gēge jiào Xiǎo Huá, jiějie jiǎo Xiǎo Jūn.
2. 我 认识 你妈妈 很 高兴.
   Wǒ rènshi nǐ māma hěn gāoxìng.
3. 她的 男 朋友 不 是 汤姆, 是 大卫.
   Tāde nán péngyou bú shì Tāngmǔ, shì Dàwèi.
4. 你的 中国 朋友 叫 什么 名字?
   Nǐde Zhōngguó péngyou jiào shénme míngzi?
5. 我 爸爸 妈妈 都 姓 黄.
   Wǒ bàba māma dōu xìng Huáng.

CULTURAL INSIGHTS

Like English names, Chinese names also consists of two parts—a given name and a family name. In Chinese however, the family name precedes, instead of following, the given name. Traditionally, the given name consists of two characters, one of which is the generation name and the other one is what may be called the distinguishing given name. The generation name is shared by all the siblings in the family and all the people in the lineage who belong to the same generation. For example, in a Kong family with four children named Kong Ling Qi, Kong Ling Hua, Kong Ling Fei and Kong Ling Tao, Kong is the family name, Ling is the generation name that identifies where the siblings belong on the genealogical ladder and Qi, Hua, Fei and Tao are that part of the given name that distinguishes the siblings one from another. In addition, all the cousins of the children on the father's side will have Ling as part of their given name. Their names will also begin with Kong Ling. In contemporary China and particularly in the urban area, more and more parents are breaking away from the tradition by leaving out the generation name. It has almost become a trendy thing for parents to give their children a one-character given name. If you recall the syllabic structure and limited possibility of sound combinations in Chinese discussed in the chapter on Chinese phonetics, it is not difficult to imagine that there are numerous namesakes in China. United Press International (UPI) recently reported that a survey conducted by the Chinese Character Reform Committee revealed the severity of the problems: 4,800 people named 梁淑珍 (Liáng Shù Zhēn) shared the exact same characters in the city of Shenyang alone. If there are so many namesakes with a two-character given name, the situation with a one-character given name is even worse. Now the Chinese government is calling on parents to give a two-character given name to their children to cut down the number of namesakes. When choosing a two-character given name, parents, particularly those in the urban area again, are no longer bound by the generation names that their ancestors or lineage elders prescribed for their children. They are free to pick any name to their liking.

Unlike people in the West, Chinese people are not very comfortable calling each other by their first or given names. First names are reserved only for family members and a selected number of really close friends. Professional colleagues are seldom "on the first-name basis," even though they may be very close. Intimacy between them is not indicated by the use of the first name, but by other means. One of these means is to prefix the word 老 (lǎo *old*) or 小 (xiǎo *young*) to the family name such as 老王 (Lǎo Wáng) and 小马 (Xiǎo Mǎ). 老 (lǎo) is generally used for middle-aged or old people, while 小 (xiǎo) is used for young people. Since Chinese people are not used to addressing people other than their family members or very close friends by their given names, they are usually content with knowing the family name of the people they meet for the first time. Very often they do not even bother to ask their given name after they asked "您贵姓" (nín guì xìng) or "你姓什么" (nǐ xìng shénme). What's the use of knowing somebody's first name if you are never going to use it?

LESSON

3

PLACES

SENTENCE PATTERNS

请问, ...?　　　　　　　　　　　　　　May I please ask, ...?
Qǐngwèn, ...?

中国　银行　在　哪儿?　　　　　　　　Where is the Bank of China?
Zhōngguó Yínháng zài nǎr?

你在哪儿工作?　　　　　　　　　　　　Where do you work?
Nǐ zài nǎr　gōngzuò?

你妈妈在家吗?　　　　　　　　　　　　Is your mother home?
Nǐ māma zài jiā ma?

中国城　　有中国　餐馆.　　　　　　　There are Chinese restaurants in Chinatown.
Zhōngguóchéng yǒu Zhōngguó cānguǎn.

哪儿有　厕所?　　　　　　　　　　　　Where can I find a restroom?
Nǎr　yǒu cèsuǒ?

这儿有　中国　餐馆　吗?　　　　　　　Is there a Chinese restaurant here?
Zhèr　yǒu Zhōngguó cānguǎn ma?

你去哪儿?　　　　　　　　　　　　　　Where are you going?
Nǐ qù nǎr?

23

CONVERSATIONS

A: 请问， 你工作 吗?
Qǐngwèn, nǐ gōngzuò ma?

May I please ask, do you work?

B: 工作。
Gōngzuò.

Yes, I do.

A: 你的单位 在哪儿?
Nǐde dānwèi zài nǎr?

Where is your workplace?

B: 我的 单位 在北京。
Wǒde dānwèi zài Běijīng.

My workplace is in Beijing.

A: 你妈妈 在家吗?
Nǐ māma zài jiā ma?

Is your mother home?

B: 不在。
Bú zài.

No, she is not.

A: 她在 哪儿?
Tā zài nǎr?

Where is she?

B: 她在学校。
Tā zài xuéxiào.

She is at school.

A: 请问， 中国 银行 在哪儿?
Qǐngwèn, Zhōngguó Yínháng zài nǎr?

Excuse me, where is the Bank of China?

B: 中国 银行 在中国城。
Zhōngguó Yínháng zài Zhōngguóchéng.

The Bank of China is in Chinatown.

A: 中国城 远 吗?
Zhōngguóchéng yuǎn ma?

Is Chinatown far?

B: 不太远。
Bú tài yuǎn.

Not too far.

A: 请问， 你在哪儿工作?
Qǐngwèn, nǐ zài nǎr gōngzuò?

Excuse me, where do you work?

B: 我 在公司 工作。
Wǒ zài gōngsī gōngzuò.

I work in a company.

A: 你在 什么 公司 工作?
Nǐ zài shénme gōngsī gōngzuò?

What company do you work for?

B: 我 在电话 公司 工作。
Wǒ zài diànhuà gōngsī gōngzuò.

I work for the telephone company.

A: 请问， 你在哪儿住?
Qǐngwèn, nǐ zài nǎr zhù?

Excuse me, where do you live?

B: 我 在曼哈顿 住。
Wǒ zài Mànhādùn zhù.

I live in Manhattan.

A: 曼哈顿 在哪儿?   Where is Manhattan?
 Mànhǎdùn zài nǎr?

B: 曼哈顿 在纽约。   It is in New York.
 Mànhǎdùn zài Niǔ Yuē.

A: 你学 中文 吗?   Do you study Chinese?
 Nǐ xué Zhōngwén ma?

B: 学。   Yes, I do.
 Xué.

A: 你在哪儿学 中文?   Where do you study Chinese?
 Nǐ zài nǎr xué Zhōngwén?

B: 我 在纽约 大学学 中文。   I study Chinese at New York University.
 Wǒ zài Niǔ Yuē Dàxué xué Zhōngwén.

A: 你的中文 老师是中国人 吗?   Is your Chinese teacher Chinese?
 Nǐde Zhōngwén lǎoshī shì Zhōngguórén ma?

B: 是。   Yes.
 Shì.

A: 他叫 什么 名字?   What is his name?
 Tā jiào shénme míngzi?

B: 他叫 李华。   His name is Li Hua.
 Tā jiào Lǐ Huá.

A: 请问, 这儿有 厕所吗?   Excuse me, is there a restroom here?
 Qǐngwèn, zhèr yǒu cèsuǒ ma?

B: 有, 在 那儿。   Yes, it's over there.
 Yǒu, zài nàr.

A: 谢谢。   Thank you.
 Xièxie.

B: 不 客气。   You are welcome.
 Bú kèqi.

A: 请问, 这儿有 中国 餐馆 吗?   Excuse me, is there a Chinese restaurant
 Qǐngwèn, zhèr yǒu Zhōngguó cānguǎn ma?   here?

B: 没有。   No, there is not.
 Méiyǒu.

A: 哪儿有 中国 餐馆?   Where can I find a Chinese restaurant?
 Nǎr yǒu Zhōngguó cānguǎn?

B: 中国城 有 中国 餐馆。   There are Chinese restaurants in Chinatown.
 Zhōngguóchéng yǒu Zhōngguó cānguǎn.

A: 中国城 有 日本餐馆 吗?   Are there Japanese restaurants in
 Zhōngguóchéng yǒu Rìběn cānguǎn ma?   Chinatown?

B: 没有。   No, there are not.
 Méi yǒu.

WORDS AND EXPRESSIONS

<u>Nouns</u>

单位	dānwèi	workplace
家	jiā	home, family
电话	diànhuà	telephone
大学	dàxué	university
人	rén	person, people
厕所	cèsuǒ	restroom
城	chéng	town, city
曼哈顿	Mànhādùn	Manhattan
纽约	Niǔ Yuē	New York

<u>Verbs</u>

工作	gōngzuò	work
住	zhù	live
学	xué	study

<u>Adjectives</u>

远	yuǎn	far

<u>Prepositions</u>

在	zài	in, at

<u>Adverbs</u>

这儿	zhèr	here
那儿	nàr	there
太	tài	too

<u>Interrogatives</u>

哪儿	nǎr	what place

<u>Expressions</u>

请问	qǐngwèn	May I ask ...

SUPPLEMENTARY WORDS AND EXPRESSIONS

商店	shāngdiàn	store
电影院	diànyǐngyuàn	movie theater

医院	yīyuàn	hospital
邮局	yóujú	post office
公园	gōngyuán	park
图书馆	túshūguǎn	library
办公室	bàngōngshì	office
公安局	gōng'ānjú	police station
博物馆	bówùguǎn	museum
教堂	jiàotáng	church
汽车站	qìchēzhàn	bus stop
火车站	huǒchēzhàn	train station
飞机场	fēijīchǎng	airport
饭店	fàndiàn	hotel

北京	Běijīng	Beijing
上海	Shànghǎi	Shanghai
南京	Nánjīng	Nanjing
旧金山	Jiùjīnshān	San Francisco
洛杉矶	Luòshānjī	Los Angeles
加州	Jiāzhōu	California

LANGUAGE POINTS

1. 请问 (qǐngwèn)

请问 (qǐngwèn) is a polite attention-getter. It literally means *may I please ask*. However confusion may arise due to its frequent translation into *excuse me* in English. To translate the expression into *excuse me* is fine in this context, but to apply it to situations where you caused somebody inconvenience such as stepping on his toes is totally wrong. In other words, 请问 (qǐngwèn) is only equivalent to one of the meanings of *excuse me* in English. It is generally used when you would like to ask somebody his or her name, direction or a question.

2. 中国银行在哪儿 (Zhōngguó Yínháng zài nǎr)

The pattern used to ask where something or some place is "_____ 在哪儿 (zài nǎr)?" In this pattern, 在 (zài) is a preposition, meaning *in* or *at*, and 哪儿 (nǎr) means *what place*. 中国银行在哪儿 (Zhōngguó Yínháng zài nǎr) literally means "the Bank of China is in what place". It would be wrong to add 是 (shì) in the sentence (中国银行是在哪儿 Zhōngguó Yínháng shì zài nǎr), although you may be tempted to do so as an English speaker. If you recall, we only use 是 (shì) when the words at either side of it are both nouns and have the same referent.

Note also that the noun placed at the beginning of the pattern is specific and definite. This is the most important way in Chinese to indicate specificity and definiteness. Thus in

27

书 在 哪 儿? Shū zài nǎr?	Where is the book?
餐 馆 在 哪 儿? Cānguǎn zài nǎr?	Where is the restaurant?
厕 所 在 哪 儿? Cèsuǒ zài nǎr?	Where is the restroom?

书 (shū *book*), 餐 馆 (cānguǎn *restaurant*) and 厕 所 (cèsuǒ *restroom*) refer to a specific book, restaurant and restroom instead of unspecified, general or indefinite ones.

3. 你在哪儿工作 (nǐ zài nǎr gōngzuò)

This sentence consists of three parts: subject 你 (nǐ *you*), adverbial phrase 在 哪 儿 (zài nǎr *where*) and verb 工 作 (gōngzuò *work*). The only difference between English and Chinese in this sentence is that the adverbial of place precedes the verb in Chinese instead of following it as in English.

4. 你 在 什 么 公 司 工 作 (Nǐ zài shénme gōngsī gōngzuò)?

This sentence may be translated idiomatically into English as *what company do you work for*, but the preposition actually used is 在 (zài), which means *in* or *at*. To the Chinese, you always work IN a company, nor FOR a company. If you really want to say *for a company*, you'll have to use another preposition 给 (gěi), but that is not as common as 在 (zài), which is what most people would use.

5. 中 国 城 有 中 国 银 行 (Zhōngguóchéng yǒu Zhōngguó Yínháng)

This is a so-called existential sentence similar to the "there is/are" structure in English. The pattern for existential sentences in Chinese is Adverbial of place + 有 (yǒu, *there is/are*) + Subject. Again the adverbial of place precedes, instead of follows, the verb 有 (yǒu). *There is a Bank of China in Chinatown* is thus expressed in Chinese as 中 国 城 有 中 国 银 行 (Zhōngguóchéng yǒu Zhōngguó Yínháng).

Please note that whenever 在 (zài) appears at the beginning of an existential sentence, it is usually dropped. The result of the deletion in the following sentences is:

(在) 这 儿 有 日 本 餐 馆. (Zài) zhèr yǒu Rìběn cānguǎn.	There is a Japanese restaurant here.
(在) 那 儿 有 女 厕 所. (Zài) nàr yǒu nǚ cèsuǒ.	There is a lady's room there.
(在) 学 校 有 学 生. (Zài) xuéxiào yǒu xuésheng.	There are students in the school.

If we compare this pattern with the pattern in 银行在哪儿 (yínháng zài nǎr), we'll find that the noun phrase in the former is not specified or definite, whereas the noun phrase in the latter is definite and specified, as discussed earlier on. This word order feature conforms to the tendency of human languages to place definite or specified items at or towards the beginning of the sentence, and indefinite or unspecified items at or towards the end of the sentence. It appears abrupt, bearing no cohesive tie with the previous discourse and leaving little room for the listener to make necessary connections and respond. The awkwardness immediately disappears as soon as we push the indefinite item towards the end of the sentence by adding *there is* before it. The following are perfect English existential sentences:

> There is a book on the desk.
> Compare: A book is on the desk.

> There are many universities in Beijing.
> Compare: Many universities are in Beijing.

This principal is even more strictly adhered to in Chinese because it does not have the flexibility of an article system to indicate definteness except by word order whereby a definite item is placed first in the sentence, and an indefinite item is placed later in the sentence.

6. 哪儿有中国银行 (nǎr yǒu Zhōngguó Yínháng)

If you have read the last point, it won't be difficulty to understand the question "哪儿有中国银行 (nǎr yǒu Zhōngguó Yínháng)". The pattern explained in 2 is used when we need to know where something or some place is, whereas the pattern illustrated in this question is used when we want to get confirmation whether there is something or some place in some particular place. Sometimes, however, we simply want to know where (i.e. in any place) we can find a certain object or place. In this case, we are actually questioning the first part of the pattern: location + 有 (yǒu) + object". Since we are questioning a location, the interrogative word that we use is naturally 哪儿 (nǎr). Thus we have 哪儿有中国银行 (nǎr yǒu Zhōngguó Yínháng). To respond to the question, all we need to do is to supply the answer where the interrogative word is in the question such as 中国城有中国银行 (Zhōngguóchéng yǒu Zhōngguó Yínháng).

Again, keep in mind that 在 (zài), which would otherwise precede 哪儿 (nǎr), is dropped because it would appear at the beginning of an existential sentence.

EXERCISES

I. Answer the following questions:

1. 你在哪儿住?
   Nǐ zài nǎr   zhù?

2. 你工作 吗? 你在哪儿工作?
   Nǐ gōngzuò ma? Nǐ zài nǎr gōngzuò?
3. 你的单位 叫 什 么 名字?
   Nǐde dānwèi jiào shénme míngzi?
4. 你的单位 远 吗?
   Nǐde dānwèi yuǎn ma?
5. 你在哪儿学 中文?
   Nǐ zǎi nǎr xué Zhōngwén?
6. 纽 约 有 中国城 吗?
   Niǔ Yuē yóu Zhōngguóchéng ma?
7. 哪 儿有 日 本 城?
   Nǎr yǒu Rìběnchéng?
8. 曼哈顿 在哪儿?
   Mànhǎdùn zài nǎr?
9. 你妈妈在 医 院 工 作 吗?
   Nǐ māma zài yīyuàn gōngzuò ma?
10. 你的学 校 有 中国 老师吗?
    Nǐde xuéxiào yǒu Zhōngguó lǎoshī ma?

II. Fill in the blanks with appropriate words:

1. 你家 _____ 哪 儿?
   Nǐ jiā_____ nǎr?
2. _____ 有 医 院?
   _____ yǒu yīyuàn?
3. 这 儿 _____ 中文 学校 吗?
   Zhèr _____ Zhōngwén xuéxiào ma?
4. 你在 _____ 学 中文?
   Nǐ zài _____ xué Zhōngwén?
5. 那 儿 _____ 有 日 本 餐馆.
   Nàr _____ yǒu Rìběn cānguǎn.
6. 女 厕所 _____ 那 儿.
   Nǚ cèsuǒ _____ nàr.
7. 我 的 男 朋友 在上海 _____ .
   Wǒde nán péngyou zài Shànghǎi _____ .
8. _____ 在哪儿?
   _____ zài nǎr?
9. 哪 儿 _____ 银 行?
   Nǎr _____ yínháng?
10. 你去 _____ ?
    Nǐ qù _____ ?

III. Translate the following into Chinese:

1. Excuse me, where is the men's room?

2. Excuse me, is there an American town in Beijing?
3. My wife works in a school.
4. His girlfriend studies at Nanjing University.
5. There is no Chinese restaurant here.
6. My mother is not a doctor. She is a teacher.
7. Our Chinese teacher lives in San Francisco.
8. My mother is not home.
9. Are your parents going to the restaurant?
10. The hospital is not there.

IV. Translate the following into English:

1. 北京 没有 美国 银行.
   Běijīng méiyǒu Měiguó yínháng.
2. 我 在学校 工作. 我 太太也在学校 工作.
   Wǒ zài xuéxiào gōngzuò. Wǒ tàitai yě zài xuéxiào gōngzuò.
3. 纽约 没有 日本城. 洛杉矶 有.
   Niǔ Yuē méiyǒu Rìběnchéng. Luòshānjī yǒu.
4. 请问, 火车站 在哪儿?
   Qǐngwèn, huǒchēzhàn zài nǎr?
5. 请问, 哪儿有 商店?
   Qǐng wèn, nǎr yǒu shāngdiàn?
6. 你们的学校 叫 什么 名字?
   Nǐmende xuéxiào jiào shénme míngzi?
7. 纽约 的中国城 有 日本 餐馆 吗?
   Niǔ Yuē de Zhōngguóchéng yǒu Rìběn cānguǎn ma?
8. 我 不知道 厕所在哪儿. 他知道.
   Wǒ bù zhīdao cèsuǒ zài nǎr. Tā zhīdao.
9. 你去哪儿? 我 去飞机场.
   Nǐ qù nǎr? Wǒ qù fēijīchǎng.
10. 我 爸爸妈妈在加州 住.
    Wǒ bàba māma zài Jiāzhōu zhù.

V. Write a paragraph introducing yourself (who you are, what your name is, where you work or study, etc.).

CULTURAL INSIGHTS

It won't take observant travelers to China very long to find the attention given by the Chinese to *danwei*. When you make a phone call to a business, a hospital, a factory, a school, or a government office, chances are that you will be asked to identify yourself first. When you do this, what the party at the other end of the line expects to hear is what *danwei* you work for. If you need to visit some *danwei* for business purposes, you would be asked to produce an introduction letter from your *danwei*, without which nobody would even talk to you. Until a few years ago, such a *danwei* introduction letter was indispensable whenever you wanted to check into a hotel or buy a soft seat train ticket or a plane ticket.

The Chinese are obsessed with *danwei* for a simple reason. It is an inescapable part of their life. To be exact, the *danwei* holds the reins of their life. As a basic organizational unit in the urban sector, the *danwei* is not only the place where people report to work, but also the focal point in their domestic and social life. Many of the functions that are deemed social, individual, domestic and governmental in other societies are assumed by the *danwei*.

In most cases, the *danwei* provides housing for its employees, often on its premises. Unless you are very wealthy, which most Chinese are not, and can afford to buy a private apartment that has become available in recent years, you are at the mercy of your *danwei*. Many young people have to shelve their plans for marriage simply because they have not been assigned an apartment due to their lack of seniority. Since the *danwei* is the ultimate owner of the residential units, it collects rents and utility payments from its employees, often by deducting them from the employees' salary.

The *danwei* is the primary enforcer of the government's public policies. Take for example the family planning program, particularly the single-birth policy. The *danwei* gives rewards to those who comply and metes out punishment to those who don't. The *danwei* very often makes sure that newlyweds time their childbearing schedule so that it won't exceed the quota allocated them for the number of births in a given period. It is also the responsibility of the *danwei* to distribute and monitor the use of contraceptive devices.

The *danwei* is also bound up with just about any other aspect of employees' domestic life. It runs nurseries, day care centers, and even schools. The *danwei* has to give its stamp of approval before one registers with the government for a marriage certificate. When there is a domestic dispute, the *danwei* often serves as the mediator or arbitrator. More importantly, the *danwei* is the one that pays your medical bills, partially or fully depending on the nature of its ownership.

Since the decollectivization and privatization in the rural areas that started towards the end of the 70s, prices of staple food and meat have shot up. The increase brought about a chain reaction in the increase of the cost of consumer products and services. As a result, the government has been subsidizing the urban residents. Various types of subsidies for grain, oil, pork, transportation, traveling and even personal hygienic activities such as haircut are administered and dispensed through the *danwei*.

Deregulation and privatization in recent years are creating a polarity of wealth in the population. Many people, especially those who are in "nonprofit" *danweis*, such as schools, and government departments are increasingly feeling uneasy as their friends and relatives in other "profit" *danweis* or the private sector are getting rich. These non-profit *danweis* have been under tremendous pressure to improve the life of their employees by putting more money into their pocket in the form of bonuses on a regular basis. The additional money is usually generated by operating some sideline businesses. It is commonplace nowadays to see schools running stores and government services running shops.

It is evident that the *danwei* is a self-contained or even self-sufficient community in the true sense of the word. As such, it has become an effective means of social control by the state to limit the mobility and maintain social stability in the urban sector. You depend on your *danwei* not just for a living, you depend on your *danwei* when you need to get married, when you are ready to have a child, when you are sick and when you need to receive government benefits. You even depend on your *danwei* when you want to resign your job and take up another one at a different *danwei*. This is because if your current *danwei* does not grant you an approval by releasing your personnel dossier that it keeps for each of its employees, you are not going anywhere even though there is an enticing offer from another *danwei*.

LESSON

4

FAMILY

SENTENCE PATTERNS

你家有几口人？
Nǐ jiā yǒu jǐ kǒu rén?

How many people are there in your family?

他们是谁？
Tāmen shì shuí?

Who are they?

你爸爸作什么工作？
Nǐ bàba zuò shénme gōngzuò?

What work does your father do?

你有几本中文书？
Nǐ yǒu jǐ běn Zhōngwén shū?

How many Chinese books do you have?

她有多少学生？
Tā yǒu duōshao xuésheng?

How many students does she have?

他在哪个学校工作？
Tā zài nǎ ge xuéxiào gōngzuò?

Which school does he work in?

你女儿是不是大学生？
Nǐ nǚ'ér shì bu shì dàxuéshēng?

Is your daughter a college student?

你有没有孩子？
Nǐ yǒu méiyǒu háizi?

Do you have any children?

CONVERSATIONS

A: 你家有 几 口 人?
Nǐ jiā yǒu jǐ kǒu rén?

How many people are there in your family?

B: 我 家有 五 口 人。
Wǒ jiā yǒu wǔ kǒu rén.

There are five people in my family.

A: 他们 是谁?
Tāmen shì shuí?

Who are they?

B: 他们 是我 爸爸, 我 妈妈,
Tā men shì wǒ bàba, wǒ māma,
我 姐姐, 我 弟弟 和 我。
wǒ jiějie, wǒ dìdi hé wǒ.

They are my father, my mother, my older sister, my younger brother and myself.

A: 你家有 几 口 人?
Nǐ jiā yǒu jǐ kǒu rén?

How many people are there in your family?

B: 我 家有 四 口 人。
Wǒ jiā yǒu sì kǒu rén.

There are four people in my family.

A: 他们 是谁?
Tāmen shì shuí?

Who are they?

B: 他们 是 我 太太, 我 女儿,
Tāmen shì wǒ tàitai, wǒ nǚ'ér,
我 儿子 和 我。
wǒ érzi hé wǒ.

They are my wife, my daughter, my son and myself..

A: 你女儿 是 不 是 大学生?
Nǐ nǚ'ér shì bu shì dàxuésheng?

Is your daughter a college student?

B: 不 是。 她 是 中学生。
Bú shì. Tā shì zhōngxuésheng.

No, she is not. She is a middle school student.

A: 你儿子 呢?
Nǐ érzi ne?

What about your son?

B: 他 是 小学生。
Tā shì xiǎoxuésheng.

He is an elementary school student.

A: 你有 没有 孩子?
Nǐ yǒu méiyou háizi?

Do you have any children?

B: 有。
Yǒu.

Yes, I do.

A: 你有 几 个孩子?
Nǐ yǒu jǐ ge háizi?

How many children do you have?

B: 我 有 两 个孩子。一个男孩,
Wǒ yǒu liǎng ge háizi. Yí ge nánhái,
一个女孩。
yí ge nǚhái.

I have two, one boy and one girl.

35

A: 你 太太 在 什么 单位 工作?
Nǐ tàitai zài shénme dānwèi gōngzuò?

Where does your wife work?

B: 她 在 学校 工作.
Tā zài xuéxiào gōngzuò.

She works in a school.

A: 她 作 什么 工作?
Tā zuò shénme gōngzuò?

What work does she do?

B: 她 是 老师.
Tā shì lǎoshī.

She is a teacher.

A: 她 忙 不忙?
Tā máng bu máng?

Is she busy?

B: 她 很 忙.
Tā hěn máng.

Yes, she is.

A: 她 有 多少 学生?
Tā yǒu duōshao xuésheng?

How many students does she have?

B: 她 有 五十 个 学生.
Tā yǒu wǔshí ge xuésheng.

She has fifty students.

A: 你 有 哥哥 吗?
Nǐ yǒu gēge ma?

Do you have older brothers?

B: 有.
Yǒu.

Yes, I do.

A: 你 有 几个 哥哥?
Nǐ yǒu jǐ ge gēge?

How many older brothers do you have?

B: 我 有 一个 哥哥.
Wǒ yǒu yí ge gēge.

I have one older brother.

A: 你 哥哥 工作 吗?
Nǐ gēge gōngzuò ma?

Does your older brother work?

B: 他 不工作, 他 是 学生.
Tā bù gōngzuò, tā shì xuésheng.

No, he is a student.

A: 他 在 哪个 学校 学习?
Tā zài nǎ ge xuéxiào xuéxí?

Which school does he study in?

B: 他 在 纽约 大学 学习.
Tā zài Niǔ Yuē Dàxué xuéxí.

He studies at New York University.

A: 他 学 什么?
Tā xué shénme?

What does he study?

B: 他 学 历史.
Tā xué lìshǐ.

He studies history.

A: 他 喜欢 历史 吗?
Tā xǐhuan lìshǐ ma?

Does he like history?

B: 很 喜欢.
Hěn xǐhuan.

Very much.

36

WORDS AND EXPRESSIONS

Nouns

历史	lìshǐ	history
男孩	nánhái	boy
女孩	nǚhái	girl
大学生	dàxuésheng	university/college student
中学生	zhōngxuésheng	secondary school student
小学生	xiǎoxuésheng	elementary school student

Verbs

作	zuò	do
学习	xuéxí	study

Interrogatives

几	jǐ	question word about numbers
多少	duōshao	question word about numbers
谁	shuí	who
哪	nǎ	which

Numerals

零	líng	zero
一	yī	one
二	èr	two
三	sān	three
四	sì	four
五	wǔ	five
六	liù	six
七	qī	seven
八	bā	eight
九	jiǔ	nine
十	shí	ten

Conjunctions

和	hé	and

Classifiers

个	ge	
本	běn	
口	kǒu	

SUPPLEMENTARY WORDS AND EXPRESSIONS

Nouns

爷爷	yéye	paternal grandfather
奶奶	năinai	paternal grandmother
外公	wàigōng	maternal grandfather
外婆	wàipó	maternal grandmother

Numerals

百	băi	hundred
千	qiān	thousand
万	wàn	ten thousand

LANGUAGE POINTS

1. How to read numbers in Chinese

　　Numbers from 0 to 10 are given in *Words and Expressions*. To read the numbers beyond 10, just insert the place name after each number such as # + place name + # + place number + # + place name, etc. The place names for tens, hundreds and thousands are: 十 (shí), 百 (băi), and 千 (qiān). Please note that there is an important difference between English and Chinese in expressing 10,000. English doesn't have a place name for it, using a composite number instead. Chinese, on the other hand, does have a place for 10,000 called 万 (wàn). Thus, a number like 12,345 should be read as 一万二千三百四十五 (yī wàn èr qiān sān băi sì shí wŭ).

　　When zero appears, the place name is not read since it does not have a value. For example 103, 4,056, and 70,809 should be read as 一百零三 (yì băi líng sān), 四千零五十六 (sì qiān líng wŭ shí liù) and 七万零八百零九 (qī wàn líng bā băi líng jiŭ).

　　Place names in Chinese beyond 10,000 are very different from English, please refer to the *Cultural Insight* section of Lesson 8 for more information.

2. Classifiers

　　Mention was made in the introductory chapter on Chinese that whenever we use a number in Chinese to quantify a noun such as *a person*, *twenty books* and *three hundred cars*, we must use a classifier between the number and the noun, somewhat similar to *a piece of paper*, *two heads of lettuce* and *three cups of coffee* in English. This similarity, however, is very limited in that these "classifiers" are only used occasionally in English, but are always present in Chinese whenever a number and a noun come together. Another major difference between the two languages is that if the "classifiers" are used in English, they are actually measure words, but for the most part in Chinese, they do not indicate any measure. They serve a special function in the language by classifying particular nouns into semantic groups. For this reason, they should be called "classifiers" rather than "measure words" as in many other textbooks. Please note that it is not true that for every noun in the language there is a specific classifier. A particular classifier is often shared by a number of nouns having the same underlying semantic feature. The most commonly used classifiers in Chinese amount to probably less than twenty. When you reach the end of this book, you may only come across seven or eight of them at the most. It may be a good exercise to ask a native speaker to give you a classifier and a number of nouns that use the classifier to see if you can find the underlying semantic feature. You may be surprised to find that most native speakers do not know the answers unless they are linguistically trained simply because they have been brought up speaking the language, not questioning about the language. Although classifiers seem to impose an extra burden on your memory, they do add precision to the language and reveal how certain things are perceived by the native speakers. Two examples would suffice. The following words use the classifier 本 (běn): *book, dictionary, photo album, magazine,* and *atlas.* What is it that they have in common? They are all bound, printed, or book-like materials. The following words use the classifier 件 (jiàn): *shirt, blouse* (in fact there is only one word in Chinese for both shirt and blouse), *sweater, blazer, jacket* and *coat.* If you think that the classifier is used for clothing, you are very close, but not exactly right, because it is not used for pants, skirt and shorts. With this clue, you may finally come to the conclusion that 件 (jiàn) is used for clothing that you wear on the upper part of your body.

What happens if you do not use a classifier between a number and a noun? In most cases, native speakers simply do not understand you. This is because they are linguistically programmed to expect to hear something (a classifier) in that syntactic slot. What happens if you did use a classifier but it was a wrong one? In most cases, native speakers will understand you, but they will laugh, sometimes hysterically. This is because classifiers group nouns together according to certain underlying semantic features. As such they are usually associated with certain images. Some classifiers are used for animals, others indicate appearances and shapes. If you use the wrong classifier, you will conjure up wrong images that will make people laugh. In fact, the deliberate misuse of classifiers is a great source of humor in Chinese. Children make mistakes using classifiers all the time. What do you do if you want the native speakers to understand, but you don't want them to laugh when you use a wrong classifier? Fortunately, there is a way. Whenever you are stuck with any classifier, use 个 (gè) instead. This is because 个 (gè) is the most frequently used classifier in Chinese. It is used for people and most objects. Chances are the classifier that you are stuck for is 个 (gè) anyway. Second, the word 个 (gè), literally meaning *piece* or *entity,* is not associated with any particular image. When there is no image, people have no reason to laugh. In addition, native speakers often use 个 (gè) for nouns that should be used with some other specific classifiers. Please also note that 个 is usually pronounced in the neutral tone.

3. 你家有几口人 (nǐ jiā yǒu jǐ kǒu rén)

In most cases, the classifier 个 (gè) is used for people (e.g. older brother, teacher, student, doctor, and lawyer) when they are preceded by a number such as *three people, four teachers,* and *two hundred students.* However when we talk about the number of people in our family, we always use the classifier 口 (kǒu) instead. For example: 我家有五口人 (wǒ jiā yǒu wǔ kǒu rén). The word 口 (kǒu) means *mouth* in literary Chinese. When used for the number of people in the family, it actually implies that there are a certain number of mouths to feed in the family.

4. The pronunciation of the number one

Number one is pronounced in the first tone (yī) when used as a pure number as in telephone numbers, ID numbers, zip codes, etc. When used in conjunction with a classifier and consequently a noun to indicate its quantity, it is pronounced in the second tone (yí) when followed by a fourth tone word, and in the fourth tone (yì) when followed by a first, second, third or neutral tone. Compare:

| 一 个 哥 哥 | one brother | 一 本 书 | one book |
| yí ge gēge | | yì běn shū | |

5. The pronunciation of the number two

Number two can be pronounced in two ways in Chinese and each one of them is written differently: èr (二) and liǎng (两). Generally, two is pronounced as èr when it is used as a meaningless number such as in a telephone number, zip code, social security number or an ID number. two is meaningless in that it does not stand for a quantitative value, but rather a differentiating sign. Thus, a zip code with a higher number is not better than or superior to one with a lower number. two is pronounced liǎng when it is meaningful. This happens when two is used to indicate a quantitative value of a noun such as two students and two books. Please note that when we use a number with a noun, we must use a classifier. *Two students* and *two books* in Chinese are actually 两 个 学 生 (liǎng ge xuésheng) and 两 本 书 (liǎng běn shū). In other words, two is always pronounced *liǎng* whenever a classifier is used after it.

6. 几 (jǐ) and 多少 (duōshao)

To ask questions about numbers, Chinese uses 几 (jǐ) and 多少 (duōshao). Although these two expressions are often translated into *how many* or *how much* in English, they are also used to ask questions about things that involve numbers such as telephone numbers, social security numbers, zip codes and so on. These are usually asked in English using *what: what is your telephone number, zip code* and so on.

几 (jǐ) and 多少 (duōshao) differ from each other in the following important ways.

First of all, there is some kind of assumption or expectation on the part of the questioner in using 几 (jǐ) that the answer will be a small number, usually not exceeding ten, or the answer is a number from a range of given choices. Such assumptions or expectations are not suggested by 多少 (duōshao), which is open or neutral. 多少 (duōshao) can be used to ask about a large number as well as a small number. So if you assume or expect the answers to the following questions will be small, you can safely ask using 几 (jǐ):

| 你 家 有 几 口 人? | How many people are there in your family? |
| Nǐ jiā yǒu jǐ kǒu rén? | |

40

你有 几本 中文　书?   How many Chinese books do you have?
Nǐ yǒu jǐ běn Zhōngwén shū?

中国城　　有 几个日本餐馆?   How many Japanese restaurants are there in
Zhōngguóchéng yǒu jǐ ge Rìběn cānguan?   Chinatown?

However, if the number is large or if you are not sure, it would be better to use 多少 (duōshao) to avoid awkwardness or even offense. It may be all right for someone to ask you 你有几本中文书 (nǐ yǒu jǐ běn Zhōngwén shū *How many Chinese books do you have*), knowing that you may not have many Chinese books, but it is inappropriate, even insulting, to ask a Chinese professor 你有几本中文书 (nǐ yǒu jǐ běn Zhōngwén shū *How many Chinese books do you have*), because you are suggesting he does not have many Chinese books. For this reason, whenever you know the answer won't be a small number such as students in a school or books in a library, or when you are not sure about the possible answer such as the number of employees in a company, it is better to use 多少 (duōshao) instead of 几 (jǐ).

There is an added advantage of using 多少 (duōshao). That is, when you use 多少 (duōshao) in the question, the classifier, whatever it is, can be left out. This option does not exist for 几 (jǐ). Compare the following:

你们 学校　的 图书馆 有   How many Chinese books does your
Nǐmen xuéxiào de túshūguǎn yǒu   library have?
多少 中文　书?
duōshao Zhōngwén shū?

你有 几本 中文　　书?   How many Chinese books do you have?
Nǐ yǒu jǐ běn Zhōngwén shū?

你们 公司有 多少 人?   How many people does your company have?
Nǐmen gōngsī yǒu duōshao ren?

你们 公司有 几个人?   How many people does your company have?
Nǐmen gōngsī yǒu jǐ ge ren?

Keep in mind that the classifier is optional after 多少 (duōshao), but obligatory after 几 (jǐ).

There are occasions, however, when only 几 (jǐ) can be used. This happens when we ask time (since we are only dealing with twelve numbers), days of the week (since we are only dealing with seven, or six to be exact, numbers) and the dates (again we are only dealing with a handful of given numbers).

7. 你女儿是不是大学生 (nǐ nǚ'ér shì bú shì dàxuésheng)

Yes/no questions in Chinese can be formed in two ways. In addition to the use of the sentence-final particle *ma*, yes/no questions can also be indicated by repeating the verb/adjective using its negative form. Compare:

你工作 吗? Nǐ gōngzuò ma?	Do you work?
你 工 作 不工作? Nǐ gōngzuò bu gōngzuò?	Do you work?
你忙 吗? Nǐ máng ma?	Are you busy?
你忙 不忙? Nǐ máng bu máng?	Are you busy?
他 是 中国人 吗? Tā shì Zhōngguórén ma?	Is he Chinese?
他 是 不 是 中 国 人? Tā shì bu shì Zhōngguórén?	Is he Chinese?

As compared with *ma*, the affirmative and negative form of the verb/adjective is more favored not only because it is more colloquial and informal, but also because it unequivocally tells the listener up front that "this is a question, be prepared to give an answer." This is particularly so with a long sentence. With *ma*, the listener has to wait until the end to know if the speaker is asking a question or is simply making a statement. By the time the end of the sentence is reached, the listener already may have forgotten already what was asked at the beginning. An added advantage of using the affirmative and negative form of the verb/adjective is that the questioner clearly states the wording of the yes/no answer. For example:

你学 不学 中文? Nǐ xué bu xué Zhōngwén?	Do you study Chinese?

The listener just has to answer 学 (xué) or 不学 (bù xué).

Please note the following:

A. The negative word for 有 (yǒu) is 没 (méi), not 不 (bù), e.g.

你有 没有 男 朋友? Nǐ yǒu méiyǒu nán péngyou?	Do you have a boyfriend?
这儿有 没有 医院? Zhèr yǒu méiyǒu yīyuàn?	Is there a hospital here?

B. When the affirmative and negative form of the verb/adjective is used, *ma* cannot be used any more. This is because both of these two forms serve the same function of indicating the question status. To use both forms would be redundant and violate the single-signal principle.

C. The affirmative and negative form of the verb/adjective cannot be used when the verb or the adjective has a modifier. For example, it is not correct to say:

42

你妈妈也去不去中国?
Nǐ māma yě qù bu qù Zhōngguó?

Is your mother also going to China?

We have to say:

你妈妈也去中国　吗?
Nǐ māma yě qù Zhōngguó ma?

Is your mother also going to China?

8. 他在哪个学校学习 (tā zài nǎ ge xúxiào xuéxí)

Besides number, a number of other words also require the presence of classifiers when they are used with nouns. These include the demonstrative pronouns 这 (zhè *this*), 那 (nà *that*), the interrogative word 哪 (nǎ *na*) and the pronoun 每 (měi *each*). These words require the use of classifiers because they are ultimately veiled forms of numbers. When we use these words, don't we really mean *this one*, *that one*, *which one* and *each one*? Let's now look at the following examples in which these words are used with classifiers:

这 个 商店　叫 什么 名字?
Zhè ge shāngdiàn jiào shénme míngzi?

What's the name of this store?

我 不 认识 那个人。
Wǒ bú rènshi nà ge rén.

I don't know that man.

哪 本 书 是 你的?
Nǎ běn shū shì nǐde?

Which book is yours?

9. 学习 (xuéxí) and 学 (xué)

学习 (xuéxí) and 学 (xué) both mean *study*. Although they can be used interchangeably from time to time, there are two differences between them. While 学 (xué) is always a verb, 学习 (xuéxí) can be used both as a verb and as a noun. For example:

他学习中文。
Tā xuéxí Zhōngwén.

He studies Chinese.

他的学习很 好。
Tāde xuéxí hěn hǎo.

His study is very good.

When both 学习 (xuéxí) and 学 (xué) are used as verbs, 学 (xué) is a transitive verb (one that takes an object) and 学习 (xuéxí) can be used both transitively or intransitively (i.e. taking no object). Compare:

我 哥哥 学 (习) 中文。
Wǒ gēge xué (xi) Zhōngwén.

My older brother studies Chinese.

他在纽 约 大学 学习。
Tā zài Niǔ Yuē Dàxué xuéxí.

He studies at New York University.

43

In the second sentence, it is not grammatical to use 学 (xué) for 学习 (xuéxí).

10. 大学 (dàxué), 中学 (zhōngxué) and 小学 (xiǎoxué)

The differentiation of places of learning into universities, secondary schools and elementary schools is indicated in Chinese through the use of such adjectives as 大 (dà *big*), 中 (zhōng *zhong*) and 小 (xiǎo *small*) with 学 (xué), which is short for 学校 (xuéxiào *school*). While 大学 (dàxué) and 小学 (xiǎoxué) are universities and elementary schools, 中学 (zhōngxué) comprises both junior highs and high schools. Students in these schools are called 大学生 (dàxuésheng), 中学生 (zhōngxuésheng) and 小学生 (xiǎoxuésheng) respectively.

EXERCISES

I. Answer the following questions:

1. 你家有几口人？
   Nǐ jiā yǒu jǐ kǒu rén?
2. 他们是谁？
   Tāmen shì shuí?
3. 你爸爸工作吗？他在哪儿工作？
   Nǐ bàba gōngzuò ma? Tā zài nǎr gōngzuò?
4. 你妈妈工作吗？她在哪儿工作？
   Nǐ māma gōngzuò ma? Tā zài nǎr gōngzuò?
5. 你是学生吗？你在哪个学校学习？
   Nǐ shì xuésheng ma? Nǐ zài nǎ ge xuéxiào xuéxí?
6. 你在学校学什么？
   Nǐ zài xuéxiào xué shénme?
7. 你有哥哥吗？你有几个哥哥？
   Nǐ yǒu gēge ma? Nǐ yǒu jǐ ge gēge?
8. 你有几本中文书？
   Nǐ yǒu jǐ běn Zhōngwén shū?
9. 你们学校有多少学生？
   Nǐmen xuéxiào yǒu duōshao xuésheng?
10. 你们学校有中国学生吗？有多少中国学生？
    Nǐmen xuéxiào yǒu Zhōngguó xuésheng ma? Yǒu duōshao Zhōngguó xuésheng?

II. Write the following numbers in pinyin:

32
854
3,020
5,600
4,798

98,765
10,304

III. See if you can figure out the underlying semantic feature for the following classifiers in
Chinese from the nouns given that use these classifiers:

张 (zhāng)   stamp, picture, desk, table, bed, map, paper, ticket
条 (tiáo)   river, pants, street, tie, scarf, road, fish, bench
块 (kuài)   soap, cake, watch, brick, candy, loaf of bread
枝 (zhī)   pencil, pen, chopstick, cigarette, flower
只 (zhī)   cat, puppy, chicken, mouse, duck, tiger

IV. Rewrite the following yes/no questions using the affirmative and negative form of the
verb/adjective:

1. 你是 中国人   吗?
   Nǐ shì Zhōngguórén ma?
2. 她有 孩子吗?
   Tā yǒu háizi ma?
3. 你爸爸妈妈 去银行 吗?
   Nǐ bàba māma qù yínháng ma?
4. 这儿有 厕所吗?
   Zhèr yǒu cècuǒ ma?
5. 你姓 王   吗?
   Nǐ xìng Wáng ma?
6. 他在 家吗?
   Tā zài jiā ma?
7. 他们 学中文   吗?
   Tāmen xué Zhōngwén ma?
8. 你的中文   老师是中国人   吗?
   Nǐde Zhōngwén lǎoshī shì Zhōngguórén ma?
9. 这   是你的书吗?
   Zhè shì nǐde shū ma?
10. 你姐姐是大学生   吗?
    Nǐ jiějie shì dàxuésheng ma?

IV. Translate the following into Chinese:
1. There are four people in my family. They are my wife, my son, my daughter and myself.
2. How many Chinese books does your Chinese teacher have?
3. How many people are there in Shanghai?
4. My wife does not work at a company. She is a school teacher.
5. I don't know that person. Do you know him?
6. My older sister is not a high school student. She is a college student.
7. What does your older sister study at college?
8. Which company do you work for?

45

9. There are 1,500 students in our school.
10. Does your younger sister have a boyfriend?

V. Translate the following into English:

1. 我 在北京 大学 学习美国 历史.
   Wǒ zài Běijīng Dàxué xuéxí Měiguó lìshǐ.
2. 他们 学校 有 两 个中国 老师.
   Tāmen xuéxiào yǒu liǎng ge Zhōngguó lǎoshī.
3. 他们 公司 很 大, 有 一千 个人.
   Tāmen gōngsī hěn dà, yǒu yì qiān ge rén.
4. 你有 几个中国 朋友?
   Nǐ yǒu jǐ ge Zhōngguó péngyou?
5. 我的男 朋友 不喜欢 学中文, 他喜欢 学 历史.
   Wǒde nán péngyou bù xǐhuan xué Zhōngwén, tā xǐhuan xué lìshǐ.
6. 我妈妈 在家工作.
   Wǒ māma zài jiā gōngzuò.
7. 你知道上海 有 多少 大学吗?
   Nǐ zhīdao Shànghǎi yǒu duōshao dàxué ma?
8. 那个 人 的哥哥是我们 的 中文 老师.
   Nà ge rén de gēge shì wǒmende Zhōngwén lǎoshī.
9. 我 家有 八口 人. 你家呢?
   Wǒ jiā yǒu bā kǒu rén. Nǐ jiā ne?
10. 他 是加州 大学 的学生.
   Tā shì Jiāzhōu Dàxué de xuésheng.

VI. Write about yourself and your family. Include such information as the number of people in your family, who they are, what they do, where they work, where they live. You can substitute English for occupation or place names in Chinese that you don't know.

CULTURAL INSIGHTS

Family has been the cornerstone of the Chinese society, both in the past and at present. To understand Chinese society, one has to understand the Chinese family. The family and the broader kinship organization play an extraordinarily important part in Chinese life. Family is held so important to the Chinese that it is considered inseparable from the state even in the literal sense of the word. The word for state in Chinese—*guojia*—is composed of *guo* (state) and *jia* (family). This is not just a linguistic coincidence. In traditional China, the state and the society were basically modeled on the domestic organization in terms of the hierarchy and overreaching relationships. The type of the relationship of subordination between the father and the son was also expected between the emperor and his subjects.

Family has always been the center of loyalty for individuals in China. Children are taught from the very beginning to have filial piety towards their parents and respect towards other senior members in the extended family. Such education and socialization prepare them from an early age in such a way that they would become, outside their family, loyal subjects to the ruler and good citizens in society. Members of a family in traditional China were even responsible for each other's behaviors. Infraction of law by one member would bring punishment to all the other members. Such severity of punishment served as a major deterrent for the recurrence of the infraction by the member. If the crime warranted the death penalty, a whole family could be exterminated. Faced with such severe consequence, the family would impose strict internal discipline on its members, a move certainly welcomed by the ruler.

Families in China differ from those in the West in an important way. In China, the ultimate goal of an individual is to perpetuate his family, whereas in the West, families exist to support the individuals. For this reason, in China family interests come before the individuals' interest. Where family interests are at stake, individual interests must be suppressed or compromised. This explains the prevalent practice of arranged marriage and child betrothal in traditional China. Since the purpose of marriage was to procreate, not to love, romance and affection became irrelevant and divorces were few and far between.

Family in China functions as a collective security system, which provides help to the sick, disabled, and unemployed. It is also a cornerstone of social policy in the country. Only those that have no families to turn to for support can count on the assistance from the state, unlike many countries in the world, particularly in the West where the obligation between parents and children is uni-directional. Parents are responsible for bringing up their children, but children are not obligated to support their parents later on. In China however, the obligation is mutual. Parents are responsible for the upbringing of their children and the children are obligated to take care of their parents in their old age. This is not just a moral issue. It is required by law as it is clearly stipulated in the Chinese constitution. It is inconceivable and incomprehensible to the Chinese to see how people in the West, particularly those well-to-do, put their aged parents in nursing homes. To them, it is simply an unforgivable sin.

The Chinese family is very often thought of as being large, consisting of several generations living under the same roof. This is nothing more than a pure myth. Chinese families have always been small, containing less then ten people in most cases. Part of the reason for this pervading myth stems from the literary portrayal of prominent families. In traditional China, the large family was the ideal, but few people except those that possessed ample wealth could attain it. Those who could afford to support a large family were usually landlords and wealthy businessmen, gentry and high ranking officials. Landless peasants could not even afford to marry and start a family, to say nothing of maintaining a large family. In contemporary China, urban families are usually of the nuclear type, consisting of parents and their children only. In rural China, both traditionally and at present, families go through a developmental cycle that consists of the following stages: nuclear (parents with their unmarried children), stem (parents with one of their married sons) and joint (parents with more than one married son). The cycle is propelled and maintained by the inevitable family division that takes places when the family reaches the joint stage.

Marriage in China has always been patrilocal, meaning that daughters leave their parental home upon marriage and sons bring their wives into the family. This is because sons bear the ultimate responsibility of taking care of the aged parents and continuing the family line. For this reason, sons are preferred to daughters. For the same reason, relatives by marriage are not of equal status either. Those on the husband's side enjoy higher status and more privileges than the ones on the wife's side. In the urban area, the economics of housing is beginning to affect post-marital residence. Due to the shortage of housing, couples are now willing and ready to move in with the wife's parents if they have space to spare.

Although tremendous changes have taken place since China entered its modern period in terms of the elimination of arranged marriage, child betrothal and concubinage, the liberalization of the divorce law, and the recent institution of the single birth program, basic characteristics of the family still remain. These include the emphasis on filial piety, preference of sons to daughters, and patrilocal marriage. In the countryside, where most Chinese live, family retains the traditional corporate quality and remains an economic unit. It was true in the collective period that ended in the late 1970s, and it is still true today. In the collective period, farmers' income was computed and distributed on the basis of the work performed by the whole family. Following the reform, land has been contracted to the household rather than individuals. Outside the family, individuals simply do not have a viable place.

5

TIME

SENTENCE PATTERNS

现在 几点? Xiànzài jǐ diǎn?	What time is it?
对不起. Duìbuqǐ.	Sorry.
没 关系. Méi guānxi.	That's all right.
你每 天 几点 上班? Nǐ měi tiān jǐ diǎn shàngbān?	What time do you go to work every day?
你每 天 什么 时间 下班? Nǐ měi tiān shénme shíjiān xiàbān?	What time do you get off work every day?
我 有时 五 点 下班, 有时 Wǒ yǒushí wǔ diǎn xiàbān, yǒushí 五 点 半 下班. wǔ diǎn bàn xiàbān.	Sometimes I get off work at 5, sometimes at 5:30.
今天 星期 几? Jīntiān xīngqī jǐ?	What day is today?

你 星 期 几 有 中 文　课?
Nǐ xīngqī jǐ yǒu Zhōngwén kè?

What day do you have your Chinese class?

今天　几 号?
Jīntiān jǐ hào?

What's the date today?

你 什 么　时 候 开 始 学 日 语?
Nǐ shénme shíhou kāishǐ xué Rìyǔ?

When are you starting to learn Japanese?

CONVERSATIONS

A: 请 问,　现 在 几 点?
Qǐngwèn, xiànzài jǐ diǎn?

Excuse me, what time is it?

B: 现 在 七 点 三 十 分。
Xiànzài qī diǎn sānshí fēn.

It is 7:30.

A: 谢 谢。
Xièxie.

Thank you.

B: 不 客 气。
Bú kèqi.

You are welcome.

A: 请 问,　现 在 几 点?
Qǐngwèn, xiànzài jǐ diǎn?

Excuse me, what time is it?

B: 对 不 起, 我 没 有 表, 我 不 知 道。
Duìbuqǐ,　wǒ méiyǒu biǎo, wǒ bù zhīdao.

Sorry, I don't have a watch. I don't know.

A: 没 关 系。
Méi guānxi.

That's all right.

A: 你 每 天 几 点 上 班?
Nǐ měi tiān jǐ diǎn shàngbān?

What time do you go to work every day?

B: 我 每 天 八 点 上 班。
Wǒ měi tiān bā diǎn shàngbān.

I go to work at 8 every day.

A: 你 每 天 什 么　时 间 下 班?
Nǐ měi tiān shénme shíjiān xiàbān?

What time do you get off work every day?

B: 我 有 时 五 点 下 班, 有 时
Wǒ yǒushí wǔ diǎn xiàbān,　yǒushí
五 点 半 下 班。
wǔ diǎn bàn xiàbān.

I sometimes get off work at 5, sometimes at 5:30.

A: 你今天上午　作什么？
Nǐ jīntiān shàngwǔ zuò shénme?

What are you going to do this morning?

B: 我今天上午　在家看书。
Wǒ jīntiān shàngwǔ zài jiā kàn shū.

I'm going to read at home.

A: 下午呢？
Xiàwǔ ne?

How about this afternoon?

B: 下午我去学校。
Xiàwǔ wǒ qù xuéxiào.

I'm going to school this afternoon.

A: 你昨天晚上　在不在家？
Nǐ zuótiān wǎnshang zài bu zài jiā?

Were you home last night?

B: 不在。
Bú zài.

No, I was not.

A: 你在哪儿？
Nǐ zài nǎr?

Where were you?

B: 我在图书馆。
Wǒ zài túshūguǎn.

I was in the library.

A: 今天星期几？
Jīntiān xīngqī jǐ?

What day is today?

B: 今天星期三。
Jīntiān xīngqī sān.

Today is Wednesday.

A: 今天几号？
Jīntiān jǐ hào?

What is the date today?

B: 今天二十八号。
Jīntiān èrshí bā hào.

Today is the 28th.

A: 你的生日　是几月几号？
Nǐde shēngrì shì jǐ yuè jǐ hào?

When is your birthday?

B: 我的生日是十二月二十四号。
Wǒde shēngri shì shíèr yuè èrshísì hào.

My birthday is December 24.

A: 你星期几有中文　课？
Nǐ xīngqī jǐ yǒu Zhōngwén ke?

What day do you have your Chinese class?

B: 我星期一、三、五有中文　课。
Wǒ xīngqī yī, sān, wǔ yǒu Zhōngwén kè.

I have my Chinese class on Monday, Wednesday and Friday.

A: 你什么　时候开始学日语？
Nǐ shénme shíhou kāishǐ xué Rìyǔ?

When are you starting to learn Japanese?

B: 明年。
Míngnián.

Next year.

WORDS AND EXPRESSIONS

Nouns

现在	xiànzài	now
点	diǎn	o'clock
分	fēn	minute
半	bàn	half
今天	jīntiān	today
明天	míngtiān	tomorrow
昨天	zuótiān	yesterday
天	tiān	day
时间	shíjiān	time
时候	shíhou	time
星期	xīngqī	week
号	hào	number
月	yuè	month
明年	míngnián	next year
生日	shēngrì	birthday
日语	Rìyǔ	Japanese
课	kè	class, lesson

Verbs

上班	shàngbān	go to work
下班	xiàbān	get off work
开始	kāishǐ	begin

Adjectives

每	měi	every, each

Expressions

有时... 有时	yǒushí ... yǒushí	sometimes ... sometimes
对不起	duìbuqǐ	sorry
没关系	méi guānxi	that's all right

SUPPLEMENTARY WORDS AND EXPRESSIONS

Nouns

手表	shǒubiǎo	watch
早上	zǎoshang	early morning

上午	shàngwǔ	morning
中午	zhōngwǔ	noon
下午	xiàwǔ	afternoon
晚上	wǎnshang	evening
夜里	yèlǐ	night
早饭	zǎofàn	breakfast
中饭	zhōngfàn	lunch
晚饭	wǎnfàn	dinner
今年	jīnnián	this year
去年	qùnián	last year
周末	zhōumò	weekend

Verbs

起床	qǐ chuáng	get up
睡觉	shuìjiào	sleep
看书	kànshū	read
结束	jiéshù	end

Pronouns

那	nà	that

Adverbs

一般	yìbān	generally, usually

LANGUAGE POINTS

1. 几 (jǐ)

Remember 几 (jǐ) is the interrogative word used to ask questions about numbers. 几 (jǐ) is therefore used to ask about time, days of the week and dates since they are all expressed in numbers.

2. To tell the time

To tell the time, we use (diǎn *o'clock*) and (fēn *minute*). For example, the following times should be read as:

7:00	七点 (qī diǎn)
8:15	八点十五 (分) (bā diǎn shíwǔ fēn)
9:40	九点四十 (分) (jiǔ diǎn sìshí fēn)
10:05	十点零五 (分) (shí diǎn líng wǔ fēn)
11:30	十一点三十 (分) (shíyī diǎn sānshí fēn)

53

In all these expressions, 分 (fēn *minute*) can be left out. Also, 11:30 can also be read as 十 一 点 半 (shíyī diǎn bàn *half past 11*).

3. 对 不 起 (duìbuqǐ) and 没 关 系 (méi guānxi)

对 不 起 (duìbuqǐ) is the most common expression of apology that can be used on all the occasions when an apology is called for. The most common response is 没 有 关 系 (méiyǒu guānxi) and the verb 有 (yǒu) is often left out. 关 系 (guānxi) in this expression means *significance*. 没 关 系 (méi guānxi) means therefore that there is no significance. If there is no significance, it doesn't matter.

4. Word order involving several temporal units

Temporal units in Chinese indicating the time, the day, the week, the month and so on invariably follow each other according to their temporal scope. The general rule is that the unit that commands a larger scope precedes the one that commands a smaller scope. Thus, the proper temporal sequence in Chinese is *year-month-day-part of the day* (such as morning or afternoon) *-time*. This is exactly the reverse of English, where the smaller unit precedes the larger unit with the only exception of the relative positioning of month and day, which is the same as Chinese. In 你 每 天 几 点 上 班? (Nǐ měitiān jǐ diǎn shàngbān *What time do you go to work every day?*), 每 天 (měitiān *every day*) commands a larger scope than 几 点 (jǐ diǎn *what time*), which is part of 每 天 (měitiān *every day*). It is therefore placed before 几 点 (jǐ diǎn).

Word order involving several spatial units parallels that with several temporal units, where larger places precede smaller places. To indicate a complete address, Chinese would start with the country followed by province, city, district, street, building number and finally the apartment number. This again is the reverse of the order in English.

5. Word order involving adverbials

One of the cardinal principles that govern word order in Chinese is that the modifier precedes the modified. For example, attributes, be they individual words, phrases or clauses, always come before nouns, and adverbs always come before adjectives, verbs, and other adverbs. Many of the adverbials that we are going to encounter in this book have to do with time or place. They are usually placed immediately before the verb as in:

你 每 天 几 点 起 床?   What time do you get up every day?
Nǐ měitiān jǐ diǎn qǐ chuáng?

我 在 中 国 学 中 文.   I study Chinese in China.
Wǒ zài Zhōngguó xué Zhōngwén.

This is one of the major difficulties for beginning students of Chinese in speaking, if not in writing, because adverbials of time and place usually follow, instead of preceding, verbs in English. Try to get used to this usage.

6. Days of the week and names of months

Days of the week in Chinese are easy to learn, as they are numbered except Sunday. The week in Chinese begins with Monday rather than Sunday as it does English (doesn't the Bible say that Sunday is the seventh day of the week?). Thus we have 星 期 一 (xīngqī yī), 星 期 二 (xīngqī èr), 星 期 三 (xīngqī sān), 星 期 四 (xīngqī sì), 星 期 五 (xīngqī wǔ), 星 期 六 (xīngqī liù), and 星 期 天 (xīngqī tiān). The word 星 期 (xīngqī) means *week*, so don't mistake the above as week one, two and so on.

Like days of the week, months in Chinese are also numbered. But unlike those, numbers are placed before, rather than after, the word 月 (yuè *month*): 一 月 (yī yuè *January*), 二 月 (èr yuè *February*), 三 月 (sān yuè *March*), 四 月 (sì yuè *April*), 五 月 (wǔ yuè *May*), 六 月 (liù yuè *June*), 七 月 (qī yuè *July*), 八 月 (bā yuè *August*), 九 月 (jiǔ yuè *September*) 十 月, (shí yuè *October*), 十 一 月 (shíyī yuè *November*) and 十 二 月 (shí'èr yuè *December*).

7. Asking dates

To ask a particular date in Chinese is literally asking what is the month and what is the number of the day in the month. We are again dealing with numbers. So we need to use the interrogative word 几 (jǐ) as in 今 天 几 月 几 号? (Jīntiān jǐ yuè jǐ hào *What is the date for today?*) In addition, we usually know what month we are in before we ask the question. For this reason, people usually leave out 几 月 (jǐ yuè) in the question. But we must include 几 月 (jǐ yuè) when we ask when is someone's birthday, since we have no idea what month his or her birthday is in.

8. 什 么 时 间 (shénme shíjiān) and 什 么 时 候 (shénme shíhou)

什 么 时 间 (shénme shíjiān), like 几 点 (jǐ diǎn), is similar to *what time* in English. It is used to ask a specific time. The answer must be a clock time, such as 7 o'clock or 8:30. 什 么 时 候 (shénme shíhou) is similar to *when* in English in that the answer can be a clock time, or a general time such as *tomorrow*, *next week*, or even *next year*. Thus 什 么 时 候 (shénme shíhou) can often be used in place of 什 么 时 间 (shénme shíjiān), but the reverse is not true when the expected answer is a general time.

EXERCISES

I. Answer the following questions:

1. 现 在 几 点?
   Xiànzài jǐ diǎn?
2. 今 天 星 期 几?
   Jīntiān xīngqī jǐ?
3. 今 天 几 号?
   Jīntiān jǐ hào?
4. 你 的 生 日 是 几 月 几 号?
   Nǐde shēngrì shì jǐ yuè jǐ hào?

5. 你妈妈 的 生日 是 几月 几号?
   Nǐ māma de shéngrì shì jǐ yuè jǐ hào?
6. 今天 是星期 天 吗?
   Jīntiān shì xīngqī tiān ma?
7. 你 明天 晚上 作 什么?
   Nǐ míngtiān wǎnshang zuò shénme?
8. 你 星期 六 下午 在哪儿?
   Nǐ xīngqī liù xiàwu zài nǎr?
9. 你 星期 几 有 中文 课?
   Nǐ xīngqī jǐ yǒu Zhōngwén kè?
10. 这 个 星期 五 是 几号?
    Zhè ge xīngqī wǔ shì jǐ hào?

II. Say the following times in Chinese:

7:05	12:30	4:15	9:43	10:59
3:28	6:32	1:30	8:04	11:16

III. Ask questions about the underlined parts in the following sentences:

1. 今天 星期四.
   Jīntiān xīngqī sì.
2. 昨天 四月 五号.
   Zuótiān sì yuè wǔ hào.
3. 他 明天 来。
   Tā míngtiān lái.
4. 我 的 美国 朋友 今年 八月 去北京。
   Wǒde Měiguó péngyou jīnnián bā yuè qù Běijīng.
5. 今天 是二月 二十三号, 星期 四。
   Jīntiān shì èr yuè èrshí sān hào, xīngqī sì.

IV. Translate the following into Chinese:

1. Where were you last night?
2. Sorry. I don't have a watch. I don't know what time it is now.
3. On what days of the week do you have your Chinese class?
4. What time do you get off work this afternoon?
5. I usually eat dinner at a restaurant Saturday evening.
6. My father gets up at six every day.
7. I don't eat breakfast.
8. It is not good not to eat breakfast.
9. What are you going to do tomorrow afternoon?
10. When are you going to go to China? - June next year.

V. Translate the following into English:

1. 我 妈妈 早上　 一般 不 吃早饭.
   Wǒ māma zǎoshang yìbān bù chī zǎofàn.

2. 她 中午　 有时 在 公司 吃饭, 有时 在家 吃饭。
   Tā zhōngwǔ yǒushí zài gōngsī chīfàn, yǒushí zài jiā chīfàn.

3. 下 星期 三 是 我 太太的 生日.
   Xià xīngqī sān shì wǒ tàitai de shēngrì.

4. 我 明天　 上午　 九点 去 银行。
   Wǒ míngtiān shàngwǔ jiǔdiǎn qù yínháng.

5. 你的 银行 在 哪儿?
   Nǐde yínháng zài nǎr?

VI. State the birthdays of your family members in complete sentences.

VII. Write your daily schedule such as when you get up, eat breakfast, go to work, have lunch, get off work, go home, have dinner and go to bed. You may also indicate things (e.g. having breakfast) that you don't do.

CULTURAL INSIGHTS

People of different cultures have different perceptions and categorizations of time. As a result, the way they use time may also be different.

Time is very often expressed in spatial terms. When asked to visualize the movement of time from past to present and then to future, most American students would say time moves horizontally from left to right, with left being the past, the midpoint that meets the eye the present and the right being the future. In Chinese however, time is perceived of as moving vertically from top to bottom, with the top being the past, the midpoint at the level of the eye the present and the bottom being the future. This explains the logic of these Chinese temporary expressions 上午 (shàngwǔ *morning*), 上个星期 (shàng ge xīngqī *last week*), and 上个月 (shàng ge yuè *last month*), where 上 (shàng) means "up," and 下午 (xiàwǔ *afternoon*), 下个星期 (xià ge xīngqī *next week*), and 下个月 (xià ge yuè *next month*), where 下 (xià) means "down."

For the English word "morning," there are two equivalents in Chinese: 早上 (zǎoshang) and 上午 (shàngwǔ). The difference between these two terms is that 早上 (zǎoshang) is the early part of the morning that usually lasts until one goes to work. When people meet each other during this part of the day, they often greet each other by saying 你早 (nǐ zǎo *Good morning*) or simply 早 (zǎo *Morning*), which literally means "You are early." 上午 (shàngwǔ) is that part of the day that extends to lunch time. In the West, noon is a point of time such that as soon as the clock strikes 12, it is afternoon. That's why we don't often hear expressions like *this noon, yesterday's noon* and so on. On the contrary, noon is a period of time in China that can extend two or three hours covering the time when people stop morning work, go home, prepare lunch, eat lunch, take a nap and head back to afternoon work. With the exception of stores, essential services and factory operations that cannot stop, government offices, schools and companies would come to a halt during this time so that people could go home to eat lunch (the most important meal of the day for most people), and take a nap. A few years ago, the Chinese government imposed a ban on this midday break by limiting the lunch time allocation and thus eliminating the indispensable nap. This measure caused havoc in the population and created a major culturally conditioned physiological breakdown. The midday break is so culturally ingrained and biologically programmed that people simply could not do without it. When forced to abandon this time-honored indulgence, people would either fall asleep or doze off on the job. Heated debates arose and various theories were advanced. One argument for the midday break was that the Chinese diet, which is made of low calorie foods such as pork and vegetables, is not as sustaining as the Western diet, which is rich in beef and dairy products. Another theory along the same line was that Chinese people spent more time shopping for and preparing food. This time-consuming endeavor was compounded by the lack of convenient household appliances such as the refrigerator and the microwave. By the time people finished their lunch, they were exhausted and desperately needed a nap to recoup their energy. Although no consensus of opinion was reached, the government gave up and people went back to their nap. Interestingly enough, with the recent economic boom and increasing privatization in China, more and more people are voluntarily giving up their nap and making use of the precious midday time. It seems that economic incentives are the only force that could thwart any customary or even biological practice.

Throughout China, there is only one time zone. The standard time is called 北京时间 (Běijīng Shíjiān *Beijing Time*). With only one time zone in such a vast country, people adapt themselves by adjusting their work schedule constantly. Thus, they may have a different schedule depending on the time of the year.

The sight of people armed with and driven by an appointment book common in the West is rare in China. People there are more relaxed and generous with time. They usually plan their activities as they go. Seldom do people plan something down to the minute several weeks or months ahead. Although things are beginning to change due to the increase of telephones, people still visit each other without giving notice. When this happens, you are not supposed to turn away the unexpected guest or guests even though the visit may come at an awkward or inconvenient time. To do so would usually generate hard feelings and offend people. On the other hand, unexpected visitors would often find an empty house after they traveled from one end of the town to the other to see a friend.

LESSON

6

NATIONALITIES & LANGUAGES

SENTENCE PATTERNS

你是哪国 人？
Nǐ shì nǎ guó rén?

Where are you from/What is your nationality?

你是哪儿人？
Nǐ shì nǎr rén?

Where are you from/Where is your hometown?

你会说 中文 吗？
Nǐ huì shuō Zhōngwén ma?

Do you speak Chinese?

会 一点儿.
Huì yìdiǎnr.

A little.

"Mandarin" 用 中文 怎么 说？
"Mandarin" yòng Zhōngwén zěnme shuō?

How do you say "Mandarin" in Chinese?

"Nánjīng huà" 是 什么 意思？
"Nánjīnghuà" shì shěnme yìsi?

What does "Nánjīng hua" mean?

我 不懂 你的话.
Wǒ bù dǒng nǐde huà.

I don't understand what you say.

请 慢 一点儿说.
Qǐng màn yìdiǎnr shuō.

Please speak a little slowly.

CONVERSATIONS

A: 你是中国人吗？
Nǐ shì Zhōngguórén ma?

Are you Chinese?

B: 是。你也是中国人吗？
Shì. Nǐ yě shì Zhōngguórén ma?

Yes, are you also Chinese?

A: 我不是，我是日本人。
Wǒ bú shì, wǒ shì Rìběnrén.

No, I am not. I am Japanese.

A: 你是哪国人？
Nǐ shì nǎ guó rén?

Where are you from/What is your nationality?

B: 我是中国人。
Wǒ shì Zhōngguórén.

I am Chinese.

A: 你太太呢？
Nǐ tàitai ne?

What about your wife?

B: 她是英国人。
Tā shì Yīngguórén.

She is English.

A: 你从哪儿来？
Nǐ cóng nǎr lái?

Where did you come from?

B: 我从法国来。
Wǒ cóng Fǎguó lái.

I came from France.

A: 你是法国人吗？
Nǐ shì Fǎguórén ma?

Are you French?

B: 不是。我是德国人。
Bú shì. Wǒ shì Déguórén.

No, I am not. I am German.

A: 对不起。
Duìbuqǐ.

I'm sorry.

B: 没关系。
Méi guānxi.

That's all right.

A: 你是哪儿人？
Nǐ shì nǎr rén?

Where are you from/Where is your hometown?

B: 我是上海人。
Wǒ shì Shànghǎirén.

I am from Shanghai.

A: 你太太也是上海人吗？
Nǐ tàitai yě shì Shànghǎirén ma?

Is your wife also from Shanghai?

B: 不是。她是广州人。
Bú shì. Tā shì Guǎngzhōurén.

No, she is from Guangzhou.

A: 你会说广东话吗？
Nǐ huì shuō Guǎngdōng huà ma?

Do you speak Cantonese?

B: 我　懂　广东　　话，但是　　　　　I understand Cantonese, but I don't speak it.
　Wǒ dǒng Guǎngdōng huà, dàn shì
　不 会 说。
　bú huì shuō.

A: 你 太 太 会 说　上 海　　话 吗？　　Does your wife speak Shanghai dialect?
　Nǐ tàitai huì shuō Shànghǎi huà ma?

B: 她 会。　　　　　　　　　　　　　Yes, she does.
　Tā huì.

A: 你 爸 爸 会 说　英 语 吗？　　　　Does your father speak English?
　Nǐ bàba huì shuō Yīngyǔ ma?

B: 会。　　　　　　　　　　　　　　Yes, he does.
　Huì.

A: 你 妈 妈 呢？　　　　　　　　　　What about your mother?
　Nǐ māma ne?

B: 她 不 会。　　　　　　　　　　　No, she doesn't.
　Tā bú huì.

A: 你 太 太 呢？　　　　　　　　　　What about your wife?
　Nǐ tàitai ne?

B: 她 会 一 点 儿。　　　　　　　　She speaks a little.
　Tā huì yìdiǎnr.

A: 你 会 说　几 种　语 言？　　　　How many languages do you speak?
　Nǐ huì shuō jǐ zhǒng yǔyán?

B: 我　会 说　四 种　语 言。　　　　I speak four languages.
　Wǒ huì shuō sì zhǒng yǔyán.

A: 哪 四 种？　　　　　　　　　　Which four?
　Nǎ sì zhǒng?

B: 英 语，法 语，西 班 牙 语 和　　English, French, Spanish and a little Chinese.
　Yīngyǔ, Fǎyǔ, Xībānyáyú hé
　一 点 儿 中 文。
　yìdiǎnr Zhōngwén.

A: 请 问，　　"Mandarin" 用　中 文　　Excuse me, how do you say "Mandarin" in
　Qǐngwèn, "Mandarin" yòng Zhōngwén　　Chinese?
　怎 么 说？
　zěnme shuō?

B: "Mandarin" 用　中 文　　说 是　　"Mandarin" in Chinese is "pǔtōnghuà."
　"Mandarin" yòng Zhōngwén shuō shì
　普 通 话。
　pǔtōnghuà.

A: "南 京　话 " 是 什 么　意 思？　　What is the meaning of "Nanjing hua?"
　"Nánjīng huà" shì shénme yìsi?

B: "南 京 话 " 的 意 思 是　　　　　"Nanjing hua" means "Nanjing dialect."
"Nánjīng huà" de yìsi　shì
"Nanjing dialect"。
"Nanjing dialect".

A: 谢 谢。　　　　　　　　　　Thank you.
Xièxie.

B: 不 客 气。　　　　　　　　　You're welcome.
Bú kèqi.

A: 请 问,　　中 国 、银 行　　Excuse me, where is the Bank of China?
Qǐngwèn, Zhōngguó yínháng
在 哪 儿?
zài nǎr?

B: 对 不 起,我 不 懂　你 的 话,　Sorry. I don't understand what you say.
Duìbuqǐ,　wǒ bù dǒng nǐde　huà,　Could you please say it again?
请 再 说 一 遍。
qǐng zài shuō yíbiàn.

A: 你 知 道 中 国　银 行　　Do you know where the Bank of China is?
Nǐ zhīdao Zhōngguó yínháng
在 哪 儿 吗?
zài nǎr　ma?

B: 知 道。中 国　银 行 在　　Yes, the Bank of China is in Chinatown.
Zhīdao. Zhōngguó yínháng zài
中 国　城。
Zhōngguóchéng.

A: 谢 谢。　　　　　　　　　　Thank you.
Xièxie.

B: 不 谢。　　　　　　　　　　Don't mention it.
Bú xiè.

A: 请 问,　男 厕 所 在 哪 儿?　Excuse me, where is the men's room?
Qǐngwèn, nán cèsuǒ zài nǎr?

B: 我 是 广 东 人,　我 的 国 语　I am Cantonese. My Mandarin is not very
Wǒ shì Guǎngdōngrén. Wǒde guóyǔ　good. Please speak a little slowly.
不 好。请 你 慢 一 点 儿 说。
bù hǎo. Qǐng nǐ　màn yìdiǎnr　shuō.

A: 对 不 起,男 厕 所 在 哪 儿?　Sorry. Where is the men's room?
Duìbuqǐ, nán cèsuǒ zài nǎr?

B: 在 五 楼。　　　　　　　　On the fifth floor.
Zài wǔ lóu.

A: 谢 谢。　　　　　　　　　　Thank you.
Xièxie.

B: 不 客 气。　　　　　　　　You're welcome.
Bú kèqi.

A: 香港人　　说 什么 话?
Xiāng Gǎngrén shuō shénme huà?

B: 香港人　　说 广东　　话。
Xiāng Gǎngrén shuō Guǎngdōng huà.

A: 你会 不会 说 广东　　话?
Nǐ huì bu huì shuō Guǎngdōng huà?

B: 我 懂 广东　　话, 但是 我 不
Wǒ dǒng Guǎngdōng huà, dànshì wǒ bú
会 说。
huì shuō.

What dialect do people in Hong Kong speak?

People in Hong Kong speak Cantonese.

Do you speak Cantonese?

I understand Cantonese, but I don't speak it.

WORDS AND EXPRESSIONS

Nouns

国	guó	country
英 语	Yīngyǔ	English language
英 国	Yīngguó	England
法 国	Fǎguó	France
德 国	Déguó	Germany
法 语	Fǎyǔ	French language
西 班 牙语	Xībānyáyǔ	Spanish language
广 州	Guǎngzhōu	Canton (the city)
广 东	Guǎngdōng	Canton (the province)
香 港	Xiāng Gǎng	Hong Kong
语 言	yǔyán	language
普 通 话	pǔtōnghuà	Mandarin
国 语	guóyǔ	Mandarin
意 思	yìsi	meaning
话	huà	speech, dialect
楼	lóu	floor, building

Verbs

会	huì	know how to, to be able to
说	shuō	speak, say
用	yòng	use
懂	dǒng	understand

Adverbs

慢	màn	slowly
再	zài	again
只	zhǐ	only

63

一遍	yíbiàn	once
一 点 儿	yìdiǎnr	a little

Prepositions
从	cóng	from

Classifiers
种	zhǒng	kind, type

Interrogatives
怎 么	zěnme	how

SUPPLEMENTARY WORDS AND EXPRESSIONS

Nouns
外 国	wàiguó	foreign country
外 国 人	wàiguórén	foreigner
外 语	wàiyǔ	foreign language
字	zì	Chinese character
四 川	Sìchuān	Sichuan (Sezchuan)
报 纸	bàozhǐ	newspaper
杂 志	zázhì	magazine
新 闻	xīnwén	news
电 视	diànshì	television
课 文	kèwén	text
会 话	huìhuà	conversation
生 词	shēngcí	new word
语 法	yǔfǎ	grammar
句 子	jùzi	sentence
练 习	liànxí	exercise
书 法	shūfǎ	calligraphy
词 典	cídiǎn	dictionary

Verbs
教	jiāo	teach
写	xiě	write
听	tīng	listen
翻 译	fānyì	translate
回 答	huídá	answer

LANGUAGE POINTS

1. Nationality terms

It is easy to form nationality terms in Chinese. All you need to do is to add the word 人 (rén) after the name of the country, such as:

美国 (Měiguó *America*)　　　美国人 (Měiguórén *American*)
中国 (Zhōngguó *China*)　　　中国人 (Zhōngguórén *Chinese*)
英国 (Yīngguó *England*)　　　英国人 (Yīngguórén *English*)
法国 (Fǎguó *France*)　　　　法国人 (Fǎguórén *French*)
德国 (Déguó *Germany*)　　　德国人 (Déguórén *German*)

国 (guó) in all these expressions simply means *country*.

If the name of a country consists of more than one syllable, the word 国 (guó) is usually not used. For example:

加拿大 (Jiā'nádà *Canada*)　　　加拿大人 (Jiā'nádàrén *Canadian*)
日本 (Rìběn *Japan*)　　　　　日本人 (Rìběnrén *Japanese*)
意大利 (Yìdàlì *Italy*)　　　　意大利人 (Yìdàlìrén *Italian*)
越南 (Yuènán *Vietnam*)　　　越南人 (Yuènánrén *Vietnamese*)
西班牙 (Xībānyá *Spain*)　　　西班牙人 (Xībānyárén *Spanish*)

The word 人 (rén) can also be used after a specific location within a country to mean a native of that place. For example:

北京 (Běijīng *Beijing*)　　　　北京人 (Běijīngrén *Beijing native*)
上海 (Shànghǎi *Shanghai*)　　上海人 (Shànghǎirén *Shanghai native*)
纽约 (Niǔ Yuē *New York*)　　　纽约人 (Niǔ Yuērén *New Yorker*)
香港 (Xiāng Gǎng *Hong Kong*)　香港人 (Xiāng Gǎngrén *Hong Kong native*)
台湾 (Táiwān *Taiwan*)　　　　台湾人 (Táiwānrén *Taiwanese*)

To ask where someone is from, we use 你是哪国人 (nǐ shì nǎ guó rén), which literally means *which country person are you*. The interrogative word 哪 (nǎ *which*) is used because we are asking the other person to choose from a range of possible answers.

It is to be noted that to the Chinese, 中国人 (Zhōngguóren), 英国人 (Yīngguórén), 日本人 (Rìběnrén) and so on refer to a person's ethnic background, having nothing to do with his or her own citizenship. Thus a person of Chinese descent is always 中国人 (Zhōngguórén), even though he or she may have been born in a foreign country or become a citizen of a foreign country through immigration.

2. 你是哪儿人 (nǐ shì nǎr rén)?

This expression, meaning literally *you are what place person*, is used when you know a person's nationality and you want to know where in that country the person is from. The response takes such forms: 我是纽约人 (wǒ shì Niǔ Yuērén *I'm a New Yorker*), 我是加州人 (wǒ shì Jiāzhōurén *I am a Californian*), 我是杭州人 (wǒ shì Hángzhōurén *I am from Hangzhou*).

2. 你会说中文吗 (nǐ huì shuō Zhōngwén ma)?

会 (huì) is not necessary in English when you ask somebody if he can speak a certain language, but it is usually used in Chinese. It means *know how to* and is used for things and skills that are acquired through learning such as language, driving, swimming, and cooking.

3. Mandarin 用中文怎么说 (Mandarin yòng Zhōngwén zěnme shuō)?

This is a useful expression used when you want to ask someone how to say something in Chinese. In the expression, the verb 说 (shuō) is modified by two adverbials 用中文 (yòng Zhōngwén *using Chinese*) and 怎么 (zěnme *how*). As such, they are placed before the verb. 用 (yòng) in 用中文 (yòng Zhōngwén) means *to use*. You may want to take the phrase to mean *using Chinese* or *in Chinese*. The item of interest - *Mandarin* - is placed first as is often in Chinese, although it is the object of the verb 说 (shuō). The subject is not present in the sentence because it is generic. It would be *you, I* or *one*. The response pattern for this question is Mandarin 用中文说是普通话 (Mandarin yòng Zhōngwén shuō shì pǔtōng huà).

4. Nánjīng huà 是什么意思 (Nánjīng huà shì shénme yìsi)?

This is the flip side of the above question, used when you heard a Chinese expression, but did not know what it meant. The answer to this question is Nánjīng huà 的意思是 Nánjīng dialect (Nánjīng huà de yìsi shì Nanjing dialect). Literally it is *Nanjing hua's meaning is Nanjing dialect*.

EXERCISES

I. Answer the following questions:

1. 你是哪国人?
   Nǐ shì nǎ guó rén?
2. 你是哪儿人?
   Nǐ shì nǎr rén?
3. 你会说什么语言?
   Nǐ huì shuō shénme yǔyán?
4. 你会说西班牙语吗?
   Nǐ huì shuo Xībānyáyǔ ma?
5. 你妈妈会说几种语言?
   Nǐ māma huì shuō jǐ zhǒng yǔyán?

6. 你 的 中 文　老师 会 说　英语　吗？
   Nǐde Zhōngwén lǎoshī huì shuō Yīngyǔ ma?

7. 德国 人 说　什 么　语言？
   Déguórén shuō shénme yǔyán?

8. 香 港 人　说 什 么　话？
   Xiāng Gǎngrén shuō shénme huà?

9. "Doctor" 用　中 文　怎 么 说？
   "Doctor" yòng Zhōngwén zěnme shuō?

10. "Cānguǎn" 是 什 么　意 思？
    "Cānguǎn" shì shénme yìsi?

II. 用 中 文 怎 么 说 (yòng Zhōngwén zěnme shuō):

bank	friend	house	bathroom	noon
birthday	lunch	college	high school student	doctor

III. 它 们 是 什 么 意 思 (tāmen shì shénme yìsi)?

Xībānyáyǔ	guóyǔ	pǔtōnghuà	Yàzhōu	Fēizhōurén
shāngdiàn	Nánjīnghuà	hěn shǎo	dǒng	Fǎguó cānguǎn

IV. Fill in the blanks with appropriate words:

1. 你 会 说　法语 ＿＿＿＿＿？
   Nǐ huì shuō fǎyǔ ＿＿＿＿＿？

2. 你 姐姐 会 说　几 ＿＿＿＿＿ 语 言？
   Nǐ jiějie huì shuō ji ＿＿＿＿＿ yǔyán?

3. 你 的 朋友 ＿＿＿＿＿ 哪 儿 来？
   Nǐde péngyou ＿＿＿＿＿ nǎr lái?

4. 他 会 说 ＿＿＿＿＿ 西 班 牙 语。
   Tā huì shuō ＿＿＿＿＿ Xībānyáyǔ.

5. 对 不 起, 我 不 懂　你 的 ＿＿＿＿＿。
   Duìbuqǐ, wǒ bù dǒng nǐde ＿＿＿＿＿.

6. 请　慢 ＿＿＿＿＿ 说。
   Qǐng màn ＿＿＿＿＿ shuō.

7. 她 从　上 海 ＿＿＿＿＿。 她 是 上 海 人。
   Tā cóng Shànghǎi ＿＿＿＿＿. Tā shì Shànghǎirén.

8. 南 京 人 说 ＿＿＿＿＿ 话？
   Nánjīngrén shuō ＿＿＿＿＿ huà?

9. 你 懂 不 ＿＿＿＿＿ 我 的 话？
   Nǐ dǒng bù ＿＿＿＿＿ wǒde huà?

10. 你 妈 妈 ＿＿＿＿＿ 说　法 语 吗？
    Nǐ māma ＿＿＿＿＿ shuō Fǎyǔ ma?

V. Translate the following into Chinese:

1. Excuse me, do you know how to say "speak slowly" in Chinese?
2. Excuse me, what does "qìchē" mean?
3. "Qìchē" means "car".
4. My Chinese teacher doesn't speak English.
5. He came from Germany, but he doesn't speak German.
6. She speaks a little Spanish.
7. People in Hong Kong speak Cantonese.
8. Who speaks French?
9. He is from Shanghai, but he doesn't speak Shanghai dialect.
10. How do you write this character?

VI. Translate the following into English:

1. 我 是 英国人， 我 太太是 法国人。
   Wǒ shì Yīngguórén, wǒ tàitai shì Fǎguórén.
2. 上 海 人 不懂 广 东 话。
   Shànghǎirén bù dǒng Guǎngdōng huà.
3. 我 的 男 朋友 会 说 四 种 语言, 我 只会 说 英语。
   Wǒde nán péngyou huì shuō sì zhǒng yǔyán, wǒ zhǐ huì shuō Yīngyǔ.
4. 你说 什么? 我 不懂. 请 再说 一遍。
   Nǐ shuō shénme? Wǒ bù dǒng. Qǐng zài shuō yí biàn.
5. 我 懂 台 湾 话, 可是 不会说。
   Wǒ dǒng Táiwān huà, kěshì bú huì shuō.
6. 他 的 广 东 话很 好, 但是 国语 不太 好。
   Tāde Guǎngdōng huà hěn hao, dànshì guóyǔ bú tài hǎo.
7. 请问, 谁 会说 英语?
   Qǐngwèn, shuí huì shuō Yīngyǔ?
8. 你知道 不知道 "公园" 是什么 意思?
   Nǐ zhīdao bu zhīdao "gōngyuán" shì shénme yìsi?
9. 她 的 话, 我 只懂 一点 儿。
   Tāde huà, wǒ zhǐ dǒng yìdiǎnr.
10. 对 不 起, 我 不会说 四 川 话。
    Duìbuqǐ, wǒ bú huì shuō Sìchuān huà.

VII. Each sentence below contains a mistake. Find and correct it:
1. 你有 几 中文 书?
   Nǐ yǒu jǐ Zhōngwén shū?
2. 你认识不 认识那 医生?
   Nǐ rènshi bu rènshi nà yīsheng?
3. 他 每天 上班 在 八点。
   Tā měitiān shàngbān zài bā diǎn.
4. 你是 不是 学生 吗?
   Nǐ shì bu shì xuésheng ma?

5. 他 有　姐 姐, 不 有　哥 哥.
　　Tā yǒu jiějie,　bù yǒu gēge.
6. 我　有　二 个 中 国　　朋 友.
　　Wǒ yǒu èr ge Zhōngguó péngyou.
7. 请 问,　中 国　　城　是 哪 儿?
　　Qǐngwèn, Zhōngguó chéng shì nǎr?
8. 他 工 作　在 餐 馆.
　　Tā gōngzuò zài cānguǎn.
9. 王　　太 太 不 去 银 行　今 天.
　　Wáng Tàitai bú qù yínhang jīntiān.
10. 你 们 学 校　的 图 书 馆　　有 几 本 书?
　　Nǐmen xuéxiào de túshūguǎn (library) yǒu jǐ běn shū?

CULTURAL INSIGHTS

　　As with any other language, Chinese is an abstract amalgam. It is realized in a variety of representations called *fangyan* (regional speech or dialect). Unlike many other languages, dialects of Chinese can be so drastically different that they are not mutually intelligible. There are places in China where people do not understand each other even though they only live a few miles apart. Since association and banding had never been encouraged in traditional China because they tended to breed the seeds of discontent or rebellion, the difficulty with which people had in communicating with each other had been a godsend opportunity for emperors to exercise effective social control over the population, much like the "confusion of tongues" described in the biblical story of the Tower of Babel. Due to the mutual intelligibility, different dialect groups in China are often conceived by scholars outside China as being different languages, but Chinese scholars have been vehemently denying this claim.

　　There are seven major dialect groups in China, which are distributed over different geographic areas of the country. Each of these dialect groups has its own variations and local subdialects. The most widely used dialect of Chinese is Mandarin. It is spoken by 70% of the population in northern and parts of southern China that account for three quarters of the country. Mandarin itself has a number of subvarieties. The standard form of Mandarin is based on the northern Mandarin with the Beijing phonological system as its norm. This standard form is used on television, radio and other official and administrative occasions. It is the dialect that children throughout the country go to school learning. As such it is understood by 94% of the population. Other dialects include *Wu* (spoken by 8% of the population), *Gan* (2%), *Hakka* (4%), *Xiang* (5%), *Min/Fukienese* (4%) and *Yue/Catonese* (5%). Of these seven major dialects, only Mandarin is indigenous and homogenous, i.e. it evolved locally in northern China over thousands of years. The other six dialects are spoken primarily in central and southeastern China. They are the result of southward migration of population since the very beginning of Chinese history.

The mutual unintelligibility of dialects had much to do with the segregation of the population in traditional China. Due to an elaborate system of administration, local governors and generals were often given unbridled power, which enabled them to exercise tight control of the people in their jurisdiction. Such tight control resulted in a practical segregation: there was little mobility and interaction between people who belonged to different political and administrative entities. As a result, the differences in their speech became more and more divergent.

Another reason that contributed to the divergence of dialects has to do with the preference of agriculture and suppression of trade and commerce by the government in traditional China. Under such a government policy, people were tied down to their land and dreaded venturing out unless there was a war or some other natural calamity.

Natural barriers such as rivers and mountains further restricted the interaction between people. These boundaries often mark the boundaries of dialect groups, particularly when they coincide with the boundaries of the units of political administration.

Although Mandarin has become the official dialect, the use of local dialects is not totally discouraged by the government. In fact, with its countenance, dialects in some places are actually thriving. Shanghai is a typical example. It is one of the few places that still maintains radio and television programs in the local dialect. The prestige of the dialect is closely related to the sense of superiority felt by Shanghai natives to people elsewhere. It used to be the case that if you didn't speak Shanghai dialect, you would get indifferent services while visiting there. To overcome this, outsiders had to learn Shanghai dialect, at least a few phrases for the occasion before they ventured into the city. Mobility has vastly increased following the reform efforts in recent years in Shanghai and other places. A recent survey showed that currently there is an annual influx of 3 million migrant workers in Shanghai seeking short-term work and taking up temporary residence. To accommodate such a large population and serve as the major center of trade and finance, Mandarin has inevitably emerged as the lingua franca.

7

MONEY & SHOPPING

SENTENCE PATTERNS

你要买 什么?
Nǐ yào mǎi shénme?

What do you want to buy?

这 件 衣服 多少 钱?
Zhè jiàn yīfu duōshao qián?

How much is this piece of clothing?

你们 收 不 收 美元?
Nǐmen shōu bu shōu Měiyuán?

Do you accept U.S. dollars?

这 件 毛衣 怎么样?
Zhè jiàn máoyī zěnmeyàng?

What do you think of this sweater?

我 觉得 很 好。
Wǒ juéde hěn hǎo.

I think it's very good.

第一百货 公司的 东西 最 多。
Dì yī bǎihuògōngsī de dōngxi zuì duō.

The First Department store has the most stuff.

你能 告诉我 在 哪儿能 换
Nǐ néng gàosu wǒ zài nǎr néng huàn
美元 吗?
Měiyuán ma?

Can you tell me where I can change U.S. dollars?

一美元 换 多少 人民币?
Yì Měiyuān huàn duōshao Rénmínbì?

How much Rénmínbì does one U.S. dollar convert to?

请 等 一下儿。　　　　　　　Just a minute.
Qǐng děng yíxiàr.

我 能 看看 吗?　　　　　　　Can I take a look?
Wó néng kànkan ma?

太 贵 了。　　　　　　　　　It's too expensive.
Tài guì le.

听说 上海 的东西 很 贵。　I heard that things in Shanghai are very
Tīngshuō Shànghǎi de dōngxi hěn guì.　expensive.

要 看 什么 店。　　　　　　It depends on what store.
Yào kàn shénme diàn.

有的 店 东西 贵, 有的 店 东西　Some stores are expensive, some stores are
Yǒude diàn dōngxi guì, yǒude diàn dōngxi　very cheap.
很 便宜。
hěn piányi.

多少 钱 一张?　　　　　　　How much is a piece?
Duōshao qián yì zhāng?

CONVERSATIONS

A: 你去哪儿?　　　　　　　　Where are you going?
　 Nǐ qù nǎr?

B: 我 去买 东西。　　　　　　I'm going shopping.
　 Wǒ qù mǎi dōngxi.

A: 你去哪儿买 东西?　　　　Where are you going shopping?
　 Nǐ qù nǎr mǎi dōngxi?

B: 我 去百货 公司 买 东西。　I'm going shopping at the the department
　 Wǒ qù bǎihuògōngsī mǎi dōngxi.　store.

A: 你要 买 什么?　　　　　　What do you want to buy?
　 Nǐ yào mǎi shénme?

B: 我 要 买 衣服。你知道 哪个　I'm going to buy clothes. Do you know
　 Wǒ yào mǎi yīfu.　Nǐ zhīdao nǎ ge　which department store has the most stuff?
　 百货 公司 的 东西 最多?
　 bǎihuògōngsī de dōngxi zuì duō?

A: 第一百货公司 的东西 最多。　The First Department store has the most
　 Dì yī bǎihuògōngsī de dōngxi zuì duō.　stuff.

A: 你们 收 不收 美元?
Nǐmen shōu bu shōu Měiyuán?

Do you accept US dollars?

B: 对不起, 我们 不 收 美元.
Duìbuqǐ, wǒmen bù shōu Měiyuán.
我们 只 收 人民币.
Wǒmen zhǐ shōu Rénmínbì.

Sorry, we don't accept U.S. dollars.
We only accept Renminbi.

A: 你能 告诉我 在哪儿能 换
Nǐ néng gàosu wǒ zài nǎr néng huàn
美元 吗?
Měiyuán ma?

Can you tell me where I can change U.S. dollars?

B: 你可以 在银行 换, 也可以在
Nǐ kěyǐ zài yínháng huàn, yě kěyǐ zài
饭店 换.
fàndiàn huàn.

You can change them at the bank or at the hotel.

A: 谢谢.
Xièxie.

Thank you.

B: 不 客气.
Bú kèqi.

You are welcome.

A: 这儿 能 换 美元 吗?
Zhèr néng huàn Měiyuán ma?

Can I exchange U.S. dollars here?

B: 能. 你要 换 多少?
Néng. Nǐ yào huàn duōshao?

Yes, how much do you want to exchange?

A: 一美元 今天 能 换 多少
Yì Měiyuán jīntiān néng huàn duōshao
人民币?
Rénmínbì?

How much Renminbi does one U.S. dollar convert to today?

B: 一美元 今天 能 换 八块
Yì Měiyuán jīntiān néng huàn bā kuài
人民币.
Rénmínbì.

One U.S. dollar converts to 8 *kuai* Renminbi.

A: 我 换 三百 美元.
Wǒ huàn sān bǎi Měiyuán.

I want to change $300.

B: 好, 请 等 一下儿. 这 是 两 千
Hǎo, qǐng děng yíxiàr. Zhè shì liǎng qiān
四百 块 人民币.
sì bǎi kuài Rénmínbì.

OK. Just a minute. This is 2400 *kuai*.

A: 谢谢.
Xièxie.

Thank you.

A: 你买什么?
Nǐ mǎi shénme?

What do you want to buy?

B: 这件 大衣多少 钱?
Zhè jiàn dàyī duōshao qián?

How much is this coat?

A: 两 百 五 十 块。　　　　　　　　　250 kuai.
　　Liǎng bǎi wǔshí kuài.

B: 我 能 不 能 看看?　　　　　　　Can I take a look?
　　Wǒ néng bu néng kànkan?

A: 当然 可以。　　　　　　　　　　Sure.
　　Dāngrǎn kěyǐ.

B: 我 能 试试 吗?　　　　　　　　Can I try it on?
　　Wǒ néng shìshi ma?

A: 没 问题。　　　　　　　　　　　No problem.
　　Méi wèntí.

A: 请问, 那 条 裤子 多少 钱?　　Excuse me, how much is that pair of pants?
　　Qǐngwèn, nà tiáo kùzi duōshao qián?

B: 一百块。　　　　　　　　　　　100 kuai.
　　Yì bǎi kuài.

A: 太贵了。有 没有 便宜一点儿 的?　Too expensive. Do you have anything
　　Tài guì le. Yǒu méiyǒu piányi yìdiǎnr de?　cheaper?

B: 有, 你看看 这 条。　　　　　　Yes, take a look at this pair.
　　Yǒu, nǐ kànkan zhè tiáo.

A: 谢谢。　　　　　　　　　　　　Thank you.
　　Xièxie.

A: 听说 上海 的 东西 很 贵。　　I heard that things in Shanghai are very
　　Tīngshuō Shànghǎi de dōngxi hěn guì.　expensive.

B: 不 一定, 要 看 什么 店。有的　Not necessarily. It depends on the store.
　　Bù yídìng, yào kàn shénme diàn. Yǒude　Some stores are expensive, some are very
　　店 东西 贵, 有的 店 东西 很　cheap.
　　diàn dōngxi guì, yǒude diàn dōngxi hěn
　　便宜。
　　piányì.

A: 什么 店 东西 贵, 什么 店　Which stores are expensive and which stores
　　Shénme diàn dōngxi guì, shénme diàn　are cheap?
　　东西 便宜?
　　dōngxi piányì?

B: 大店 的 东西 贵, 小 店 的 东西　Big stores are expensive, small ones are not.
　　Dà diàn de dōngxi guì, xiǎo diàn de dōngxi
　　不 太 贵。
　　bú tài guì.

A: 你们 卖 不 卖 邮票?　　　　　Do you sell stamps?
　　Nǐmen mài bu mài yóupiào?

B: 卖。你 要 几 张?　　　　　　　Yes. How many do you want?
　　Mài. Nǐ yào jǐ zhāng?

A: 多少 钱 一张?
Duōshao qián yì zhāng?

How much is one?

B: 两 毛 一张.
Liǎng máo yì zhāng.

20 cents each.

A: 我 要 十五张. 一共 多少 钱?
Wǒ yǎo shíwǔ zhāng. Yígòng duōshao qián?

I want 15. How much altogether?

B: 一共 三块.
Yígòng sān kuài.

3 *kuai* altogether.

A: 这 件 毛衣 怎么样?
Zhè jiàn máoyī zěnmeyàng?

What do you think of this sweater?

B: 很 好看.
Hěn hǎo kàn.

Looks very good.

A: 长 不 长?
Cháng bu cháng?

Is it long?

B: 我 觉得 不长.
Wǒ juéde bù cháng.

I don't think it's long.

A: 颜色 怎么样?
Yánsè zěnmeyàng?

What do you think of its color?

B: 颜色 也 不错. 多少 钱?
Yánsè yě bú cuò. Duōshao qián?

The color is also good. How much is it?

A: 一百二十块.
Yì bǎi èrshí kuài.

120 *kuai*.

B: 我 觉得 不太 贵, 你 看 呢?
Wǒ juéde bú tài guì, nǐ kàn ne?

I don't think it's expensive. What do you think?

A: 我 看 也 很好.
Wǒ kàn yě hěn hǎo.

I also think it's good.

WORDS AND EXPRESSIONS

<u>Nouns</u>

钱	qián	money
东西	dōngxi	things, stuff
百货公司	bǎihuògōngsī	department store
衣服	yīfu	clothes, clothing
毛衣	máoyī	sweater
大衣	dàyī	coat
裤子	kùzi	pants
颜色	yánsè	color
邮票	yóupiào	stamps
美元	Měiyuán	U.S. dollars

人民币	Rénmínbì	Renminbi
块	kuài	monetary unit
毛	máo	monetary unit
分	fēn	monetary unit

Verbs

买	mǎi	buy
卖	mài	sell
要	yào	want
收	shōu	accept
能	néng	can
可以	kěyǐ	may
换	huàn	change, exchange
试	shì	try
告诉	gàosu	tell
等	děng	wait
觉得	juéde	feel, think

Adjectives

多	duō	many, much
贵	guì	expensive
便宜	piányi	cheap
长	cháng	long

Adverbs

| 最 | zuì | most |
| 一共 | yígòng | altogether |

Numbers

| 第 | dì | ordinal number indicator |

Classifiers

张	zhāng	
条	tiáo	
件	jiàn	

Expressions

当然	dāngrán	of course
听说	tīngshuō	it is said
有的…… 有的	yǒude ... yǒude	some ... others ...
要看	yàokàn	It depends.
不一定	bù yídìng	not necessarily

76

SUPPLEMENTARY WORDS AND EXPRESSIONS

Nouns

售货员	shòuhuòyuán	sales clerk
顾客	gùkè	customer
市场	shìchǎng	market
鞋子	xiézi	shoes
帽子	màozi	hat
袜子	wàzi	socks
衬衫	chènshān	shirt, blouse
咖啡	kāfēi	coffee
服装店	fúzhuāngdiàn	clothing store
鞋店	xiédiàn	shoe store
书店	shūdiàn	bookstore
纪念品	jìniànpǐn	souvenir
工艺品	gōngyìpǐn	handicraft product
价格	jiàgé	price
信用卡	xìnyòngkǎ	credit card
支票	zhīpiào	check

Verbs

付	fù	pay
穿	chuān	wear, put on
开门	kāi mén	open (for business)
关门	guān mén	close (for business)

Adjectives

合适	héshì	suitable
短	duǎn	short
肥	féi	loose
瘦	shòu	tight
少	shǎo	few or little

Classifiers

双	shuāng	pair
杯	bēi	cup

LANGUAGE POINTS

1. 东西 (dōngxi)

东西 (dōngxi), a combination of two opposite words 东 (dōng) and 西 (xī), is used in the sense of things or stuff. It always refers to physical and tangible objects, often used after certain verbs to avoid making specific references. Here are some examples:

买东西 mǎidōngxi	buy things	卖东西 mài dōngxi	sell things
吃东西 chī dōngxi	eat something	喝东西 hē dōngxi	drink something
写东西 xiě dōngxi	do some writing	听东西 tīng dōngxi	listen to something
洗东西 xǐ dōngxi	do some washing	看东西 kàn dōngxi	read something

2. 要 (yào)

Used in conjunction with another verb, 要 (yào) functions as a modal verb with the meaning of *to be going to, would like,* or *want.* For example:

他星期五 要 去中国.
Tā xīngqi wǔ yào qù Zhōngguó.　　He is going to China on Friday

你要 买 什么?
Nǐ yào mǎi shénme?　　What do you want to buy?

你要 换 多少 钱?
Nǐ yào huàn duōshao qián?　　How much money do you want to change?

3. 第一百货公司 (dì yī bǎihuògōngsī)

As compared with English, ordinal numbers (such as first, second, and third) are much easier to form from cardinal numbers (such as one, two, and three). We simply prefix the word 第 (dì) before the cardinal number. Keep in mind that like cardinal numbers, ordinal numbers also require the presence of classifiers when used with nouns. See for example:

第一个人　　the first person
dì yī　ge rén

第五本书　　the fifth book
dì wǔ běn shū

第十件 大衣　　the tenth coat
dì shí jiàn dàyī

4. 第 一 百 货 公 司 的 东 西 最 多 (dì yī bǎihuògōngsī de dōngxi zuì duō)

多 (duō *many* or *much*) and 少 (shǎo *few* or *little*) are seldom used as predicatives in English. That's why we don't often hear people say *my money is little* and *his money is much* or *people in that city are many* and *people in this city are few*. The more frequent forms in English are *I have little money, he has a lot of money, there are many people in that city,* and *there are few people in this city.*

In Chinese, however, it is commonplace to use 多 (duō) and 少 (shǎo) as predicatives such as:

我 的 钱 很 少, 她 的 钱 很 多。
Wǒde qián hěn shǎo, tāde qián hěn duō.

I have little money, she has a lot of money.

这 个 学 校 的 学生 很 多,
Zhè ge xuéxiào de xuésheng hěn duō,

There are many students in this school, but very few students in that school.

那 个 学 校 的 学生 很 少.
nà ge xuéxiào de xuésheng hěn shǎo.

5. Formation of superlatives

It is very simple to form superlative adjectives in Chinese: prefix the word 最 (zuì) to the adjectives. Here are some more examples:

最 好	best	最 高 兴	happiest
zuì hǎo		zuì gāoxìng	
最 忙	busiest	最 累	most tired
zuì máng		zuì lèi	
最 少	least	最 慢	slowest
zuì shǎo		zuì màn	

6. 能 (néng) and 可 以 (kěyǐ)

能 (néng) and 可 以 (kěyǐ) are modal verbs in Chinese similar to *can* and *may* in English. They should be used in conjunction with another verb. 能 (néng) is usually used in questions and 可 以 (kěyǐ) in answers. For example:

A: 你 能 告 诉 我 在 哪 儿 能 换
Nǐ néng gàosu wǒ zài nǎr néng huàn
美 元 吗?
Měiyuán ma?

Can you tell me where I can change U.S. dollars?

B: 你 可 以 在 银 行 换, 也 可 以 在
Nǐ kěyǐ zài yínháng huàn, yě kěyǐ zài
饭 店 换.
fàndiàn huàn.

You can change them at the bank or at the hotel.

79

A: 我 能 不 能 看看?　　　　　　Can I take a look?
　　Wǒ néng bu néng kànkan?
B: 当然 可以.　　　　　　　　　Sure.
　　Dāngrán kěyǐ.

7. Monetary units in Chinese

There are three monetary units in the Chinese currency 人民币 (rénmínbì): 元 (yuán) / 块(kuài), 角 (jiǎo)/毛 (máo) and 分 (fēn). The difference between 元 (yuán) and 块 (kuài), and between 角 (jiǎo) and 毛 (máo) is that 元 (yuán) and 角 (jiǎo) are formal and written expressions, whereas 块 (kuài) and 毛 (máo) are spoken and everyday forms. One 元 (yuán)/ 块 (kuài) consists of 10 角 (jiǎo)/ 毛 (máo) and one 角 (jiǎo)/ 毛 (máo) consists of 10 分 (fēn) in turn. Comparison should be made with the U.S. monetary system where there are only two formal units: dollar and cents. We may say 99 cents in English, but we can never say 99 分 (fēn) in Chinese simply because there is an additional unit for 10 cents in Chinese. The correct form of 99 cents in Chinese is 9 毛 (máo) 9 分 (fēn).

8. 件 (jiàn) and 条 (tiáo)

It was mentioned in Lesson 4 that 件 (jiàn) and 条 (tiáo) are classifiers for clothing. The interesting difference between them is that 件 (jiàn) is used for clothing that we wear on the upper part of our body such as *shirt*, *blouse*, *coat* and *jacket* and 条 (tiáo) is used for clothing that we wear on the lower part of our body such as *pants*, *shorts*, *skirt*, and *underwear*. Besides clothing, 条 (tiáo) is also used for things that are narrow and long such as *river*, *belt*, *scarf*, *tie*, *street*, *banner* and *fish*.

9. 等一下儿 (děng yíxiàr)

一下 儿 (yíxiàr) in 等 一 下 儿 (děngyí xiàr) indicates that the action expressed by the verb is informal, brief or tentative. For example:

你来一下儿.　　　　　　Come over for a minute.
Nǐ lái yíxiàr.

我 看 一下儿.　　　　　　Let me take a look.
Wǒ kàn yí xiàr.

请 坐 一下儿.　　　　　　Please have a seat.
Qíng zuò yí xiàr.

The same idea can be expressed by the following two alternative patterns: 1) duplication of the verb, and 2) duplication of the verb while inserting 一 (yí) in between. Compare:

我 看 一下儿.　　　　　　Let me take a look.
Wǒ kàn yíxiàr.

我 看看.　　　　　　　Let me take a look.
Wǒ kànkan.

我 看 一 看.　　　　　　Let me take a look.
Wǒ kàn yí kàn.

Motion verbs such as 来 (lái) and 去 (qù) usually can only use the form with 一 下 儿 (yíxiàr).

10. 这 件 衣服 多少钱 (zhè jiàn yīfu duōshao qián)?
　　This sentence illustrates the standard form of asking price, where the item of interest (clothing or anything else) is placed first followed by 多少钱 (duōshao qián). If the item of interest is not defined by a demonstrative pronoun such as 这 (zhè) or 那 (nà), a number with a classifier can be attached at the end of the question to indicate the unit. For example:

鞋子多少 钱 一双?　　　How much is a pair of shoes?
Xiézi duōshao qián yì shuāng?

咖啡多少 钱 一杯?　　　How much is a cup of coffee?
Kāfēi duōshao qián yì bēi?

邮票 多少 钱 一张?　　　How much is a stamp?
Yóupiào duōshao qián yì zhāng?

11. 太贵 了(tài guì le)
　　Particle 了 (le) is often used in conjunction with 太 (tài) after an adjective to soften the tone if the adjective conveys a negative meaning such as 贵 (guì). In addition, *too*, which is the seeming equivalent of 太 (tài) in Chinese, usually carries a negative tone, meaning *excessively* such as *too good (to be true)* and *too fast (to be safe)*, whereas 太 (tài) in Chinese is not always so. See for example:

太 好了.　　　　　　　It's great.
Tài hǎo le.

我 太高兴 了.　　　　　I'm elated.
Wǒ tài gāoxìng le.

12. 听说上海的 东西很贵 (tīngshuō Shànghǎi de dōngxi hěn guì)
　　听说 (tīngshuō) is equivalent to *I heard, I learned, it is said* or *they say* in English. If the subject is the first person pronoun 我 (wǒ), it is often left out:

听说 他 会说 中文.　　　I heard that he can speak Chinese.
Tīngshuō tā huì shuō Zhōngwén.

81

听说　他在纽约　住.
Tīngshuō tā zài Niǔ Yuē zhù.

I heard that he lives in New York.

听说　香港　的东西很
Tīngshuō Xiāng Gǎng de dōngxi hěn
便宜.
piányi.

They say things in Hong Kong are very cheap.

13. 要看什么店 (yào kàn shénme diàn)

"要看 (yào kàn) ..." is used in the sense of *it depends on* ... The subject is usually absent. See for example:

A: 你明天　去不去公园?
　　Nǐ míngtiān qù bu qù gōngyuán?

Are you going to the park tomorrow?

B: 要看天气怎么样.
　　Yào kàn tiānqī zěnmeyàng.

It depends on the weather

A: 你喜欢不喜欢看电视?
　　Nǐ xǐhuan bu xǐhuan kàn diànshì?

Do you like to watch TV?

B: 要看是什么电视.
　　Yào kàn shì shénme diànshì.

It depends on what is on TV.

14. 这件毛衣怎么样 (zhè jiàn máoyī zěnmeyàng)?

"Something 怎么样 (zěnmeyàng)" is a very useful expression used to solicit opinions or suggestions, meaning "How is ...?" or "What do you think of ...?" It is always placed at the end of a sentence such as:

你的中文　老师怎么样?
Nǐde Zhōngwén lǎoshī zěnmeyàng?

How is your Chinese teacher?

昨天　的电影　怎么样?
Zuótiān de diànyīng zěnmeyàng?

How was the movie yesterday?

我们去中国　城, 怎么样?
Wǒmen qù Zhōngguóchéng, zěnmeyàng?

Let's go to Chinatown, shall we?

... 怎么样 (zěnmeyàng) is very often used interchangeably with the expression 好不好 (hǎo bu hǎo).

EXERCISES

I. Answer the following questions:

1. 你的中文 书 多少 钱?
   Nǐde Zhōngwén shū duōshao qián?
2. 你有 中国 钱 吗?
   Nǐ yǒu Zhōngguó qián ma?
3. 你知道一 美元 能 换 多少 人民币 吗?
   Nǐ zhīdao yì Měiyuán néng huàn duōshao Rénmínbì ma?
4. 在 美国 能 用 日元 吗?
   Zài Měiguó nèng yòng Rìyuán ma?
5. 英国人 用 什么 钱?
   Yīngguórén yòng shénme qián?
6. 旧金山 (San Francisco) 的 东西 贵不贵?
   Jiùjīnshān   de dōngxi guì bu guì?
7. 纽约 哪个百货公司 最大?
   Niǔ Yuē nǎ ge bǎihuògōngsī zuì dà?
8. 你今天去不去百货公司? 你去买 什么?
   Nǐ jīntiān qù bu qù bǎihuògōngsī? Nǐ qù mǎi shénme?
9. 你 一般在哪儿买 衣服?
   Nǐ yìbān zài nǎr mǎi yīfu?
10. 你们那儿有 没有 中文 书店?
    Nǐmen nàr yǒu méiyǒu Zhōngwén shūdiàn?

II. Fill in the blanks with appropriate words:

1. 这 _____ 毛衣多少 钱?
   Zhè _____ máoyi duōshao qián?
2. 你们 _____ 不收 日元?
   Nǐmen _____ bu shōu Rìyuán?
3. _____ 有 美国 银行?
   _____ yǒu Měiguó yínháng?
4. 这 个店 的东西不贵, 很 _____ 。
   Zhè ge diàn de dōngxi bú guì, hěn _____ .
5. 你要 换 _____ 美元?
   Nǐ yào huàn _____ Měiyuán?

III. How do you say the following sums in Chinese using the three monetary units:

¥10	¥1.20	¥5.64	¥7.08	¥33.94
¥580	¥99.99	¥6,832.81	¥40.60	¥2,080.01

83

IV. Translate the following into Chinese:

1. Please come (here) for a minute.
2. How much is this dictionary?
3. Sorry. We only accept U.S. dollars. We don't accept Renminbi.
4. Could you tell me where I can find a shoe store?
5. Some stores accept credit cards and others don't.
6. Which department store is the largest in Beijing?
7. It depends on the price.
8. You can't change money in the stores.
9. Can I try on this pair of shoes for a minute?
10. I heard that things in Chinatown are very cheap.

V. Translate the following into English:

1. 我 没 有 美元, 我 只 有 日元。
   Wǒ méi yǒu Měiyuán, wǒ zhǐ yǒu Rìyuán.
2. 昨天 一美元 能 换 八块 人民币。
   Zuótiān yì Měiyuán néng huàn bā kuài Rénmínbì.
3. 那 个 书店 的 英语 书 最多。
   Nà ge shūdiàn de Yīngyǔ shū zuì duō.
4. 很 多人 喜欢 去上海 买 东西。
   Hěn duō rén xǐhuan qù Shànghǎi mǎi dōngxi.
5. 美国 的 商店 卖 很 多 中国 的 东西。
   Měiguó de shāngdiàn mài hěn duō Zhōngguó de dōngxi.
6. 这 条 裤子太长 了, 有 没 有 短 一 点 儿 的?
   Zhè tiáo kùzi tài cháng le, yǒu méiyǒu duǎn yìdiǎnr de?
7. 你 的 大 衣 多 少 钱?
   Nǐde dàyī duōshao qián?
8. 听说 日本东西 很 贵。
   Tīngshuō Rìběn dōngxi hěn guì.
9. 能 不 能 去中国 要 看 我 有 没 有 钱。
   Néng bu néng qù Zhōngguó yào kàn wǒ yǒu méiyǒu qián.
10. 便宜的东西 不 一 定 好。
    Piányide dōngxi bù yídìng hǎo.

CULTURAL INSIGHTS

The debate about the causal relationship between language and thought has been of perennial interest among linguists, anthropologists, psychologists and philosophers. No consensus has been reached due to the circular nature of evidencing. Thought is not empirically observable except through language and the effect of language is manifested again in language. However the correlation between aspects of language and thought is indisputable. The absence of a linguistic mechanism is often accompanied by an absence of a conceptual scheme. Comparison between English and Chinese in terms of the way in which questions about ordinal numbers are formed illustrate a good case in point.

Unlike English where ordinal numbers can be morphologically very different from cardinal numbers, ordinal numbers in Chinese bear close formal resemblance to cardinal numbers in a consistent way. They are formed by prefixing the word *di* before the cardinal numbers such as *di yi* (first), *di er* (second), *di san* (third), etc. *Di* serves a function similar to *-th* at the end of cardinal numbers in English. However, the similarity quickly ends when we ask questions about ordinal numbers in Chinese and English.

It is extremely difficult in English to form a question that elicits an unambiguous answer in the form of an ordinal number. Try to formulate a natural question to the following sentence that elicit the answer "the 40th":

Ronald Reagan was the 40th President of the United States.

Native speakers of English would find the task impossible to accomplish other than to express it in a two-step process such as *George Washington was the first President of the United States, what about Reagan?* Some of the attempts resulted in awkward questions like *Which President was Reagan?* (the answer is not necessarily *the 40th*, it could very well be *he was the one with an actor's background*).

Questions about ordinal numbers, however, do not present any problem in Chinese. To ask a question about an ordinal number in Chinese, all you need to do is to use *ji*, the question word about numbers, after the ordinal number indicator *di* such as *di ji ge ren* and *di ji ben shu* (No translation is attempted since it is impossible to translate).

What should interest us is not why it is difficult in English to ask questions about ordinal numbers, but rather why it is that it never bothers English speakers to ask such questions. Does it mean that order and sequence are important to the Chinese, but not to the speakers of English? It is true that order and sequence in the form of seniority, seating arrangement and so on are of consequence to the Chinese who are a number-conscious people, but no one would accept the claim that they are not important to speakers of English. The reason that English speakers never agonize about how to ask such questions is simply that it never occurs to them to ask such questions. Language is the tool through which thinking is conducted. A linguistic gap necessarily creates a conceptual gap. To explore gaps such as this in linguistic mechanism in relation to conceptual schemes in various language would be a worthwhile pursuit.

Language is often thought of as being a mirror that reflects the external reality. Nothing, in fact, could be further from the truth. Language is a mirror, but it is a "fun house" mirror distorting our perception of the external reality. The external reality is cut up and classified differently in different languages. The classic example is the color system. While some languages have up to 20 terms for primary colors, others have only two. Units of numbers in Chinese, as compared with those in English provide another example, where they often do not correspond to each other:

billion			million			thousand		hundreds	tens	ones	*English*
yi			wan				qian	bai	shi	ge	*Chinese*
3	2	1	9	8	7	6	5	4	3	2	1	

The above number is read in Chinese as *san qian liang bai yi shi jiu yi ba qian qi bai liu shi wu wan si qian san bai er shi yi.*

8

FOOD & EATING

SENTENCE PATTERNS

月 宫 好象 不 错.
Yuè Gōng hǎoxiàng bú cuò.

The Moon Palace seems very good.

月 宫 的什么 菜 有名?
Yuè Gōng de shénme cài yǒumíng?

What are the specialty dishes at the Moon Palace?

你们 要 米饭 还是 要 面条?
Nǐmen yào mǐfàn háishi yào miàntiáo?

Do you want rice or noodle?

我 都 不要.
Wǒ dōu bú yào.

I want neither.

你 吃 过 北京 烤鸭 吗?
Nǐ chī guo Běijīng kǎoyā ma?

Have you ever had Beijing Duck?

你 有 没有 喝过 青岛 啤酒?
Nǐ yǒu méiyǒu hē guo Qīngdǎo píjiǔ?

Have you ever had Qingdao beer?

CONVERSATIONS

A: 你们 饿 不 饿?
   Nǐmen è bu è?

Are you hungry?

B: 我 有 点儿 饿。
   Wǒ yǒudiǎnr è.

I'm a little hungry.

C: 我 很 饿。
   Wǒ hěn è.

I'm very hungry.

A: 我们 去吃 中国 菜, 怎么样?
   Wǒmen qù chī Zhōngguó cài, zěnmeyàng?

Shall we go and have Chinese food?

B: 当然 好。我们 去哪儿吃?
   Dāngrán hǎo. Wǒmen qù nǎr chī?

Great idea. Where shall we go?

A: 去 中国城, 好 不 好?
   Qù Zhōngguóchéng, hǎo bu hǎo?

Let's go to Chinatown, shall we?

B: 好。 你 知道 中国城 哪家
   Hǎo. Nǐ zhīdao Zhōngguóchéng nǎ jiā
   餐馆 好 吗?
   cānguǎn hǎo ma?

Do you know which restaurant in Chinatown is good?

A: 月 宫 好象 不错。
   Yuè Gōng hǎoxiàng bú cuò.

The Moon Palace seems very good.

B: 月 宫 的什么 菜有名?
   Yuè Gōng de shénme cài yǒumíng?

What are the specialty dishes at the Moon Palace?

A: 月 宫 的烤鸭和海鲜 有名。
   Yuè Gōng de kǎoyā hé hǎixiān yǒumíng.

The roast duck and seafood there are famous.

A: 几 位?
   Jǐ wèi?

How many people?

B: 三 位。
   Sān wèi.

Three.

A: 请 这儿坐。这 是 菜单。
   Qǐng zhèr zuò. Zhè shì càidān.

Please sit here. This is the menu.

B: 谢 谢。
   Xièxie.

Thank you.

A: 你们 要 什么 菜?
   Nǐmen yào shénme cài?

What dish do you want to order?

B: 我们 要 一个酸 辣汤, 一个
   Wǒmen yào yí ge suān là tāng, yí ge
   木 须 肉, 一个烤鸭和一个素菜。
   mùxū ròu, yí ge kǎoyā hé yí ge sùcài.

We want a sweet and sour soup, a *muxu* (mushu) pork, a roast duck and a vegetable.

A: 你们 要 喝点儿什么?
   Nǐmen yào hē diǎnr shénme?

What would you like to drink?

B: 你们 有 什么?
   Nǐmen yǒu shénme?

What do you have?

A: 我们 有白酒, 红酒 和啤酒。
   Wǒmen yǒu báijiǔ, hóngjiǔ hé píjiǔ.

We have liquor, wine, and beer.

B: 你们 有 没有 青岛 啤酒?
   Nǐmen yǒu méiyǒu Qīngdǎo píjiǔ?

Do you have Qingdao beer?

A: 有，要几瓶？
Yǒu, yào jǐ píng?

Yes, how many bottles?

B: 我们 要 五瓶。
Wǒmen yào wǔ píng.

We want five bottles.

A: 你们 要 米饭 还是 要 面条？
Nǐmen yào mǐfàn háishi yào miàntiáo?

Do you want rice or noodles?

B: 我 要 米饭。
Wǒ yào mǐfàn.

I want rice.

C: 我 要 面条。
Wǒ yào miàntiáo.

I want noodles.

D: 我 都 不要。能 不能 给我 面包？
Wǒ dōu bú yào. Néng bu néng gěi wǒ miànbāo?

I want neither. Can you give me bread?

A: 当然 可以。
Dāngrán kěyǐ.

Of course.

A: 你能 不能 喝酒？
Nǐ néng bu néng hē jiǔ?

Can you drink?

B: 要看 什么 酒。
Yàokàn shénme jiǔ.

It depends on what drink.

A: 你能 喝什么 酒？
Nǐ néng hē shénme jiǔ?

What can you drink?

B: 我 能 喝啤酒。
Wǒ néng hē píjiǔ.

I can drink beer.

A: 你能 喝多少 啤酒？
Nǐ néng hē duōshao píjiǔ?

How much beer can you drink?

B: 我 能 喝两 瓶。
Wǒ néng hē liǎng píng.

I can drink two bottles.

A: 你吃过北京 烤鸭吗？
Nǐ chī guo Běijīng kǎoyā ma?

Have you had Beijing Duck before?

B: 没有。这 是第一次。
Méiyǒu. Zhè shì dì yī cì.

No, this is the first time.

A: 味道 怎么样？
Wèidào zěnmeyàng?

How does it taste?

B: 味道 好极了。
Wèidào hǎo jíle.

It is simply great.

A: 你有 没有 喝过青岛 啤酒？
Nǐ yǒu méiyǒu hē guo Qīngdǎo píjiǔ?

Have you had Qingdao Beer before?

B: 喝过。
Hē guo.

Yes.

A: 你觉得怎么样？
Nǐ juéde zěnmeyàng?

What do you think of it?

B: 青岛 啤酒很 好 喝。
Qīngdǎo píjiǔ hěn hǎo hē.

Qingdao Beer tastes very good.

89

A: 你 最 喜欢 吃 中国　 的 什么　菜?
　 Nǐ zuì xǐhuan chī Zhōngguó de shénme cài?

What Chinese dish do you like to eat the most?

B: 我 最 喜欢 吃 四川 菜。
　 Wǒ zuì xǐhuan chī Sìchuān cài.

I like to eat the Sichuan (Sezchuan) dish the most.

A: 听说　四川 菜 很 辣。
　 Tīngshuō Sìchuān cài hěn là.

I heard that the Sichuan (Sezchuan) dish is very spicy.

B: 对, 但是 很 好 吃。
　 Duì, dànshi hěn hǎo chī.

Right, but it is delicious.

A: 我们的　菜 怎么 样?
　 Wǒmende cài zěnmeyàng?

How is our food?

B: 很 好 吃。
　 Hěn hǎo chī.

Delicious.

A: 谢谢。这 是 帐单。
　 Xièxie. Zhè shì zhàngdān.

Thank you. Here is the check.

B: 一共　多少　钱?
　 Yígòng duōshao qián?

How much altogether?

A: 一共　二 十 五 块。
　 Yígòng èrshiwǔ kuài.

25 dollars altogether.

B: 这 是 二 十 五 块。这 是 小费。
　 Zhè shì èrshiwǔ kuài. Zhè shì xiǎofèi.

This is 25 dollars. This is the tip.

A: 谢谢。欢迎　再 来。
　 Xièxie. Huānyíng zài lái.

Thank you. Come again.

B: 一定。
　 Yídìng.

Absolutely.

WORDS AND EXPRESSIONS

Nouns

米饭	mǐfàn	cooked rice
面包	miànbāo	bread
菜	cài	dishes
烤鸭	kǎoyā	roast duck
海鲜	hǎixiān	seafood
菜单	càidān	menu
汤	tāng	soup
木须	mùxū	muxu (mushu)
素菜	sùcài	vegetable dish
白酒	báijiǔ	liquor
红酒	hóngjiǔ	wine
啤酒	píjiǔ	beer

瓶	píng	bottle
肉	ròu	meat
帐单	zhàngdān	check, bill
小费	xiǎofèi	tip
味道	wèidào	taste
次	cì	time (occurance)

Verbs

好象	hǎoxiàng	seem
喝	hē	drink
坐	zuò	sit
给	gěi	give
欢迎	huānyíng	welcome

Adjectives

有名	yǒumíng	famous
酸	suān	sour
辣	là	spicy
对	duì	right, correct

Adverbs

| 极了 | jíle | extremely |
| 一定 | yídìng | certainly, definitely |

Classifiers

| 位 | wèi | |
| 家 | jiā | |

Particles

| 过 | guo | |

Expressions

| 有点儿 | yǒudiǎnr | a little |

SUPPLEMENTARY WORDS AND EXPRESSIONS

Nouns

牛肉	niúròu	beef
猪肉	zhūròu	pork
羊肉	yángròu	lamb
鸡	jī	chicken

鱼	yú	fish
电影	diànyǐng	movie
茶	chá	tea
鸡蛋	jīdàn	egg
牛奶	niúnǎi	milk
饺子	jiǎozi	dumpling
包子	bāozi	steamed stuffed bun
水果	shuǐguǒ	fruit
碗	wǎn	bowl
盘子	pánzi	plate
筷子	kuàizi	chopsticks
刀	dāo	knife
叉	chā	fork
餐巾	cānjīn	napkin
糖	táng	sugar
盐	yán	salt
月宫	Yuè Gōng	Moon Palace
青岛	Qīngdǎo	Qingdao

Verbs

炒	chǎo	fry
炸	zhà	deep fry
做饭	zuòfàn	cook
请......吃饭	qǐng ... chīfàn	invite sb. to dinner

Adjectives

红	hóng	red
绿	lǜ	green
咸	xián	salty
甜	tián	sweet

LANGUAGE POINTS

1. 家 (jiā)

家 (jiā), as a classifier, is used with such words as hospital, bank, company, factory, movie theater, store and restaurant. What is common among these words is that they are all home-like (the original meaning of 家 jiā) buildings and structures.

2. 几 位 (jǐ wèi)?

几 位 (jǐ wèi) is an abbreviated form for 你们 是 几 位 客 人 (nǐmen shì jǐ wèi kèrén). 位 (wèi) is a polite classifier for people, usually used for words like *guest, teacher, customer, friend, gentleman,* and *lady.* In informal and familiar speech, 个 (gè) is used instead.

3. 你们 要 喝 点 儿 什 么 (nǐmen yào hē diǎnr shénme)?

点 儿 (diǎnr) is short for 一点 儿 (yìdiǎnr). When the number is one, we often leave it out. For example:

我 有 个 问题。 Wǒ yǒu ge wèntí.	I have a question.
她 要 买 件 大衣。 Tā yào mǎi jiàn dàyī.	She wants to buy a coat.
我 有点 儿 饿。 Wǒ yǒudiǎnr è.	I'm a little hungry.

4. 你们 要 米饭 还是 要 面条 (nǐmen yào mǐfàn háishi yào miàntiáo)?

This is an alternative question involving a choice. The question is indicated by 还 是 (háishi), which is placed between the two choices. Please note that 还 是 (háishi) used in the sense of *or* is an interrogative expression. As such, it can only be used in questions. In other words, 还 是 (háishi) can never be used in affirmative sentences in the sense of *or.* The Chinese word for *or* in affirmative sentences like *he is coming either today or tomorrow* is 或 (huò) or 或 者 (huò zhě).

There are three possible answers to an alternative question: 1) making one choice, 2) accepting both choices, and 3) rejecting both choices. See the following illustrations:

你喜欢 法国 电影 还是美国 电影?
Nǐ xǐhuan Fǎguó diànyǐng háishi Měiguó diànyǐng?
Do you like French movies or American movies?

我 喜欢美国 电影 / 我 喜欢 法国 电影.
Wǒ xǐhuan Měiguó diànyǐng. Wǒ xǐhuan Fǎguó diànyǐng.
I like American movies. / I like French movies.

我 都 喜欢。 Wǒ dōu xǐhuan.	I like both.
我 都 不喜欢。 Wǒ dōu bù xǐhuan.	I like neither.

93

In the second and third answers, 都 (dōu) is used to indicate inclusiveness, positive or negative. This is different from English, where *both* is used in affirmative responses whereas *neither* is used in negative responses.

5. 你吃过北京烤鸭吗 (nǐ chī guo Běijīng kǎoyā ma)?
    The grammatical particle 过 (guo) is used after a verb to indicate an action that took place at an unspecified time in the past. The emphasis is on the experience rather than the result or completion of the action. It can often be translated into the perfect tense (such as *I have done ... before, he has been to ...before*, and *they have seen ...before*). See the following examples:

我 爸爸 去 过 北京.
Wǒ bàba   qù guo Běijīng.
          My father has been to Beijing.

他吃 过 法国 菜.
Tā chī guo Fǎguó cài.
          He has had French food.

他们 学 过 中文.
Tāmen xué guo Zhōngwén.
          They have studied Chinese.

    The negative of the sentence is indicated by 没有 (méiyǒu), where 有 (yǒu) is sometimes left out, instead of 不 (bù), e.g.

我 爸爸没有 去 过 北京.
Wǒ bàba   méiyǒu qù guo Běijīng.
          My father has never been to Beijing.

他没有 吃过 法国 菜.
Tā méiyǒu chī guo Fǎguó cài.
          He has never had French food.

他们 没有 学 过 中文.
Tāmen méiyǒu xué guo Zhōngwén.
          They have never studied Chinese.

    Like sentences with a present or future reference, there are two yes/no forms for sentences using 过 (guo) to indicate past experience: attaching 吗 (ma) at the end of the sentence or using 有没有 (yǒu méiyǒu) before the verb. See for example:

你爸爸 去过 北京 吗?   你爸爸 有 没有 去 过 北京?
Nǐ bāba qù guo Běijīng ma?   Nǐ bāba yǒu méiyǒu qù guo Běijīng?
       Has your father been to Beijing?

他 吃过 法国菜 吗?   他有 没有 吃 过 法国菜?
Tā chī guo Fǎguó cài ma?   Tā yǒu méiyǒu chī guo Fǎguó cài?
       Has he ever had French food?

他们 学 过 中文 　 吗？　　　他们 有 没 有 学 过 中文？
Tāmen xué guo Zhōngwén ma?　　Tāmen yǒu méiyǒu xué guo Zhōngwén?
Have they ever studied Chinese?

To give a yes answer to the above questions, simply take the verb together with 过 (guo). To give a no answer, use 没有 (méiyǒu) before the verb and 过 (guo). The following are yes/no answers to the above questions:

去 过/没有 去 过
qù guo/méiyǒu qù guo

吃 过/没有 吃 过
chī guo/méiyǒu chī guo

学 过/没有 学 过
xué guo/méiyǒu xué guo

6. 很 好 吃 (hěn hǎochī)

好 (hǎo) is often used with a verb to form an adjective, meaning *good to* ... For example:

好 喝 hǎo hē	good to drink
好 听 hǎo tīng	good to listen (used to describe music, song, voice, etc.)
好 看 hǎo kàn	pretty, interesting (used to describe people, books, movies, etc.)
好 玩 hǎo wán	fun, interesting (used to describe places, toys, etc.)

EXERCISES

I. Answer the following questions:

1. 你喜欢 吃中国　　菜还是日本菜？
   Nǐ xǐhuan chī Zhōngguó cài háishi Rìběn cài?
2. 你喝过青岛　　啤酒吗？
   Nǐ hē guo Qīngdǎo píjiǔ ma?
3. 你吃肉吗? 你 喜欢 吃什么 肉？
   Nǐ chī ròu ma? Nǐ xǐhuan chī shénme ròu?
4. 你去过中国　　吗？
   Nǐ qù guo Zhōngguó ma?

5. 你 会 不 会 做 菜? 你 会 做 什 么 菜?
   Nǐ huì bu huì zuò cài? Nǐ huì zuò shénme cài?
6. 你 家 谁 做 饭?
   Nǐ jiā shuí zuò fàn?
7. 你 能 不 能 喝 酒? 你 能 喝 什 么 酒? 你 能 喝 多 少?
   Nǐ néng bu néng hē jiǔ? Nǐ néng hē shénme jiǔ? Nǐ néng hē duōshao?
8. 纽 约 的 什 么 最 有 名?
   Niǔ Yuē de shénme zuì yǒumíng?
9. 中 国 茶 好 喝 不 好 喝? 你 喜 欢 红 茶 还 是 绿 茶?
   Zhōngguó chá hǎo hē bu hǎo hē? Nǐ xǐhuan hóngchá háishi lǜchá?
10. 你 在 学 校 工 作 还 是 在 公 司 工 作?
    Nǐ zài xuéxiào gōngzuò háishi zài gōngsī gōngzuò?

II. Fill in the blanks with appropriate words:

1. 你 是 中 国 人 _____ 美 国 人?
   Nǐ shì Zhōngguórén _____ Měiguórén?
2. 你 喜 欢 _____ 喜 欢 法 国 菜?
   Nǐ xǐhuan _____ xǐhuan Fǎguó cài?
3. 他 没 有 去 _____ 英 国.
   Tā méiyǒu qù _____ Yīngguó.
4. 日 本 音 乐 很 好 _____.
   Rìběn yīnyuè hěn hǎo _____.
5. 我 妈 妈 吃 _____ 北 京 烤 鸭.
   Wǒ māma chī _____ Běijīng kǎoyā.
6. 你 _____ 没 有 看 过 这 本 书?
   Nǐ _____ méiyǒu kàn guo zhè běn shū?
7. _____ 有 中 国 餐 馆?
   _____ yǒu Zhōngguó cānguǎn?
8. 一 共 _____ 钱?
   Yígòng _____ qián?
9. 这 _____ 餐 馆 的 菜 很 有 名。
   Zhè _____ cānguǎn de cài hěn yǒumíng.
10. 这 是 我 第 二 _____ 喝 青 岛 啤 酒。
    Zhè shì wǒ dì èr _____ hē Qīngdǎo píjiǔ.

III. First change the following sentences into yes/no questions and then change them into negative sentences:

1. 我 看 过 英 国 电 影。
   Wǒ kàn guo Yīngguó diànyǐng.
2. 她 的 老 师 学 过 德 语。
   Tāde lǎoshī xué guo Déyú.
3. 他 去 过 香 港。
   Tā qù guo Xiāng Gǎng.

4. 我的中国　朋友　来过我家.
Wǒde Zhōngguó péngyou lái guo wǒ jiā.

5. 他们 吃 过 法国菜.
Tāmen chī guo Fǎguó cài.

6. 她的男朋友　听 过 日本音乐.
Tāde nán péngyou tīng guo Rìběn yīnyuè.

7. 我 爸爸 在中国　银行 工作　过.
Wǒ bàba zài Zhōngguó yínháng gōngzuò guo.

8. 她妈妈 在 中国　换 过 钱.
Tā māma zài Zhōngguó huàn guo qián.

9. 王　老师 在那个商店　买 过 东西.
Wáng Lǎoshī zài nà ge shāngdiàn mǎi guo dōngxi.

10. 我 弟弟 在加州 住 过.
Wǒ dìdi zài Jiāzhōu zhù guo.

IV. Translate the following into Chinese:

1. I'm not too hungry.
2. Peking Duck is very famous.
3. Is the men's room on the second floor or third floor?
4. Do you want coffee or tea?
5. This restaurant's dishes are delicious.
6. Have you been to the Chinatown in New York?
7. You look very tired.
8. This was my first time eating Japanese food. I found the taste was very good.
9. Restaurants in China don't accept tips.
10. What do you think if we go to see a movie?

V. Translate the following into English:

1. 你爸爸 在 大学 工作　还是在中学　工作?
Nǐ bàba zài dàxué gōngzuò háishi zài zhōngxué gōngzuò?

2. 绿茶 不好 喝, 我 喜欢 红茶.
Lǜchá bù hǎo hē, wǒ xǐhuan hóngchá.

3. 你的女朋友　是中国人　还是美国人?
Nǐde nǚ péngyou shì Zhōngguórén háishi Měiguórén?

4. 我 先生　没有 看 过 中国　电影.
Wǒ xiānsheng méiyǒu kàn guo Zhōngguó diànyǐng.

5. 广州　的 什么 菜有名?
Guǎngzhōu de shénme cài yǒumíng?

6. 我 姐姐不能 喝白酒, 能 喝一点儿 红酒.
Wǒ jiějie bù néng hē báijiǔ, néng hē yìdiǎnr hóngjiǔ.

7. 米饭和面条　我 都 不要, 我 要 面包.
Mǐfàn hé miàntiáo wǒ dōu bú yào, wǒ yào miànbāo.

8. 他家他太太做饭，我家我做饭.
   Tā jiā tā tàitai zuò fàn, wǒ jiā wǒ zuò fàn.
9. 你今天晚上 在家吃饭还是在餐馆 吃饭?
   Nǐ jīntiān wǎnshang zài jiā chī fàn háishi zài cānguǎn chī fàn?
10. 中国人 有时只吃饭,不吃菜, 美国人 有时 只吃菜, 不吃饭.
    Zhōngguórén yǒushi zhǐ chī fàn, bù chī cài, Měiguórén yǒushi zhǐ chī cài, bù chī fàn.

VI. Write five things that you have done before.

CULTURAL INSIGHTS

Few people in the world have never had some culinary experience with Chinese food. To many people, the very term China or Chinese conjures up images of savory cuisine. It is indisputable that the Chinese people attach great importance to the preparation of their food, which can reach incredible levels of sophistication, elaboration and variety. Dishes not only have to taste good, but also have to be aesthetically appealing. If you are invited by your friends in China to a meal, you can expect to see a lavish spread of food, which is the best way in Chinese culture to show hospitality to friends, particularly those coming from afar.

Meals are called *fan* in Chinese. A typical Chinese meal consists of two parts: *fan* and *cai*. *Fan* is grain or starch-based staple, which includes rice, noodle, steamed bread, steamed buns, dumplings and so on. It comes in a bowl, which is served individually. *Cai* refers to dishes, which consists of two types—*sucai* and *huncai*. *Sucai* are vegetable dishes and *huncai* are dishes with meat or fish. Dishes are usually served on a plate, which is shared. Of particular mention are the terms for the meat of various animals. In English, the term for the meat served on the table is often different from that used for the animal in the pen or the stable, a result of the Norman Conquest. In Chinese however, the terms for the meat of various animals are simply the combination of the word for the animal plus the word *rou* (meat) such as *zhu rou* (pig meat, thus pork), *niu rou* (cow meat, thus beef) and *yang rou* (sheep meat, thus lamb). They may not sound as elegant as those Norman-French terms, but they are logical and easy to remember.

You may have already noticed that the staple food and the meal, of which the staple food is a part, are both called *fan*. This is for a good reason. There is a rhetorical device in language called *synecdoche* whereby the part can be used to refer to the whole such as *roof* for the *house* and *waves* for the *ocean*. *Fan* is a good case in point. Traditionally and to a large extent still true today, *fan* is held more important than *cai* to the Chinese, providing about 75 percent of caloric intake for the population. For this reason, *fan* is often called *zhu shi* (main food) in Chinese. *Fan* is considered so important chiefly for an economic reason. It is easier to afford *fan* than *cai*. In the West, *fan* only serves as side food and may be dispensed with altogether, whereas in China, sometimes people only eat *fan* without *cai*. Since *fan* was taken so seriously, it came to be used to refer to the whole meal that includes *cai* as well. Let's use *fan the meal* and *fan the staple* to distinguish them. This explains why the Chinese do not think you have eaten even if you are full, eating a lot of dishes, but no rice or bread, because you have not eaten *fan*, a play upon words that can be interpreted as *fan the staple*.

Tang (soup) is part of *cai*, which can be of many varieties. Different from the practice in the West, *tang* is served either with the meal or at the end of the meal, but never before the meal. On formal occasions, people do drink. The word used by the Chinese for drink is a generic one—*jiu*, which simply means alcoholic beverage, covering liquor, wine, and beer. At the meal, Chinese people like to urge their guests to drink more on the belief that if they do not let their guests drink to their hearts' content, they are mistreating them. Mistreatment of guests is definitely a sin. For this reason, the hosts will go out of their way to make their guests drink more by finding all sorts of justifications. It is customary in China for a guest to tell the host that he can only drink 30 percent when he can actually drink 100 percent just to leave enough room to maneuver with the host. Failing to do so, you may become the object of repeated toasts in a shower of hospitality.

Tea is an everyday drink for which there is a national taste. This native product is served on all occasions. Visitors to someone's house will be served tea without asking. Chinese teas fall into the following general types: green tea, black tea (which is actually called red tea in China), jasmine tea, and *wulong* tea, each of which can be further divided. The classification is often based on the manner in which a particular kind of tea is produced. Green tea is unfermented, black tea is fermented, *wulong* tea is semi-fermented, and jasmine tea is made from a combination of black tea, green tea, *wulong* tea and some fragrant flowers. Although the taste for tea varies from individual to individual, generally people in southern China prefer green tea, whereas those in northern China prefer jasmine tea. *Wulong* tea is the favorite in areas of Guangdong and Fujian. This geographical preference may have to do with the climatic conditions. Green tea is popular in the warm south because it is soothing and jasmine tea is favored in the cold north because it adds heat to the body temperature.

9

TRAVEL

SENTENCE PATTERNS

你每天 怎么去上班?
Nǐ měitiān zěnme qù shàngbān?

How do you go to work every day?

我 每天 坐地铁去上班.
Wǒ měitiān zuò dìtiě qù shàngbān.

I go to work by subway every day.

从 南京 路坐 地铁到 火车站
Cóng Nánjīng Lù zuò dìtiě dào huǒchēzhàn
要 多少 时间?
yào duōshao shíjiān?

How long does it take to go from Nanjing Road to the train station by subway?

你们 去华盛顿 作什么?
Nǐmen qù Huáshèngdùn zuò shénme?

Why are you going to Washington?

我们 去玩.
Wǒmen qù wán.

We are going there for pleasure.

你家离学校 远 不远?
Nǐ jiā lí xuéxiào yuǎn bu yuǎn?

Is your home far from the school?

我 有时 骑自行车 去上学,
Wǒ yǒushí qí zìxíngchē qù shàng xué,
有时 走去上学.
yǒushí zǒu qù shàng xué.

Sometimes I go to school by bike, sometimes I go there on foot.

你今年 在哪儿过 圣诞节?
Nǐ jīnnián zài nǎr guò Shèngdànjié?

Where are you going to spend your Christmas this year?

我 想 坐飞机去。
Wǒ xiǎng zuò fēijī qù.

I'd like to go by plane.

你去洛杉矶 住 哪儿?
Nǐ qù Luòshānjī zhù nǎr?

Where are you going to stay in Los Angeles?

旅馆 好不好 找?
Lǚguǎn hǎo bu hǎo zhǎo?

Is it easy to find a hotel?

你一定要 去玩玩。
Nǐ yídìng yào qù wánwan.

You must go there for a visit.

你去过 中国 几次?
Nǐ qù guo Zhōngguó jǐ cì?

How many times have you been to China?

你去过中国 的什么 地方?
Nǐ qù guo Zhōngguó de shénme dìfang?

Where in China have you been to?

CONVERSATIONS

A: 你在哪儿工作?
Nǐ zài nǎr gōngzuò?

Where do you work?

B: 我 在中国 银行 工作.
Wǒ zài Zhōngguó yínháng gōngzuò.

I work at the Bank of China.

A: 你每天 怎么去上班?
Nǐ měitiān zěnme qù shàng bān?

How do you get to work every day?

B: 我 每天 坐地铁去上班.
Wǒ měitiān zuò dìtiě qù shàngbān.

I get to work by subway every day.

A: 你太太每天 也坐 地铁去
Nǐ tàitai měitiān yě zuò dìtiě qù
上班吗?
shàngbān ma?

Does you wife also get to work by subway every day?

B: 她不坐 地铁, 她坐 汽车.
Tā bú zuò dìtiě, tā zuò qìchē.

She does not take the subway. She takes the bus.

A: 上海 有 地铁吗?
Shànghǎi yǒu dìtiě ma?

Are there subways in Shanghai?

B: 有.
Yǒu.

Yes.

A: 从　南京路　坐地铁到火车站
Cóng Nánjīng Lù zuò dìtiě dào huǒchēzhàn
要 多少　时间？
yào duōshao shí jiān?

How long does it take to go from Nanjing Road to the train station by subway?

B: 大概 五分钟。
Dàgài wǔ fēnzhōng.

About five minutes.

A: 上海　有 几路 地铁？
Shànghǎi yǒu jǐ lù dìtiě?

How many subway lines are there in Shanghai?

B: 上海　只有 一路地铁。
Shànghǎi zhǐ yǒu yí lù dìtiě.

There is only one subway line in Shanghai.

A: 这 个周末　你去哪儿？
Zhè ge zhōumò nǐ qù nǎr?

Where are you going to go this weekend?

B: 我 和我 太太去华盛顿。
Wǒ hé wǒ tàitai qù Huáshèngdùn.

My wife and I are going to Washington.

A: 你们 去华盛顿　作 什么？
Nǐmen qù Huáshèngdùn zuò shénme?

Why are you going there?

B: 我们　去玩。
Wǒmen qù wán.

We are going there for pleasure.

A: 你们　怎么去？
Nǐmen zěnme qù?

How are you going to go?

B: 我们　开 车 去。
Wǒmen kāi chē qù.

We are driving there.

A: 从　纽约　开车 到 华盛顿
Cóng Niǔ Yuē kāi chē dào Huáshèngdùn
要 几个小时？
yào jǐ ge xiǎoshí?

How long does it take to drive from New York to Washington?

B: 大概 要 四个小时。
Dàgài yào sì ge xiǎoshí.

It takes about four hours.

A: 你家离学校　远 不远？
Nǐ jiā lí xuéxiào yuǎn bu yuǎn?

Is your home far from the school?

B: 不 太远。 坐 汽车只要十分钟。
Bú tài yuǎn. Zuò qìchē zhǐyào shífēnzhōng.

Not too far. It only takes about ten minutes by bus.

A: 你每天　怎么去上学？
Nǐ měitián zěnme qù shàngxué?

How do you go to school every day?

B: 我 有时 骑自行车 去, 有时 走去.
Wǒ yǒushí qí zixíngchē qù, yǒushí zǒu qù.

Sometimes I go there by bike, sometimes on foot.

A: 你骑自行车要 多少　时间？
Nǐ qí zixíngchē yào duōshao shíjiān?

How long does it take you to go by bike?

B: 骑自行车 要 十五 分钟。
Qí zixíngchē yào shíwǔ fēnzhōng.

It takes about 15 minutes to go by bike.

A: 走 呢？
Zǒu ne?

What about walking?

B: 走 要 三十 分钟.
Zǒu yào sānshí fēnzhōng.

It takes about 30 minutes.

A: 你今年 在哪儿过 圣诞节?
Nǐ jīnnián zài nǎr guò Shēngdànjié?

Where are you going to spend your Christmas this year?

B: 我 去加州.
Wǒ qù Jiāzhōu.

I'm going to California.

A: 你去加州 的什么 地方?
Nǐ qù Jiāzhōu de shénme dìfang?

Where in California are you going?

B: 我 去洛杉矶.
Wǒ qù Luòshānjī.

I'm going to Los Angeles.

A: 你怎么 去?
Nǐ zěnme qù?

How are you going?

B: 我 想 坐飞机去, 可是飞机票
Wǒ xiǎn zuò fēijī qù, kěshì fēijī piào
很 贵, 我 可能 坐 火车 去.
hěn guì, wǒ kěnéng zuò huǒchē qù.

I'd like to go by plane, but I may take the the train, because the plane ticket is very expensive.

A: 你去洛杉矶 住 哪儿?
Nǐ qù Luòshānjī zhù nǎr?

Where are you going to stay in Los Angeles?

B: 我 住 旅馆.
Wǒ zhù lǚguǎn.

I'm going to stay in a hotel.

A: 旅馆 好找 不好 找?
Lǚguǎn hǎo zhǎo bu hǎo zhǎo?

Is it easy to find a hotel?

B: 好 找. 洛杉矶有 很 多 旅馆.
Hǎo zhǎo. Luòshānjī yǒu hěn duō lǚguǎn.

Yes, there are many hotels in Los Angeles.

A: 你去过中国 吗?
Nǐ qù guo Zhōngguó ma?

Have you been to China?

B: 去 过.
Qù guo.

Yes.

A: 你去过 几次?
Nǐ qù guo jǐ cì?

How many times have you been there?

B: 我 去过 两 次.
Wǒ qù guo liǎng cì.

I've been there twice.

A: 你去过 中国 的什么 地方?
Nǐ qù guo Zhōngguó de shénme dìfang?

Where in China have you been to?

B: 我去 过 中国 的北京, 上海,
Wǒ qù guo Zhōngguó de Běijīng, Shànghǎi,
苏州, 杭州 和 广州.
Sūzhōu, Hángzhōu hé Guǎngzhōu.

I've been to Beijing, Shanghai, Suzhou, Hangzhou and Guangzhou.

A: 你最喜欢 哪个 地方?
Nǐ zuì xǐhuan nǎ ge dìfang?

Which place do you like the best?

B: 我 最喜欢 苏州 和杭州.
Wǒ zuì xǐhuan Sūzhōu hé Hángzhōu.

I like Suzhou and Hangzhou the best. Do you know? Chinese people often say, "up

你知道 吗? 中国人 常 说,
Nǐ zhīdao ma? Zhōngguórén cháng shuō,
"上 有 天堂, 下 有 苏 杭".
"Shàng yǒu tiāntáng, xià yǒu Sū Háng."

above there is paradise, down below there is Suzhou and Hangzhou.

WORDS AND EXPRESSIONS

Nouns

车	chē	vehicle
路	lù	road, route
小时	xiǎoshí	hour
分钟	fēnzhōng	minute
年	nián	year
圣诞节	Shèngdànjié	Christmas
飞机	fēijī	airplane
地铁	dìtiě	subway
自行车	zìxíngchē	bicycle
旅馆	lǚguǎn	hotel
地方	dìfang	place
票	piào	ticket
天堂	tiāntáng	paradise
华盛顿	Huáshèngdùn	Washington
苏州	Sūzhōu	Suzhou
杭州	Hángzhōu	Hangzhou

Verbs

开	kāi	operate, drive
骑	qí	ride
走	zǒu	walk
玩	wán	play
上学	shàngxué	go to school
想	xiǎng	would like
过	guò	celebrate, spend (holiday)
找	zhǎo	look for, find
可能	kěnéng	maybe

Adverbs

大概	dàgài	probably
常	cháng	often
上	shàng	up
下	xià	down

<u>Prepositions</u>

从 ...... 到	cóng ... dào ...	from ... to ...
离	lí	away from

SUPPLEMENTARY WORDS AND EXPRESSIONS

<u>Nouns</u>

出租汽车	chūzū qìchē	taxi
电车	diànchē	trolley-bus
街	jiē	street
警察	jǐngchá	police, policeman
护照	hùzhào	passport
签证	qiānzhèng	visa
旅行	lǚxíng	travel
旅行社	lǚxíngshè	travel agency
行李	xíngli	luggage
船	chuán	boat, ship
海关	hǎiguān	customs
导游	dǎoyóu	guide
市中心	shì zhōngxīn	city center, downtown
亚洲	Yàzhōu	Asia
欧洲	Oūzhōu	Europe
美洲	Měizhōu	America (continent)
非洲	Fēizhōu	Africa
澳州	Aòzhōu	Australia

<u>Adjectives</u>

新	xīn	new
近	jìn	close

LANGUAGE POINTS

1. 你每天怎么去上班 (Nǐ měitiān zěnme qù shàngbān)?

怎么 (zěnme) in the question serves as an adverbial of manner. As such, it is placed before the verb together with 每天 (měitiān), which is an adverbial of time. Similarly we can say:

你明天 怎么来? Nǐ míngtiān zěnme lái?	How are you coming tomorrow?

这 个 字 怎 么 写?　　　　　　　How do you write this character?
Zhè ge zì zěnme xiě?

"English" 用 中 文　怎 么 说?　　How do you say "English" in Chinese?
"English" yòng Zhōngwén zěnme shuō?

2. 我 每 天 坐 地 铁 去 上 班 (Wǒ měitiān zuò dìtiě qù shàngbān)

　　To answer the question "你 每 天 怎 么 去 上 班" (Nǐ měitiān zěnme qù shàngbān), all you need to do is to specify, where the question word is, the means such as taking a bus, train, taxi, riding a bicycle or walking.

3. 从 南 京 路 坐 地 铁 到 火 车 站 要 多 少 时 间 (Cóng Nánjīng Lù zuò dìtiě dào huǒchēzhàn yào duōshao shíjiān)?

　　"从 ...... 到 ......" (cóng ... dào ...) is equivalent to *from ... to* in English. For example:

从　早　到　晚　　　　　　　from morning till night
cóng zǎo dào wǎn

从　学 校　到　家　　　　　from school to home
cóng xuéxiào dào jiā

从　中 国　　到 美 国　　　from China to the United States
cóng Zhōngguó dào Měiguó

　　Since Chinese strictly adheres to the principal of temporal sequence whereby what happens first is placed first, the temporal sequence in the question is 1) departing from Nanjing Road, 2) taking the subway, and 3) arriving at the train station. They thus follow each other. Sometimes however, "taking the subway" can be placed either before 1) or after 3) as in

坐　地 铁 从　南 京　路 到 火 车 站　要 多 少　时 间?
Zuò dìtiě　cóng Nánjīng Lù dào huǒchēzhàn yào duōshao shíjiān?

从　南 京　路 到 火 车 站　坐 地 铁 要 多 少　时 间?
Cóng Nánjīng Lù dào huǒchēzhàn zuò dìtiě　yào duōshao shíjiān?

　　The word 要 (yào) in Chinese has two basic meanings: 1) *want, need*, or *be going to*, and 2) *take* or *require* (time, etc.). 要 (yào) is used in the first sense when the subject is animate, be a person or personified object. 要 (yào) is used in the second sense when the subject is impersonal in the form of a process or an action. Compare:

她 明 天　要 去 中 国.　　　　She is going to China tomorrow.
Tā míngtiān yào qù Zhōngguó.

去 火 车 站　你 要 坐 汽 车.　　You need to take the bus to go to the train
Qù huǒchēzhàn nǐ yào zuò qìchē.　　station.

106

开 车 去 要 两 天。   It takes two days to drive there.
Kāi chē qù yào liǎng tiān.

4. 你们去华盛顿作什么 (Nǐmen qù Huáshèngdùn zuò shénme)?

"去 ... 作什么" (qù ... zuò shénme) is a question frequently used to ask about the purpose of going to a certain place. Although Mandarin does have a specific expression equivalent to *why* in English - 为什么 (wèi shénme), it is not as often used as this question form in this instance.

5. 我们去玩 (Wǒmen qù wán)

玩 (wán) is a difficult word to translate into English. Although dictionaries often define it as *play*, it is widely used in Chinese to mean *enjoy, have fun, have a good time, hang out,* or *do something for pleasure*. It is basically opposed to work. The various meanings of 玩 (wán) are illustrated in the following examples:

你有 时间 请 来我 家玩。   Please drop by my house when you have
Nǐ yǒu shíjiān qǐng lái wǒ jiā wán.   time.

北京 很 好 玩。   Beijing is a fun place.
Běijīng hěn hǎo wán.

这 个周末 我 去公园 玩。   I'm going to the park this weekend (to relax).
Zhè ge zhōumò wǒ qù gōngyuán wán.

6. 你家离学校远不远 (Nǐ jiā lí xuéxiào yuǎn bu yuǎn)?

"A 离 (lí) B 远 (yuǎn) /近 (jìn)" is a pattern used to indicate the distance between two places, equivalent to English *A is far from/close to B*. Since "离 (lí) B" (away from B or close to B) is an adverbial expression indicating a point of reference, it is placed before the verb, or the adjective as in this case.

Distinction should be made between 从 (cóng) and 离 (lí), which are often confused because both can be translated into English as *from*. Keep in mind that 从 (cóng) indicates a point of origin or departure, usually used with motion verbs such as 来 (lái *come*) or 去 (qù *go*). On the other hand, 离 (lí) marks a point of reference, usually used with a static verb or adjective. Compare:

他 从 美国 来。   He comes from the United States.
Tā cóng Měiguó lái.

我 家离银行 很 近。   My home is close to the bank.
Wǒ jiā lí yínháng hěn jìn.

7. 你今年在哪儿过圣诞节 (Nǐ jīnnián zài nǎr guò Shèngdànjié)?

过 (guò), meaning *spend*, *celebrate*, or *observe*, is often used in connection with holidays, festivals, birthdays and other important occasions. Although it may be glossed as *spend*, it is never used with money to mean *spend money*. See for example:

中国人　过 不 过 圣诞节?　　　　Do Chinese people celebrate Christmas?
Zhōngguórén guò bu guò Shèngdànjié?

孩子们 最 喜欢 过 年.　　　　　Children like to celebrate New Year's Day
Háizimen zuì xǐhuan guò nián.　　　the most.

你 太太 的 生日 怎么 过?　　　　How do you celebrate your wife's birthday?
Nǐ tàitai de shēngrì zěnme guò?

8. 今 年 (jīnnián)

The following are various ways to express days (today, yesterday, tomorrow), week, month and year (current, previous and next):

明天	明年	下个星期	下个月
míngtiān	míngnián	xià ge xīngqī	xià ge yuè
tomorrow	*next year*	*next week*	*next month*
今天	今年	这个星期	这个 月
jīntiān	jīnnián	zhè ge xīngqī	zhè ge yuè
today	*this year*	*this week*	*this month*
昨天	去年	上个星期	上 个 月
zuótiān	qùnián	shàng ge xīngqi	shàng ge yuè
yesterday	*last year*	*last week*	*last month*

It is clear that 天 (tiān) and 年 (nián) share the same descriptive expressions except *last year*, which is not 昨 年 (zuónián), but rather 去 年 (qùnián) and 星 期 (xīngqī) and 月 (yuè) share the same descriptive expressions.

9. 你 去 过 中国 的 什么 地方 (Nǐ qù guo Zhōngguóde shénme dìfang)?

什么 地方 (shénme dìfang) is a descriptive interrogative expression about place with the same meaning as 哪儿 (nǎr). 你 去 过 中国 的 什么 地方 (Nǐ qù guo Zhōngguóde shénme dìfang) means *where in China have you been to* (literally *you have been to China's what places*). Similarly we can say:

你 去 过 欧洲　 的 哪儿/什 么　地方?　　Where in Europe have you been to?
Nǐ qù guo Ōuzhōu de nǎr　/shénme dìfang?

10. 我 想 坐 飞 机 去 (Wǒ xiǎng zuò fēijī qù)

想 (xiǎng) in the sentence is used as a modal verb, meaning *would like*, *wish*, or *want* (usually in the negative). It is to be followed by a lexical verb. For example:

你想 吃 什么?
Nǐ xiǎng chī shénme?

What would you like to eat?

你想 不想 去看 电影?
Nǐ xiǎng bu xiǎng qù kàn diànyǐng?

Would you like to go to the movies?

他不想 去学校.
Tā bú xiǎng qù xuéxiào.

He doesn't want to go to school.

想 (xiǎng) can also be used as a lexical verb with the meaning *think, believe,* or *miss.* For example:

我 很 想 你。
Wǒ hěn xiǎng nǐ.

I miss you very much.

我 想 坐 火 车 要 六 个 小时。
Wǒ xiǎng zuò huǒchē yào liù ge xiǎoshí.

I think it takes six hours by train.

你 想 不 想 家?
Nǐ xiǎng bu xiǎng jiā?

Do you miss home?

11. 你去洛杉矶住哪儿 (Nǐ qù Luòshānjī zhù nǎr)?
The distinction in English between *to live* and *to stay* is not made in Chinese, where both are expressed by the word 住 (zhù). For example:

你们的中文 老师住 哪儿?
Nǐmende Zhōngwén lǎoshī zhù nǎr?

Where does your Chinese teacher live?

你去北京 住 哪儿?
Nǐ qù Běijīng zhù nǎr?

Where are you going to stay when you go to Beijing?

You may have noticed that the adverbial of place is placed after, instead of before, the verb and the preposition 在 (zài) is not present. This is because with certain verbs (住 zhù is one of them), the adverbial can be placed either before or after the verb. For example, we can either say 你在 哪儿住 (nǐ zài nǎr zhù) or 你住在 哪儿 (nǐ zhù zài nǎr). However, the adverbial of place must follow the verb when it is used in conjunction with the motion verbs 来 (lái *come*) and 去 (qù *go*):

你来纽 约 住 哪儿?
Nǐ lái Niǔ Yuē zhù nǎr?

Where are you going to stay when you come to New York?

你去北京 住 什么 饭店?
Nǐ qù Běijīng zhù shénme fàndiàn?

Which hotel are you going to stay in when you go to Beijing?

When the adverbial follows the verb, the preposition 在 (zài) is often left out.

12. 上有天堂, 下有苏杭 (Shàng yǒu tiāntáng, xià yǒu Sū Háng)
    This is a saying in Chinese describing the unsurpassing beauty of Suzhou and Hangzhou.
    Literally it means "up above there is paradise, down below there is Suzhou and Hangzhou."
    Notice the rhyme and the grammatical symmetry of the two lines.

EXERCISES

I. Answer the following questions:

1. 你工作 不工作? 你每天 怎么去 上班?
   Nǐ gōngzuò bu gōngzuò? Nǐ měitiān zěnme qù shàngbān?
2. 你是学生 吗? 你每天 怎么去学校?
   Nǐ shì xuésheng ma? Nǐ měitiān zěnme qù xuéxiào?
3. 你家离银行 远 不远?
   Nǐ jia lí yínháng yuǎn bu yuǎn?
4. 今年 的中国 新年 是几月几号? 你过不过? 怎么 过?
   Jīnnián de Zhōngguó xīnnián shì jǐ yuè jǐ hào? Nǐ guò bu guò? Zěnme guò?
5. 你去过 英国 吗? 你去过英国 的什么 地方?
   Nǐ qù guo Yīngguó ma? Nǐ qù guo Yīngguó de shénme dìfang?
6. 你想 不想 去中国? 你想 什么 时候去?
   Nǐ xiǎng bu xiǎng qù Zhōngguó? Nǐ xiǎng shénme shíhòu qu?
7. 从 纽约 坐飞机到华盛顿 要几个小时?
   Cóng Niǔ Yuē zuò fēijī dào Huáshèngdùn yào jǐ ge xiǎoshí?
8. 你这个周末 作什么?
   Nǐ zhè ge zhōumò zuò shénme?
9. 你去过香港 吗? 去过几次?
   Nǐ qù guo Xiāng Gǎng ma? Qù guo jǐ cì?
10. 你有没有 开过日本车?
    Nǐ yǒu méiyǒu kāi guo Rìběn chē?

II. Fill in the blanks with appropriate words:

1. 你知道 _____ 写这个字吗?
   Nǐ zhīddao _____ xiě zhè ge zì ma?
2. 你爸爸去香港 _____ 什么?
   Nǐ bàba qù Xiāng Gǎng _____ shénme?
3. 天安门 _____ 我们的 旅馆很 近. 坐 地铁只要 十分钟.
   Tiānānmén _____ wǒmende lǚguǎn hěn jìn. Zuò dìtiě zhǐ yào shí fēnzhōng.
4. 明天 是你太太的生日, 你们怎么 _____?
   Míngtiān shì nǐ tàitai de shēngrì, nǐmen zěnme _____?
5. 骑自行车去你的学校 要 _____ 时间?
   Qí zìxíngchē qù nǐde xuéxiào yào _____ shí jiān?

6. 他 去 过 法国 _____ 什 么 地 方?
   Tā qù guo Fǎguó _____ shénme dìfang?
7. 杭 州 很 好 _____。
   Hángzhōu hěn hǎo _____.
8. 我 去过 纽约 三 _____。
   Wǒ qù guo Niǔ Yuē sān _____.
9. _____ 火 车 站 去 北京 大 学 要 坐 汽 车.
   _____ huǒchēzhàn qù Běijīng Dàxué yào zuò qìchē.
10. 你 知 道 地 铁 站 在 _____ 吗?
    Nǐ zhīdao dìtiězhàn zai _____ ma?

III. Translate the following into Chinese:

1. Is it easy to find a hotel in Washington?
2. Xi'an is far from Guangzhou.
3. It takes about 20 hours to go from Beijing to Shanghai by train.
4. Are there subway lines in Nanjing?
5. Many Chinese go to work by bicycle.
6. How do you go to Guangzhou from Hong Kong?
7. She has been to Japan five times.
8. I would like to go to China next year.
9. My friend won't stay in a hotel. He will stay in my house.
10. Many Chinese people are now celebrating Christmas.

IV. Translate the following into English:

1. 这 个 周末 我 和我 太太去 公园 玩.
   Zhè ge zhōumò wǒ hé wǒ tàitai qù gōngyuán wán.
2. 我 妈妈 去过 欧洲 的 英国 和法国.
   Wǒ māma qù guo Ōuzhōu de Yīngguó hé Fǎguó.
3. 火 车 票 很 便宜, 但是 火车 很 慢.
   Huǒchē piào hěn piányi, dànshì huǒchē hěn màn.
4. 现在 旅馆 不太 好 找.
   Xiànzài lǚguǎn bú tài hǎo zhǎo.
5. 我 家离 公 司 很近, 我 走 去 上班.
   Wǒ jiā lí gōngsī hěn jìn. Wǒ zǒu qù shàngbān.
6. 从 我 家 开 车 到 公 司 要 三十 分钟.
   Cóng wǒ jiā kāi chē dào gōngsī yǎo sān shí fēnzhōng.
7. 我 想 苏州 大概 很 好 玩.
   Wǒ xiǎng Sūzhōu dàgài hěn hǎo wán.
8. 她 爸爸 去过 中国 的 很 多 地方, 他 最 喜欢 南京.
   Tā bàba qù guo Zhōngguo de hěn duō dìfang, tā zuì xǐhuan Nánjīng.
9. 你 怎 么 去 火车站?
   Nǐ zěnme qù huǒchēzhàn?

10. 我 有 时 在 家 吃 中 饭, 有 时 在 学 校 吃 中 饭.
Wǒ yǒushí zài jiā chī zhōngfàn, yǒushí zài xuéxiào chī zhōngfàn.

CULTURAL INSIGHTS

It is impossible to find an equivalent in English for the Chinese word *che*. Dictionaries often define it as *vehicle*, but it is far from being the case. In Chinese, almost anything with a wheel can be called *che*, such as the train, the bus, the car, the truck, the bicycle, the rickshaw, the cart, and even the stroller. Specific *che*'s are indicated in one of the two ways: 1) by a descriptor, and 2) by a distinguishing verb. Descriptors include the following *huoche* (train), *qiche* (motor vehicle), *zixingche* (bicycle), *mache* (horse-drawn carriage). *Qiche* itself is a generic word that covers car, truck, bus and so on, which can be further distinguished using additional descriptives such as *xiaoqiche* (car), *kache* (truck), *gonggong qiche* (bus) and so on. Specific *che's* can also be indicated by the particular verbs they are used with even when the descriptors are not present. For example, *zuo che* would mean "take the bus," *kai che* "drive a car," *qi che* "ride a bicycle," and *la che* (pull a cart).

Of all the *che's*, *zixingche* (bicycle) seldom fails to amaze travelers to China with its sheer numbers and ingenious use. Like rice, chopsticks and characters, they are part of the Chinese landscape. They fill the streets and sidewalks. Bicycles are used by Chinese people not as exercise instruments, but as an important means of transportation, much like cars to people in the West. Up until the most recent times, the number and the brand of the bicycle a family possessed were taken as the yardstick of its wealth. Small wonder that people in China treat their bicycles as much as people elsewhere treat their cars. They have to register their bicycles with the police department and there are specific traffic rules and regulations for cyclists. People take such pains to keep their bicycles in mint condition that some *danwei* give their employees extra pay earmarked specifically for bicycle maintenance. In recent years, people have been allowed to buy and own cars, but it is doubtful that cars can ever replace bicycles as the primary means of transportation in China. First of all, few people are wealthy enough to afford a car. Even if people can afford a car sometime in the future, it would be unimaginable that they can find a place to park their cars, as limited available spaces in the cities are being quickly taken over with the constructions of commercial and residential buildings. Bicycles will therefore remain an integral part of people's life for a long time to come.

Intra-city travel depends heavily on public buses and trolley-buses. They are very cheap to ride but usually crowed. It is a real adventure during rush hour to get on one. Pushing and shoving are commonplace. In recent years, private buses called *zhongba* (medium-sized bus) have appeared in the streets of China. They are more efficient and provide better services. The subway system is only found in certain major cities such as Beijing, Tianjin and Shanghai. Although subway lines and trains are limited in these places, they are very clean and well maintained.

The train remains the most popular form of public transportation for inter-city travels, as traveling by airplane is still a luxury for most people. It is by no means rare for people in China to travel on the train for days on end. Most trains are equipped with four types of seats found in separate cars. These are hard seats, soft seats, hard sleepers and soft sleepers. Hard seats are the lowest of the four classes, but are very cheap. Soft seats are usually found on trains that travel short distances. Hard sleepers are triple-deck six-bed niches with no door towards the corridor. Soft sleepers are compartments with four beds. Most train stations have a ticket window set aside for foreigners. Although there will be some extra charge, the convenience definitely outweighs the aggravation of standing in a line for hours.

SENTENCE PATTERNS

今天 多少 度？
Jīntiān duōshao dù?

What is the temperature today?

明天 没有 雨。
Míngtiān méiyǒu yǔ.

There is no rain tomorrow.

你们 那儿 昨天 下 雨 了吗？
Nǐmen nàr zuótiān xià yǔ le má?

Did it rain in your place yesterday?

下 了。
Xià le.

Yes, it did.

昨天 有 没有 下雪？
Zuótiān yǒu méiyǒu xià xuě?

Did it snow yesterday?

北京 冬天 的天气怎么样？
Běijīng dōngtiān de tiānqì zěnmeyàng?

What's the weather like in Beijing in the winter?

美国人 夏天一般作 什么？
Měiguórén xiàtiān yìbān zuò shénme?

What do American people usually do in the summer?

今天 比昨天 冷。
Jīntiān bǐ zuótiān lěng.

It is colder today than yesterday.

南京 夏天 有 多 热？
Nánjīng xiàtiān yǒu duō rè?

How hot is it in Nanjing in the summer?

114

CONVERSATIONS

A: 今天　天气怎么样?
Jīntiān tiānqì zěnmeyàng?

How is the weather today?

B: 今天　是　晴天，但是　很　冷。
Jīntiān shì qíngtiān, dànshì hěn lěng.

It is sunny today, but it is very cold.

A: 今天　多少　度?
Jīntiān duōshao dù?

What is the temperature today?

B: 今天　28 度。
Jīntiān 28 dù.

It is 28 degrees today.

A: 你知道　明天　天气怎么样　吗?
Nǐ zhīdao míngtiān tiānqì zěnmeyàng ma?

Do you know how the weather will be tomorrow?

B: 听说　有　雨。
Tīngshuō yǒu yǔ.

I heard that it will rain.

A: 大　雨还是　小　雨?
Dà yǔ háishi xiǎo yǔ?

Is the rain going to be heavy?

B: 可能　是大雨，你最好　带　伞。
Kěnéng shì dà yǔ, nǐ zuì hǎo dài sǎn.

It's probably going to be heavy. You'd better take your umbrella.

A: 谢谢。
Xièxie.

Thank you.

A: 你们　那儿昨天　下　雨了吗?
Nǐmen nàr zuótiān xià yǔ le mǎ?

Did it rain in your place yesterday?

B: 下　了。
Xià le.

Yes, it did.

A: 昨天　的雨大不大?
Zuótiān de yǔ dà bu dà?

Was the rain yesterday heavy?

B: 不　太大。
Bú tài dà.

Not too heavy.

A: 昨天　有　没有　下雪?
Zuótiān yǒu méiyǒu xià xuě?

Did it snow yesterday?

B: 没有。
Méiyǒu.

No, it didn't.

A: 北京　冬天　的天气怎么样?
Běijīng dōngtiān de tiānqì zěnmeyàng?

What's the weather like in Beijing in the winter?

B: 北京　冬天　很　冷，常常
Běijīng dōngtiān hěn lěng, chángcháng
有　大风。
yǒu dà fēng.

It's very cold and windy in Beijing in the winter.

A: 北京 冬天 常常 下雪 吗？
Běijīng dōngtiān chángcháng xià xuě ma?

Does it often snow in Beijing in the winter?

B: 对，常常 下雪。
Duì, chángcháng xià xuě.

Yes, it often snows.

A: 北京 什么 季节 最好？
Běijīng shénme jìjié zuì hǎo?

What's the best season in Beijing?

B: 北京 秋天最好，不冷 也不热。
Běijīng qiūtiān zuìhǎo, bù lěng yě bú rè.

Fall is the best in Beijing. It is neither cold nor hot.

A: 南京 夏天 热不热？
Nánjīng xiàtiān rè bu rè?

Is it hot in Nanjing in the summer?

B: 南京 夏天非常 热。
Nánjīng xiàtiān fēicháng rè.

It's very hot in Nanjing in the summer.

A: 有 多 热？
Yǒu duō rè?

How hot is it?

B: 南京 夏天 常常 有 100 度。
Nánjīng xiàtiān chángcháng yǒu 100 dù.

It often reaches 100 degrees in Nanjing in the summer.

A: 美国人 夏天一般 作 什么？
Měiguórén xiàtiān yìbān zuò shénme?

What do American people usually do in the summer?

B: 美国人 夏天常常 去度假。
Měiguórén xiàtiān chángcháng qù dù jià.

They often go on vacation in the summer.

A: 他们 一般去哪儿度假？
Tāmen yìbān qù nǎr dù jià?

Where do they usually go for vacation?

B: 有的 人 出国 旅行，有的人
Yǒude rén chūguó lǚxíng, yǒude rén
去海滩。
qù hǎitān.

Some travel abroad and some go to the beach.

A: 今天 冷 还是 昨天 冷？
Jīntiān lěng háishi zuótiān lěng?

Which day is colder, today or yesterday?

B: 今天 比昨天 冷。
Jīngtiān bǐ zuótiān lěng.

It's colder today than yesterday.

A: 今天 的风 大还是 昨天 的风 大？
Jīntiān de fēng dà háishi zuótiān de fēng dà?

Which day is windier, today or yesterday?

B: 昨天 的风 大。
Zuótiān de fēng dà.

Yesterday was windier.

A: 你喜欢 热天 还是冷 天？
Nǐ xǐhuan rè tiān háishi lěng tiān?

Do you like hot weather or cold weather?

B: 我 喜欢 冷 天。
Wǒ xǐhuan lěng tiān.

I like cold weather.

A: 为 什么？
Wèi shénme?

Why?

B: 冷　天 可以 去 滑雪，还 可以 去 溜 冰。　We can go skiing or ice skating in cold
　　Lěng tiān kěyǐ　qù huáxuě, hái kěyǐ qù liūbīng.　weather.

WORDS AND EXPRESSIONS

<u>Nouns</u>

天气	tiānqì	weather
雨	yǔ	rain
雪	xuě	snow
风	fēng	wind
季节	jìjié	season
冬天	dōngtiān	winter
夏天	xiàtiān	summer
秋天	qiūtiān	fall
春天	chūntiān	spring
度	dù	degree
伞	sǎn	umbrella
海滩	hǎitān	beach

<u>Verbs</u>

带	dài	carry
度假	dùjià	go on vacation
出	chū	go out
滑雪	huáxuě	ski
溜冰	liūbīng	ice skate

<u>Adjectives</u>

冷	lěng	cold
热	rè	hot
晴	qíng	sunny
阴	yīn	cloudy
大	dà	big
小	xiǎo	small

<u>Adverbs</u>

常常	chángcháng	often

<u>Interrogatives</u>

为什么	wèi shénme	why

Conjunctions

比	bǐ	than

Expressions

最好	zuìhǎo	best, had better

SUPPLEMENTARY WORDS AND EXPRESSIONS

Nouns

暖气	nuǎnqì	heat, heating
空调	kōngtiáo	air conditioning
云	yún	cloud
雾	wù	fog
雷	léi	thunder
闪电	shǎndiàn	lightning
台风	táifēng	typhoon
冰	bīng	ice
雨衣	yǔyī	raincoat
预报	yùbào	forecast
摄氏	shèshì	Centigrade
华氏	huáshì	Fahrenheit
东	dōng	east
南	nán	south
西	xī	west
北	běi	north

Adjectives

暖	nuǎn	warm
凉	liáng	cool

LANGUAGE POINTS

1. 今天多少度 (Jīntiān duōshao dù)?

The equivalent in Chinese to *temperature* is 温度 (wēndù). When referring to various types of temperatures, we usually use a specifying modifier with the word 温 (wēn) as in 体温 (tǐwēn *body temperature*) and 气温 (qìwēn *atmospheric temperature*). 度 (dù) in Chinese actually means *degree*. To ask about temperature, we would use 今天多少度 (jīntiān duōshao dù), since we are dealing with a number.

118

2. 了 (le) as an aspect marker

Chinese indicates a completed action with the particle 了 (le) after the verb. Compare:

我 吃早饭。 Wǒ chī zǎofàn.	I eat breakfast.
我 吃了早饭。 Wǒ chī le zǎofàn.	I ate breakfast.

我 妈妈今天下午 去银行。 Wǒ māma jīntiān xiàwǔ qù yínháng.	My mother is going to the bank this afternoon.
我 妈妈昨天 下午 去了银行。 Wǒ māma zuótiān xiàwu qù le yínháng.	My mother went to the bank yesterday afternoon.

It is important to keep in mind that the negative form of a verb with 了 (le) is not 不 (bù), but rather 没有 (méiyǒu). Once 没有 (méiyǒu) is used, 了 (le) has to be dropped from the sentence. This is because 没有 (méiyǒu) as a negative expression is only used to negate a completed action and grammatically 了 (le) plays the same role. It would be redundant to have two grammatical signals present in the same sentence for the same purpose. Compare the use of 不 (bù) and 没有 (méiyǒu) in the following sentences:

我 不吃早饭。 Wǒ bù chī zǎofàn.	I don't eat breakfast.
我 没有 吃早饭。 Wǒ méiyǒu chī zǎofàn.	I didn't eat breakfast.

我 妈妈今天下午 不去银行。 Wǒ māma jīntiān xiàwǔ bú qù yínháng.	My mother is not going to the bank this afternoon.
我 妈妈昨天 下午 没有 去 Wǒ māma zuótiān xiàwǔ méiyǒu qù 银行。 yínháng.	My mother didn't go to the bank yesterday afternoon.

Please note that 了 (le) is only used to indicate the completion of an action. It is therefore not to be used for cognitive verbs such as 认识 (rènshi *know*), 知道 (zhīdao *know*), 会 (huì *know how to*), 喜欢 (xǐhuan *like*) and so on, even though they may be used with a past reference. When these cognitive verbs are negated, we still use 不 (bù), rather than 没有 (méiyǒu). Thus, depending on the context, 我不认识他 (wǒ bù rènshi tā) can be interpreted either as *I don't know him* or *I didn't know him*. Similarly, adjectives and prepositions can only be used with 不 (bù), since they do not indicate actions. Here are a few more examples:

他现在 不在家。 Tā xiànzài bú zài jiā.	He is not home now.
他昨天 晚上 不在家。 Tā zuótiān wǎnshang bú zài jiā.	He was not home last night.

我 今天不忙。
Wǒ jīntiān bù máng.
我 昨天 不忙。
Wǒ zuótiān bù máng.

I'm not busy today.

I was not busy yesterday.

我 的 女 朋友 不 会 说 英语。
Wǒde nǔpéngyou bú huì shuō yīngyǔ.
我 的 女 朋友 去年 不 会 说
Wǒde nǔpéngyou qùnián bú huì shuō
英语。
yīngyǔ.

My girlfriend can't speak English.

My girlfriend couldn't speak English last year.

Yes/no questions involving a completed action are formed in one of the two ways:

1) Using the sentence-particle 吗 (ma):
   你买 了衣服 吗？
   Nǐ mǎi le yīfu ma?

   Did you buy the clothes?

   他去了中国   吗？
   Tā qù le Zhōngguó ma?

   Has he gone to China?

2) Using the affirmative-negative form 有没有 (yǒu méiyǒu):
   你今天有 没 有 上班？
   Nǐ jīntiān yǒu méiyǒu shàngbān?

   Did you go to work today?

   你有 没 有 吃 中饭？
   Nǐ yǒu méiyǒu chī zhōngfàn?

   Have you had your lunch?

   你有 没 有 去看 电影？
   Nǐ yǒu méiyǒu qù kàn diànyǐng?

   Did you go to see the movie?

In this connection, it may be necessary to compare the use of 了 (le) with that of 过 (guo) discussed in Lesson 8. Although both of them are used to indicated a completed action, there is an important difference between them. While 了 (le) is used for an action that is completed at a specified time, 过 (guo) is usually used for an action completed at an unspecified time in the past. 了 (le) emphasizes the action, whereas 过 (guo) emphasizes the experience and the result. Compare:

他 吃了中国   菜。
Tā chī le Zhōngguó cài.
他 吃 过 中国   菜。
Tā chī guo Zhōngguó cài.

He ate the Chinese food (just now).

He has had Chinese food (before).

我 昨天 看 了 这 本 书。
Wǒ zuótiān kàn le zhè běn shū.

I read this book yesterday.

我 看 过 这 本 书。
Wǒ kàn guo zhè běn shū.

I have read this book (sometime in the past).

我 爸爸 来 了 美国。
Wǒ bàba lái le Měiguó.

My father has come to the United States (he is still here).

我 爸爸 来 过 美国。
Wǒ bàba lái guo Měiguó.

My father has been to the United States (he is not here unless there is some qualification).

It was mentioned in the introductory chapter on Chinese that verbs in Chinese are marked by specific particles for aspect (manner in which an action takes place), but not for time (past, present or future). What 了 (le) indicates is simply the completion of an action, which can take place in the future as well as the past, although completed actions are usually associated with the past. The following is an example of 了 (le) used to indicate a completed action in the future as projected from the present time:

我 吃 了 饭 去 看 电影。
Wǒ chī le fàn qù kàn diànyǐng.

After I've finished eating, I'll go to see a movie.

5. 大雨 (dà yǔ) and 小雨 (xiǎo yǔ)

To describe the severity of a weather condition such as rain, snow or wind, Chinese uses the adjectives 大 (dà *big*) and 小 (xiǎo *small*). See for example:

大雨 (dà yǔ *heavy rain*)　　大雪 (dà xuě *heavy snow*)　　大风 (dà fēng *strong wind*)
小雨 (xiǎo yǔ *drizzle*)　　　小雪 (xiǎo xuě *light snow*)　　小风 (xiǎo fēng *breeze*)

Words like *rain* and *snow* can be used as verbs as well as nouns in English, but they are always nouns in Chinese. To indicate *to rain* and *to snow*, we usually use the verb 下 (xià *fall*) as in 下雨 (xià yǔ *to rain*) and 下雪 (xià xuě *to snow*).

6. 南京夏天有多热 (Nánjīng xiàtiān yǒu duō rè)?

To ask about the specific measure of certain conditions such as *how long*, *how cold*, etc., Chinese uses the pattern: Subject + 有多 (yǒu duō) + Adjective. For example:

纽约 的 冬天 有 多 冷?
Niǔ Yuē de dōngtiān yǒu duō lěng?

How cold is it in New York in winter?

长江 有 多 长?
Chángjiāng yǒu duō cháng?

How long is the Yangtze River?

她的 房子 有 多 大?
Tāde fángzi yǒu duō dà?

How big is her house?

你 有 多 高?
Nǐ yǒu duō gāo?

How tall are you/what's your height?

7. 今 天 比 昨 天 冷 (jīntiān bǐ zuótiān lěng)

To indicate a comparison between two items, we use the pattern "A 比 (bǐ) B + Adjective", where A is the subject and 比 (bǐ) is an adverbial of reference. As such, it is placed before the verb-like adjective. Other examples are:

纽 约 比华盛顿 大.
Niǔ Yuē bǐ Huáshèngdùn dà.

New York is larger than Washington.

上 海 的人比北京 的人 多.
Shànghǎi de rén bǐ Běijīng de rén duō.

There are more people in Shanghai than in Beijing.

这 件 大衣比那件 大衣贵.
Zhè jiàn dàyi bǐ nà jiàn dàyi guì.

This coat is more expensive than that coat.

中国 菜比日本菜好吃.
Zhōngguó cài bǐ Rìběn cài hǎochī.

Chinese food tastes better than Japanese food.

In all these sentences, there is no need for a *more* in Chinese. If there is a specific measurement in the sentence indicating how much the two items being compared differ from each other, it should be placed last in the sentence. For example:

这 件 毛衣比那件毛衣 贵 20 美元.
Zhè jiàn máoyī bǐ nà jiàn máoyī guì 20 Měiyuán.
This sweater is $20 more expensive than that sweater.

今天 的温度 比昨天 的温度 高 三 度.
Jīntiān de wēndù bǐ zuótiān de wēndù gāo sān dù.
The temperature today is 3 degrees higher than yesterday.

他 们 的 公 司 比我们的 公 司 多 100 个人.
Tāmende gōngsī bǐ wǒmende gōngsī duō 100 ge rén.
Their company has 100 more people than ours.

EXERCISES

I. Answer the following questions:

1. 今天 天气 怎么样? 昨天 呢?
Jīntiān tiānqì zěnmeyàng? Zuótiān ne?

2. 明天 有 没有 雨?
   Míngtiān yǒu méiyǒu yǔ?

3. 今天 多少 度?
   Jīntiān duōshao dù?

4. 今天 有 没有 风? 风 大不大?
   Jīntiān yǒu méiyǒu fēng? Fēng dà bu dà?

5. 你们 那儿 什么 季节 天气 最 好?
   Nǐmen nàr shénme jìjié tiānqì zuì hǎo?

6. 你们 那儿 夏天 热不热? 有 多 热?
   Nǐmen nàr xiàtiān rè bu rè? Yǒu duō rè?

7. 你们 那儿 冬天 有 没有 雪? 雪 大不大?
   Nǐmen nàr dōngtiān yǒu méiyǒu xuě? Xuě dà bu dà?

8. 你 喜欢 冷 天 还是 热天? 为 什么?
   Nǐ xǐhuan lěng tiān háishi rè tiān? Wèi shénme?

9. 你 秋天 喜欢 作 什么?
   Nǐ qiūtiān xǐhuan zuò shénme?

10. 你 今年 夏天 去不去 度假? 去 哪儿 度假?
    Nǐ jīnnián xiàtiān qù bu qù dù jià? Qù nǎr dù jià?

11. 你 上 星期天 晚上 作了 什么?
    Nǐ shàng xīngqī tiān wǎnshang zuò le shénme?

12. 你 今天 中午 有 没有 吃 中饭?
    Nǐ jīntiān zhōngwǔ yǒu méiyǒu chī zhōngfàn?

13. 你 昨天 晚上 看 了 电视 吗?
    Nǐ zuótiān wǎnshang kàn le diànshì ma?

14. 你 有 没有 学 过 法语?
    Nǐ yǒu méiyǒu xué guo Fǎyǔ?

15. 你 去过 欧洲 吗?
    Nǐ qù guo Ōuzhōu ma?

II. Change the following sentences into yes/no questions, using two alternative forms:

1. 我 太太 去了 商店。
   Wǒ tàitai qù le shāngdiàn.

2. 我们的 中文 老师 来了。
   Wǒmende Zhōngwén lǎoshī lái le.

3. 下 雨了。
   Xià yǔ le.

4. 纽 约 今年 冬天 下了 很 多 雪。
   Niǔ Yuē jīnnián dōngtiān xià le hěn duō xuě.

5. 他们 下班 了。
   Tāmen xiàbān le.

III. Change the following sentences into negatives:

1. 我 爸爸 妈妈 昨天　都 来了。
   Wǒ bàba māma zuótiān dōu lái le.
2. 星期 六晚上　　我看 了电视。
   Xīngqī liù wǎnshang wǒ kàn le diànshì.
3. 银行　　关门 了。
   Yínháng guānmén le.
4. 她用　了我的 汽车。
   Tā yòng le wǒde qìchē.
5. 我 先生　　起床 了。
   Wǒ xiānsheng qǐchuáng le.

IV. Write five things that you did yesterday. Pay attention to the indication of complete actions.

V. Correct the error contained in each of the following sentences.

1. 我 昨天 不 吃 早饭。
   Wǒ zuótiān bù chī zǎofàn.
2. 她 妈妈 今天 早上　在 了家。
   Tā māma jīntiān zǎoshang zài le jiā.
3. 你上　 星期 天 有 没有　去 教堂 (church) 吗?
   Nǐ shàng xīngqī tiān yǒu méiyǒu qù jiàotáng　　ma?
4. 他们 没有 来 了 中国。
   Tāmen méiyǒu lái le Zhōngguó.
5. 我 去年 没有 认识 她。
   Wǒ qùnián méiyǒu rènshi tā.

VI. Translate the following into Chinese:

1. What is the weather like in Shanghai in the fall?
2. Does it often rain in the summer in New York?
3. It's going to be a sunny day tomorrow.
4. Is there snow in Hangzhou? —Sometimes there is, sometimes there is not.
5. In the winter it is very windy where we live.
6. What was the temperature yesterday? —It was 53 degrees.
7. I heard that there has been a lot of snow in France this year.
8. The weather is the best in Guangzhou in the spring.
9. How heavy was the rain yesterday?
10. It sometimes snows in Nanjing in the spring.
11. My mother went to the store.
12. He didn't eat breakfast this morning.
13. Have you ever driven a Chinese car?
14. I studied ten Chinese characters last night.
15. They exchanged $500 at the Bank of China today.

VII. Translate the following into English:

1. 今天 是阴天, 很 冷, 风 很 大。
   Jīntiān shì yīntiān, hěn lěng, fēng hěn dà.
2. 今年 冬天 纽 约 的雪 大不大?
   Jīnnián dōngtiān Niǔ Yuē de xuě dà bu dà?
3. 中国人 夏天喜欢 作 什么?
   Zhōngguórén xiàtiān xǐhuan zuò shénme?
4. 很 多 美国人 冬天 喜欢去滑雪。
   Hěn duō Měiguórén dōngtiān xǐhuan qù huáxuě.
5. 去年 的冬天 不太冷, 夏天不太热。
   Qùnián de dōngtiān bú tài lěng, xiàtiān bú tài rè.
6. 我 不喜欢 北京 的春天, 风 太大。
   Wǒ bù xǐhuan Běijīng de chūntiān, fēng tài dà.
7. 昨天 的雨大还是今天 的雨大?
   Zuótiān de yǔ dà háishi jīntiān de yǔ dà?
8. 北京 大学 的学生 比 南京 大学 的学生 多。
   Běijīng Dàxué de xuésheng bǐ Nánjīng Dàxué de xuésheng duō.
9. 我 家离公司 比他家离 公司 远。
   Wǒ jiā lí gōngsī bǐ tā jiā lí gōngsī yuǎn.
10. 这 本 书比那本 书 便宜 三块 钱。
    Zhè běn shū bǐ nà běn shū piányì sān kuài qián.

VIII. Describe today's weather conditions.

IX. Write a comparative sentence for the following sentences:

1. 今天 的雪 大。昨天 的雪 不大。
   Jīntiān de xuě da. Zuótiān de xuě bú dà.
2. 她的中文 好。我的中文 不好。
   Tāde Zhōngwén hǎo. Wǒde Zhōngwén bù hǎo.
3. 红 酒好喝。白酒不好 喝。
   Hóng jiǔ hǎo hē. Bái jiǔ bù hǎo hē.
4. 飞机快。火车 不快。
   Fēijī kuài. Huǒchē bú kuài.
5. 北京 好玩。上海 不好玩。
   Běijīng hǎo wán. Shànghǎi bù hǎo wán.
6. 这 本 书 20块 钱。那本书 10块 钱。
   Zhè běn shū 20 kuài qián. Nà běn shū 10 kuài qián.
7. 我 爸爸忙。我 妈妈不忙。
   Wǒ bàba máng. Wǒ māma bù máng.
8. 纽 约 的旅馆好 找。洛杉矶 的旅馆不好 找。
   Niǔ Yuē de lǚguǎn hǎo zhǎo. Luòshānjī de lǚguǎn bù hǎo zhǎo.
9. 今天 50度。昨天 40度。
   Jīntiān 50 dù. Zuótiān 40 dù.

10. 我们 学校 有 600个学生。 他们学校 有 400 个学生。
Wǒmen xuéxiào yǒu 600 ge xuésheng. Tāmen xuéxiào yǒu 400 ge xuésheng.

CULTURAL INSIGHTS

After Russia and Canada, China is the third largest country in the world. Lying in East Asia, China shares borders with a host of countries, Mongolia to the north, Russia to the northeast, Korea to the east, Myanmar (formerly Burma), Laos and Vietnam to the south, Afghanistan, Pakistan, India, Nepal, and Bhutan to the west and southwest, Kazakhstan, Kyrgyzstan and Tajikistan to the northwest.

The administrative divisions consist of a three-tier hierarchy: 1) Central Government, 2) provinces/autonomous regions/municipalities directly under the Central Government, and 3) cities. Counties, with jurisdictions in rural areas, used to be directly under provincial administration, but are now for the most part under the administration of cities.

Under the Central Government, there are twenty-three provinces, five autonomous regions and four centrally administered municipalities. These divisions are all equal in status. Autonomous regions are so called because they enjoy some degree of independence in terms of public policy, as they are the areas with large settlements of ethnic minorities. The four centrally administered municipalities are Beijing, Shanghai, Tianjin and Chongqing. Chongqing, a southwestern city in Sichuan Province, only attained this status as recently as March 1997. With a population of more than 30 million, the newly expanded Chongqing has become the world's largest city. Outside the mainland, Hong Kong has recently been reverted to China after a 150-year lease to Britain. The return of Macao is being negotiated. Taiwan, which is regarded by Mainland China as a renegade province, is still controlled by the Nationalist government.

Provinces are divided into cities. In recent years, cities have been given additional administrative power as counties have been brought under their jurisdiction. In the urban area, cities are subdivided into two levels: districts and wards. In the rural area, they are subdivided into counties and townships. In the cities, housing is generally provided by the *danwei* in designated apartment buildings. Neighborhoods thus formed are not stratified by occupation or income and most importantly, they are closely knit face-to-face communities, which contributes to residential stability and a low level of crime.

Of particular mention are the approximately 900,000 villages in the countryside, where most Chinese live. They are usually clustered around a market town that coincides in most cases with the seat of the township. The market town further links the farmers to a larger network of the economy and society. But due to the restriction imposed through the household registration system, farmers are confined to their villages and prevented from seeking opportunities elsewhere. With the recent reform, a substantial number of rural people are venturing out of their villages and expanding their social horizons to work and engage in social life in the cities, but still they cannot be formally employed by the government or state-owned businesses or set up residence there.

The Communist Party, with a 50-million membership, exercises the ultimate and unchallenged leadership and authority over the Chinese people. Its organization and supervision penetrate all the levels of government and are present in all the institutions, organizations and state-owned businesses. A *danwei* (work unit) usually has a dual system of supervision by a Party secretary and an administrator. In some units, the Party secretary and the administrator are one and the same person. In theory, the Party secretary oversees the implementation of the Party policies and guidelines and the administrators/managers are responsible for the day-to-day-operation of their *danwei*, but in reality, many of the administrative and managerial decisions have to be cleared with, or even made by, the Party secretary. The authority of the Party is omnipresent and unchallenged.

Glossary

Character	Pinyin	English	Lesson
澳州	Aòzhōu	Australia	9
八	bā	eight	4
爸爸	bàba	father	1
百	bǎi	hundred	4
百货公司	bǎi huò gōngsi	department store	7
白酒	báijiǔ	liquor	8
半	bàn	half	5
办公室	bàngōngshì	office	3
包子	bāozi	steamed stuffed bun	8
报纸	bàozhǐ	newspaper	6
杯	bēi	cup	7
北	běi	north	10
北京	Běijīng	Beijing	3
本	běn	(classifer)	4
比	bǐ	than	10
冰	bīng	ice	10
博物馆	bówùguǎn	museum	3
不	bù	not	1
不一定	bù yídìng	not necessarily	7
菜	cài	dishes	8
菜单	càidān	menu	8
餐馆	cānguǎn	restaurant	2
餐巾	cānjīn	napkin	8
厕所	cèsuǒ	restroom	3
叉	chā	fork	8
茶	chá	tea	8
常	cháng	often	9
常常	chángchang	often	10
长	cháng	long	7
炒	chǎo	fry	8
车	chē	vehicle	9
城	chéng	town, city	3
衬衫	chènshān	shirt, blouse	7
吃	chī	eat	2
出	chū	go out	1

穿	chuān	wear, put on	7
船	chuán	boat, ship	9
春天	chūntiān	spring	10
出租汽车	chūzū qìchē	taxi	9
次	cì	time (occurrence)	8
词典	zídiǎn	dictionary	6
从	cóng	from	6
从 ...... 到	cóng ... dào ...	from ... to ...	9
错	cuò	wrong, bad	1
大	dà	big	10
大概	dàgài	probably	9
带	dài	carry	10
当然	dāngrán	of course	7
但是	dànshì	but	2
单位	dānwèi	workplace	3
刀	dāo	knife	8
导游	dǎoyóu	guide	9
大学	dàxué	university	3
大学生	dàxuésheng	college student	4
大衣	dàyī	coat	7
的	de	(possessive marker)	2
德国	Déguó	Germany	6
等	děng	wait	7
第	dì	(ordinal number indicator)	7
点	diǎn	o'clock	5
电车	diànchē	trolley-bus	9
电话	diànhuà	telephone	3
电视	diànshì	television	6
电影	diànyǐng	movie	8
电影院	diànyǐngyuàn	movie theater	3
弟弟	dìdi	younger brother	1
地方	dìfang	place	9
地铁	dìtiě	subway	9
懂	dǒng	understand	6
东	dōng	east	10
冬天	dōngtiān	winter	10
东西	dōngxi	things, stuff	7
都	dōu	both, all	2
度	dù	degree	10
度假	dùjià	go on vacation	10
短	duǎn	short	7
对	duì	right, correct	8
对不起	duìbuqǐ	sorry	5

多	duō	many, much	7
多少	duōshao	(question word for numbers)	4
二	èr	two	4
儿子	érzi	son	2
饭店	fàndiàn	hotel	3
翻译	fānyì	translate	6
法国	Fǎguó	France	6
法语	Fǎyǔ	French language	6
肥	féi	loose	7
飞机	fēijī	airplane	9
飞机场	fēijīchǎng	airport	3
非洲	Fēizhōu	Africa	9
分	fēn	minute	5
分	fēn	(monetary unit)	7
风	fēng	wind	10
分钟	fēnzhōng	minute	9
付	fù	pay	7
服装店	fúzhuāngdiàn	clothing store	7
告诉	gàosu	tell	7
高兴	gāoxìng	happy	1
个	gè	(classifier)	4
哥哥	gēge	older brother	1
给	gěi	give	8
公安局	gōng'ānjú	police station	3
工人	gōngrén	factory worker	2
公司	gōngsi	company	2
工艺品	gōngyìpǐn	handicraft product	7
公园	gōngyuán	park	3
工作	gōngzuò	work	3
广东	Guǎngdōng	Canton (the province)	6
广州	Guǎngzhōu	Canton (the city)	6
关门	guān mén	close (for business)	7
贵	guì	distinguished	2
贵	guì	expensive	7
顾客	gùkè	customer	7
过	guò	celebrate	9
国	guó	country	6
过	guo	(aspect marker)	8
国语	guóyǔ	Mandarin	6
海关	hǎiguān	customs	9

海滩	hǎitān	beach	10
海鲜	hǎixiān	seafood	8
杭州	Hángzhōu	Hangzhou	9
号	hào	number	5
好	hǎo	good	1
好象	hǎoxiàng	seem	8
和	hé	and	4
喝	hē	drink	8
很	hěn	very	1
合适	héshì	suitable	7
红	hóng	red	8
红酒	hóngjiǔ	wine	8
话	huà	speech, dialect	6
换	huàn	change, exchange	7
滑雪	huáxuě	ski	10
欢迎	huānyíng	welcome	8
华盛顿	Huáshèngdùn	Washington	9
华氏	huáshì	Fahrenheit	10
会	huì	know how to	6
回答	huídá	answer	6
会话	huìhuà	conversation	6
火车站	huǒchēzhàn	train station	3
护照	hùzhào	passport	9
几	jǐ	(question word for numbers)	4
鸡	jī	chicken	8
家	jiā	home, family	3
价格	jiàgé	price	7
件	jiàn	(classifier)	7
叫	jiào	call	2
教	jiāo	teach	6
教堂	jiàotáng	church	3
饺子	jiǎozi	dumpling	8
加州	Jiāzhōu	California	3
鸡蛋	jīdàn	egg	8
街	jiē	street	9
姐姐	jiějie	older sister	1
结束	jiéshù	end	5
季节	jìjié	season	10
极了	jíle	extremely	8
纪念品	jìniànpǐn	souvenir	7
近	jìn	close	9
警察	jǐngchá	police, policeman	9
经理	jīnglǐ	manager	2

今年	jīnnián	this year	5
今天	jīntiān	today	5
九	jiǔ	nine	4
旧金山	Jiùjīnshān	San Francisco	3
觉得	juéde	feel, think	7
句子	jùzi	sentence	6
咖啡	kāfēi	coffee	7
开	kāi	operate, drive	9
开门	kāi mén	open (for business)	7
开始	kāishǐ	begin	5
看	kàn	read, see	2
看书	kànshū	read	5
烤鸭	kǎoyā	roast duck	8
课	kè	class, lesson	5
可能	kěnéng	maybe	9
客气	kèqi	polite, formal	2
课文	kèwén	text	6
可以	kěyǐ	may	7
空调	kōngtiáo	air conditioning	10
口	kǒu	(classifier)	4
块	kuài	monetary unit	7
筷子	kuàizi	chopsticks	8
裤子	kùzi	pants	7
辣	là	spicy	8
来	lái	come	1
老板	lǎobǎn	boss	2
老师	lǎoshī	teacher	1
累	lèi	tired	1
雷	léi	thunder	10
冷	lěng	cold	10
离	lí	away from	9
凉	liáng	cool	10
练习	liànxí	exercise	6
零	líng	zero	4
历史	lìshǐ	history	4
六	liù	six	4
溜冰	liūbīng	ice skate	10
楼	lóu	floor, building	6
路	lù	road, route	9
绿	lǜ	green	8
旅馆	lǚguǎn	hotel	9
洛杉矶	Luòshānjī	Los Angeles	3

律师	lùshī	lawyer	1
旅行	lǚxíng	travel	9
旅行社	lǚxíngshè	travel agency	9
吗	ma	(particle)	1
买	mǎi	buy	7
卖	mài	sell	7
妈妈	māma	mother	1
马马虎虎	mǎma hūhu	so-so	1
慢	màn	slowly	6
曼哈顿	Mànhādūn	Manhattan	3
忙	máng	busy	1
毛	máo	(monetary unit)	7
毛衣	máoyī	sweater	7
帽子	màozi	hat	7
每	měi	every, each	5
没	méi	not	2
没关系	méi guānxi	That's all right.	5
美国	Měiguó	United States	1
妹妹	mèimei	younger sister	1
美元	Měiyuán	U.S. dollars	7
美洲	Měizhōu	America (continent)	9
们	men	(plural suffix)	2
面包	miànbāo	bread	8
面条	miàntiáo	noodle	2
米饭	mǐfàn	cooked rice	8
明年	míngnián	next year	5
明天	míngtiān	tomorrow	5
名字	míngzi	name	2
那	nà	that	5
男	nán	male	2
哪儿	nǎr	what place	3
那儿	nàr	there	3
奶奶	nǎinai	paternal grandmother	4
男孩	nánhái	boy	4
南京	Nánjīng	Nanjing	3
哪	nǎ	which	4
南	nán	south	10
呢	ne	(particle)	1
能	néng	can	7
你	nǐ	you	1
年	nián	year	9
您	nín	you (polite form)	2

牛奶	niúnǎi	milk	8
牛肉	niúròu	beef	8
纽约	Niǔ Yuē	New York	3
暖	nuǎn	warm	10
暖气	nuǎnqì	heat, heating	10
女	nǚ	female	2
女儿	nǚ'er	daughter	2
女孩	nǚhái	girl	4
欧洲	Ōuzhōu	Europe	9
盘子	pánzi	plate	8
朋友	péngyou	friend	2
便宜	piányi	cheap	7
票	piào	ticket	9
啤酒	píjiǔ	beer	8
瓶	píng	bottle	8
普通话	pǔtōnghuà	Mandarin	6
七	qī	seven	4
骑	qí	ride	9
千	qiān	thousand	4
钱	qián	money	7
签证	qiānzhèng	visa	9
汽车站	qìchēzhàn	bus stop	3
起床	qǐ chuáng	get up	5
晴	qíng	sunny	10
请......吃饭	qǐng ... chīfàn	invite sb. to dinner	8
青岛	Qīngdǎo	Qingdao	8
请问	qǐng wèn	May I ask ...	3
秋天	qiūtiān	fall	10
去	qù	go	1
去年	qùnián	last year	5
热	rè	hot	10
人	rén	person, people	2
人民币	Rénmínbì	Renminbi	7
认识	rènshi	know	1
日本	Rìběn	Japan	1
日语	Rìyǔ	Japanese	5
肉	ròu	meat	8
三	sān	three	4
伞	sǎn	umbrella	10

闪电	shǎndiàn	lightning	10
上	shàng	up	9
上班	shàngbān	go to work	5
商店	shāngdiàn	store	3
上海	Shànghǎi	Shanghai	3
上午	shàngwǔ	morning	5
上学	shàng xué	go to school	9
生词	shēngcí	new word	6
圣诞节	Shèngdànjié	Christmas	9
生日	shēngrì	birthday	5
什么	shénme	what	2
摄氏	shèshì	Centigrade	10
十	shí	ten	4
是	shì	be	1
试	shì	try	7
市场	shìchǎng	market	7
时候	shíhou	time	5
时间	shíjiān	time	5
市长	shìzhǎng	mayor	2
市中心	shì zhōngxīn	city center, downtown	9
瘦	shòu	tight	7
收	shōu	accept	7
手表	shǒubiǎo	watch	5
售货员	shòuhuòyuán	sales clerk	7
双	shuāng	pair	7
书	shū	book	2
书店	shūdiàn	bookstore	7
书法	shūfǎ	calligraphy	6
谁	shuí	who	4
水果	shuǐguǒ	fruit	8
睡觉	shuìjiào	sleep	5
说	shuō	speak, say	6
四	sì	four	4
四川	Sìchuān	Sichuan (Sezchuan)	6
酸	suán	sour	8
素菜	sùcài	vegetable dish	8
苏州	Sūzhōu	Suzhou	9
他	tā	he	1
她	tā	she	1
它	tā	it	1
太	tài	too	3
台风	táifēng	typhoon	10
糖	táng	sugar	8

汤	tāng	soup	8
天	tiān	day, weather	5
甜	tián	sweet	8
天气	tiānqì	weather	10
天堂	tiāntáng	paradise	9
条	tiáo	(classifier)	7
听	tīng	listen	6
听说	tīngshuō	it is said	7
同事	tóngshì	colleague	2
图书馆	túshūguǎn	library	3
外公	wàigōng	maternal grandfather	4
外国	wàiguó	foreign country	6
外国人	wàiguórén	foreigner	6
外婆	wàipó	maternal grandmother	4
外语	wàiyǔ	foreign language	6
碗	wǎn	bowl	8
玩	wán	play	9
万	wàn	ten thousand	4
晚饭	wǎnfàn	dinner	5
晚上	wǎnshang	evening	5
袜子	wàzi	socks	7
位	wèi	(classifier)	8
味道	wèidào	taste	8
为什么	wèishénme	why	10
问题	wèntí	question	2
我	wǒ	I	1
五	wǔ	five	4
雾	wù	fog	10
西	xī	west	10
下	xià	down, fall	9
下班	xiàbān	get off work	5
咸	xián	salty	8
想	xiǎng	would like, think	9
香港	Xiāng Gǎng	Hong Kong	6
先生	xiānsheng	Mr., husband	1
现在	xiànzài	now	5
小	xiǎo	small	10
小费	xiǎofèi	tip	8
小姐	xiǎojiě	Miss	1
小时	xiǎoshí	hour	9
小学生	xiǎoxuésheng	elementary school student	4
校长	xiàozhǎng	school principal/president	2

夏天	xiàtiān	summer	10
下午	xiàwǔ	afternoon	5
西班牙语	Xībānyáyǔ	Spanish language	6
写	xiě	write	6
鞋店	xiédiàn	shoe store	7
谢谢	xièxie	thank (you)	2
鞋子	xiézi	shoes	7
喜欢	xǐhuan	like	1
新	xīn	new	9
姓	xìng	family name	2
行李	xíngli	luggage	9
星期	xīngqī	week	5
新闻	xīnwén	news	6
信用卡	xìnyòngkǎ	credit card	7
学	xué	study	3
雪	xuě	snow	10
学生	xuésheng	student	1
学习	xuéxí	study	4
学校	xuéxiào	school	2
盐	yán	salt	8
羊肉	yángròu	lamb	8
颜色	yánsè	color	7
要	yào	want, take (time, etc)	7
要看	yàokàn	It depends.	7
亚洲	Yàzhōu	Asia	9
也	yě	also	1
夜里	yèlǐ	night	5
爷爷	yéye	paternal grandfather	4
一	yī	one	4
一般	yìbān	generally, ususally	5
一遍	yíbiàn	once	6
一点儿	yìdiǎnr	a little	6
一定	yídìng	certainly, definetely	8
衣服	yīfu	clothes	7
一共	yígòng	altogether	7
阴	yīn	cloudy	10
英国	Yīngguó	England	6
英语	Yīngyǔ	English language	6
银行	yínháng	bank	2
医生	yīshēng	doctor	1
意思	yìsi	meaning	6
医院	yīyuàn	hospital	3
用	yòng	use	6

有	yǒu	have, there is/are	2
有 的... 有 的	yǒu de ... yǒude	some ... others ...	7
有 点 儿	yǒu diǎnr	a little	8
邮 局	yóujú	post office	3
有 名	yǒumíng	famous	8
邮 票	yóupiào	stamps	7
有 时... 有 时	yǒushí ... yǒushí	sometimes ... sometimes	5
鱼	yú	fish	8
雨	yǔ	rain	10
远	yuǎn	far	3
预 报	yùbào	forecast	10
月	yuè	month	5
语 法	yǔfǎ	grammar	6
云	yún	cloud	10
语 言	yǔyán	language	6
雨 衣	yǔyī	raincoat	10
杂 志	zázhì	magazine	6
在	zài	in, at	3
再	zài	again	6
再 见	zàijiàn	good-bye	2
早 饭	zǎofàn	breakfast	5
早 上	zǎoshang	early morning	5
怎 么	zěnme	how	6
怎 么 样	zěnmeyàng	how is ...?	1
炸	zhà	deep fry	8
张	zhāng	(classifer)	7
帐 单	zhàngdàn	check, bill	8
找	zhǎo	look for, find	9
这	zhè	this	1
这 儿	zhèr	here	3
只	zhǐ	only	6
知 道	zhīdao	know	2
支 票	zhīpiào	check	7
种	zhǒng	kind, variety	6
中 饭	zhōngfàn	lunch	5
中 国	Zhōngguó	China	1
中 文	Zhōngwén	Chinese language	2
中 午	zhōngwǔ	noon	5
中 学 生	zhōngxuésheng	secondary school student	4
周 末	zhōumò	weekend	5
住	zhù	live	3
猪 肉	zhūròu	pork	8
字	zì	Chinese character	6

自行车	zìxíngchē	bicycle	9
走	zǒu	walk	9
最	zuì	most	7
最好	zuìhǎo	best, had better	10
作	zuò	do	4
坐	zuò	sit, take (the bus, etc)	8
做饭	zuòfàn	cook	8
昨天	zuótiān	yesterday	5

Key to the Exercises

Lesson 1

II.

1.

A: Zhào Xiānsheng, nǐ hǎo!
B: Huáng Xiǎojie, nǐ hǎo!
A: Nǐ máng ma?
B: Bù máng, nǐ ne?
A: Wǒ hěn máng.

2.

A: Nǐ bàba qù Zhōngguó ma?
B: Qù.
A: Nǐ māma ne?
B: Tā yě qù.

3.

A: Nǐ gēge shì lǎoshī ma?
B: Shì.
A: Nǐ mèimei yě shì lǎoshī ma?
B: Bú shì, tā shì xuésheng.

4.

A: Zhè shì Huá Xiānsheng. Zhè shì Wáng Xiǎojie.
B: Rènshi nǐ hěn gāoxìng.
C: Rènshi nǐ wǒ yě hěn gāoxìng.

III.

1. Nǐ lèi ma?
2. Hú Xiānsheng bú shì yīshēng. Tā shì lǜshī.
3. Wǒ bàba hěn máng. Wǒ māma bù máng.
4. Wǒ bú rènshi tā.
5. Tā dìdi hěn gāoxìng.
6. Zhè shì wǒ bàba.
7. Wǒ māma bú qù Zhōngguó. Tā qù Rìběn.
8. Lǐ Xiānsheng shì lǜshī. Lǐ Tàitai yě shì lǜshī.
9. Tā bàba māma lái Měiguó.
10. Nǐ gēge xǐhuan wǒ mèimei ma?

IV.

1. Nǐ mèimei lái Měiguó ma?	Shì./Bú shì.
2. Shěn xiǎojiě shì lǎoshī ma?	Shì./Bú shì.
3. Tā rènshi wǒ bàba ma?	Rènshi./Bú rènshi.
4. Nǐ māma yě shì yīshēng ma?	Yě shì./Bú shì.
5. Tā gēge hěn xǐhuan Zhōngguó ma?	Xǐhuan./Bù xǐhuan.
6. Tā shì Wáng Xiānsheng ma?	Shì./Bú shì.
7. Zhāng Xiǎojie hěn gāoxìng ma?	Tā hěn gāoxìng./Tā bù gāoxìng.
8. Tā jiějie shì xuésheng ma?	Shì./Bú shì.
9. Nǐ bàba māma hěn máng ma?	Hěn máng./Bù máng.
10. Nǐ hěn lèi ma?	Hěn lèi./Bú lèi.

Lesson 2

II.

1. Nǐ zhīdao tā nǚ pěngyou de míngzi ma?	Bù zhīdao.
2. Nǐ rènshi wǒde Zhōngwén lǎoshī ma?	Rènshi.
3. Nǐ xìng Wáng ma?	Bù, wǒ xìng Zhāng.
4. Nǐ rènshi tā ma?	Wǒ zhīdao ta, dànshì wǒ bú rènshi tā.
5. Nǐ shì Zhào Xiānsheng de tàitai ma?	Shì.
6. Rènshi nǐ hěngāoxìng.	Rènshi nǐ wǒ yě hěn gāoxìng.

III.

1. Zhè shì shénme?
2. Tā shì wǒ gēge de nǚ péngyou.
3. Wǒ zhīdào tā, dànshì wǒ bú rènshi tā.
4. Wǒ tàitai jiào Lìli.
5. Tā nǚ'er méi yǒu Zhōngguó péngyou.

IV.

1. Tā méi yǒu nǚ péngyou.
2. Wǒ bú jiào Dàwèi.
3. Wǒmende Zhōngwén lǎoshī bú xìng Wáng.
4. Wǒ māma bú gāoxìng.
5. Tā méi yǒu érzi.
6. Tā tàitai méi yǒu gēge.
7. Wǒ bú rènshi tā xiānsheng.
8. Tāmen méi yǒu Měiguó péngyou.
9. Wǒ bàba bù máng.
10. Wǒmen bú qù Zhōngguó.

V.

1. I have an older brother and also an older sister. My older brother's name is Xiao Hua and my older sister's name is Xiao Jun.

2. I'm very happy to know your mother.
3. Her boyfriend is David, not Tom.
4. What is the name of your Chinese friend?
5. The family names of both my parents are Huang.

Lesson 3
II.
1. Nǐ jiā zài nǎr?
2. Nǎr yǒu yīyuàn?
3. Zhèr yǒu Zhōngwén xuéxiào ma?
4. Nǐ zài nǎr xué Zhōngwén?
5. Nàr méi yǒu Rìběn cānguǎn.
6. Nǚ cèsuǒ zài nàr.
7. Wǒde nǚ péngyou zài Shànghǎi zhù.
8. (Any place name) zài nǎr?
9. Nǎr yǒu yínháng?
10. Nǐ qù nǎr?

III.
1. Qǐngwèn, nán cèsuǒ zài nǎr?
2. Qǐngwèn, Běijīng yǒu Měiguóchéng ma?
3. Wǒ tàitai zài xuéxiào gōngzuò.
4. Tā nǚ péngyou zài Nánjīng Dàxué xuéxi.
5. Zhèr méi yǒu Zhōngguó cānguǎn.
6. Wǒ māma bú shì yīshēng. Tā shì lǎoshī.
7. Wǒmende Zhōngwén lǎoshī zhù zài Jiùjīnshān.
8. Wǒ māma bú zài jiā.
9. Nǐ bàba māma qù cānguǎn ma?
10. Yīyuàn bú zài nàr.

IV.
1. There is no American bank in Beijing.
2. I work at a school and so does my wife.
3. There is no Japantown in New York, but there is one in Los Angeles.
4. Excuse me, where is the train station?
5. Excuse me, where can I find a store?
6. What is the name of your school?
7. Are there any Japanese restaurants in Chinatown in New York?
8. I don't know where the bathroom is, but he does.
9. Where are you going? —I'm going to the airport.
10. My parents live in California.

Lesson 4

II.

1. sān shí èr
2. bā bǎi wǔ shí sì
3. sān qiān líng èrshí
4. wǔ qiān liù bǎi
5. sì qiān qī bǎi jiǔ shí bā
6. jiǔ wàn bā qiān qī bǎi liù shí wǔ
7. yí wàn líng sān bǎi líng sì

III.

1. zhāng - objects with flat surface or sheet-like
2. tiáo - long and narrow objects
3. kuài - small dimentional objects
4. zhī - small, thin, narrow and long objects
5. zhī - animals

IV.

1. Nǐ shì bú shì Zhōngguórén?
2. Tā yǒu méiyou háizi?
3. Nǐ bàba māma qù bu qù yínháng?
4. Zhèr yǒu méiyou cècuǒ?
5. Nǐ xìng bu xìng Wáng?
6. Tā zài bu zài jiā?
7. Tāmen xué bu xué Zhōngwén?
8. Nǐde Zhōngwén lǎoshī shì shì Zhōngguórén?
9. Zhè shì bu shì nǐde shū?
10. Nǐ jiějie shì bu shì dàxuésheng?

IV.

1. Wǒ jiā yǒu sì kǒu rén. Tāmen shì wǒ tàitai, wǒ érzi, wǒ nǚ'ér hé wǒ.
2. Nǐde Zhōngwén lǎoshī yǒu duōshao Zhōngwén shū?
3. Shànghǎi yǒu duōshao rén?
4. Wǒ tàitai bú zài gōngsī gōngzuò. Tā shì xuéxiào lǎoshī.
5. Wǒ bú rènshi nà ge rén. Nǐ rènshi tā ma?
6. Wǒ jiějie bú shì zhōngxuésheng. Tā shì dàxuésheng.
7. Nǐ jiějie zài dàxué xué shénme?
8. Nǐ zài nǎ ge gōngsī gōngzuò?
9. Wǒmen xuéxiào yǒu yì qiān wǔ bǎi ge xuésheng.
10. Nǐ mèimei yǒu nán péngyou ma?

V.

1. I study American history at Beijing University.
2. There are two Chinese teachers in their school.

3. Their company is very big. There are 1,000 people there.
4. How many Chinese friends do you have?
5. My boyfriend does not like to study Chinese. He likes to study history.
6. My mother works at home.
7. Do you know how many universities there are in Shanghai?
8. That person's older brother is our Chinese teacher.
9. There are eight people in my family. How about yours?
10. He is a student at the University of California.

Lesson 5

I.

7:05	—	qī diǎn wǔ fēn	12:30	—	shí èr diǎn sānshí (fēn)
4:15	—	sì diǎn shí wǔ (fēn)	9:43	—	jiǔ diǎn sì shí sān (fēn)
10:59	—	shí diǎn wǔ shí jiǔ (fēn)	3:28	—	sān diǎn èr shí bā (fēn)
6:32	—	liù diǎn sān shí èr (fēn)	1:30	—	yì diǎn sān shí (fēn)
8:04	—	bā diǎn líng sì (fēn)	11:16	—	shí yī diǎn shí liù (fēn)

III.

1. Jīntiān xīngqī jǐ?
2. Zuótiān jǐ yuè jǐ hào?
3. Tā shénme shíhou lái?
4. Nǐde Měiguó péngyou jīnnián bā yuè qù nǎr?
5. Jīntiān shì jǐ yuè ji hào, xīngqī jǐ?

IV.

1. Nǐ zuótian wǎnshang zài nǎr?
2. Duìbuqǐ, wǒ méiyou biǎo. Wǒ bù zhīdao xiànzài jǐ diǎn.
3. Nǐ xīngqī jǐ yǒu Zhōngwén kè?
4. Nǐ jīntiān xiàwǔ jǐ diǎn xià bān?
5. Wǒ xīngqi liù wǎnshang yìbān zài cānguǎn chīfàn.
6. Wǒ bàba měi tiān liù diǎn qǐchuáng.
7. Wǒ bù chī zǎofàn.
8. Bù chī zǎofàn bù hǎo.
9. Nǐ míngtiān xiàwǔ zuò shénme?
10. Nǐ shénme shíhou qù Zhōngguó? — Míngnián liù yuè.

V.

1. My mother usually does not eat breakfast.
2. Sometimes she eats lunch at work, sometimes at home.
3. Next Wednesday is my wife's birthday.
4. I'm going to the bank at 9:00 tomorrow morning.
5. Where is your bank?

Lesson 6

IV.

1. Nǐ huì shuō fǎyǔ ma?
2. Nǐ jiějie huì shuō jǐ zhǒng yǔyán?
3. Nǐde péngyou cóng nǎr lái?
4. Tā huì shuō yìdiǎnr Xībānyáyǔ.
5. Duìbuqǐ, wǒ bù dǒng nǐde huà.
6. Qǐng màn yìdiǎnr shuō.
7. Tā cóng Shànghǎi lái. Tā shì Shànghǎirén.
8. Nánjīngrén shuō shénme huà?
9. Nǐ dǒng bù dǒng wǒde huà?
10. Nǐ māma huì shuō Fǎyǔ ma?

V.

1. Qǐngwèn, nǐ zhīdao yòng Zhōngwén zěnme shuō "speak slowly" ma?
2. Qǐngwèn, "qìchē" shì shénme yìsi?
3. "Qìchē" de yìsi shì "car".
4. Wǒde Zhōngwén lǎoshī bú huì shuō Yīngyǔ.
5. Tā cóng Déguó lái, dànshì tā bú huì shuō Déyǔ.
6. Tā huì shuō yìdiǎnr Xībānyá yǔ.
7. Xiāng Gǎng rén shuō Guǎngdōnghuà.
8. Shuí huì shuō Fǎyǔ?
9. Tā shì Shànghǎirén, dànshì tā bú shuō Shànghǎihuà.
10. Nǐ zěnme xiě zhè ge hànzì?

VI.

1. I'm English and my wife is French.
2. People in Shanghai do not understand Cantonese.
3. My boyfriend speaks four languages, but I only speak English.
4. Pardon? I don't understand. Please say it again.
5. I understand Taiwan dialect, but I don't speak it.
6. His Cantonese is very good, but his Mandarin is not.
7. Excuse me, who speaks English?
8. Do you know what "gōngyuán" means?
9. I can only understand a little of what she said.
10. Sorry, I do not speak Sichuan dialect.

VII.

1. Nǐ yǒu jǐ běn Zhōngwén shū?
2. Nǐ rènshi bu rènshi nà ge yīsheng?
3. Tā měitiān bā diǎn shàngbān .
4. Nǐ shì bu shì xuéshēng?
5. Tā yǒu jiějie, méiyou gēge.
6. Wǒ yǒu liǎng ge Zhōngguó péngyou.

7. Qǐngwèn, Zhōngguóchéng zài nǎr?
8. Tā zài cānguǎn gōngzuò.
9. Wáng Tàitai jīntiān bú qù yínháng.
10. Nǐmen xuéxiào de túshūguǎn yǒu duōshao (běn) shū?

Lesson 7
II.
1. Zhè jiàn máoyi duōshao qián?
2. Nǐmen shōu bu shōu Rìyuán?
3. Nǎr yǒu Měiguó yínháng?
4. Zhè ge diàn de dōngxi bú guì, hěn piányi.
5. Nǐ yào huàn duōshao Měiyuán?

III.
1. ¥10   — shí kuài
2. ¥1.20   — yí kuài liǎng máo
3. ¥5.64   — wǔ kuài liù máo sì (fēn)
4. ¥7.08   — qī kuài líng bā (fēn)
5. ¥33.94   — sānshí sān kuài jiǔ máo sì (fēn)
6. ¥580   — wǔ bǎi bāshí kuài
7. ¥99.99   — jiǔshí jiǔ kuài jiǔ máo jiǔ (fēn)
8. ¥6,832.81   — liù qiān bā bǎi sānshí èr kuài bā máo yī (fēn)
9. ¥40.60   — sìshí kuài liù máo
10. ¥2,080.01   — èr qiān líng bāshí kuài líng yì (fēn)

IV.
1. Qǐng lái yíxiàr.
2. Zhè běn cídiǎn duōshao qián?
3. Duìbuqǐ, wǒmen zhǐ shōu Měiyuán. Wǒmen bù shōu Rénmínbì.
4. Nǐ néng gàosù wǒ nǎr yǒu xiédiàn ma?
5. Yǒude shāngdiàn shōu xìnyòngkǎ, yǒude shāngdiàn bù shōu.
6. Běijīng nǎ ge bǎihuò gōngsī zuì dà?
7. Yào kàn jiàgé.
8. Nǐ bù néng zài shāngdiàn huàn qián.
9. Wǒ néng shì yíxiàr zhè shuāng xié ma?
10. Tīngshuō Zhōngguóchéng de dōngxi hěn piányì.

V.
1. I don't have U.S. dollars. I only have Japanese yen.
2. One U.S. dollar could convert to eight Renminbi yesterday.
3. That bookstore has the most English books.
4. Many people like to go shopping in Shanghai.
5. Stores in the United States sell a lot of Chinese products.
6. This pair of pants is too long. Do you have anything shorter?

7. How much is your overcoat?
8. I heard that things in Japan are very expensive.
9. Whether or not I can go to China depends on whether I have money.
10. Cheap stuff may not be good.

Lesson 8
II.
   1. Nǐ shì Zhōngguórén háishi Měiguórén?
   2. Nǐ xǐhuan bù xǐhuan Fǎguó cài?
   3. Tā méiyǒu qù guo Yīngguó.
   4. Rìběn yīnyuè hěn hǎo tīng.
   5. Wǒ māma chī guo Běijīng kǎoyā.
   6. Nǐ yǒu méiyǒu kàn guo zhè běn shū?
   7. Nǎr yǒu Zhōngguó cānguǎn?
   8. Yígòng duōshao qián?
   9. Zhè jiā cānguǎn de cài hěn yǒumíng.
   10. Zhè shì wǒ dì èr cì hē Qīngdǎo píjiǔ.

III.
   1. Nǐ yǒu méiyou kàn guo Yīngguó diànyǐng?/Wǒ méiyou kàn guo Yīngguó diànyǐng.
   2. Tāde lǎoshī yǒu méiyou xué guo Déyǔ?/Tāde lǎoshī méiyou xué guo Déyǔ.
   3. Tā yǒu méiyou qù guo Xiāng Gǎng?/Tā méiyou qù guo Xiāng Gǎng.
   4. Nǐde Zhōngguó péngyou yǒu méiyou lái guo nǐ jiā?/Nǐde Zhōngguó péngyou méiyou lái guo nǐ jiā.
   5. Tāmen chī guo Fǎguó cài ma?/Tāmen méiyou chī guo Fǎguó cài.
   6. Tāde nán péngyou tīng guo Rìběn yīnyuè ma?/Tāde nán péngyou méi yǒu tīng guo Rìběn yīnyuè.
   7. Nǐ bāba yǒu méiyou zài Zhōngguó yínháng gōngzuò guo?/Wǒ bāba méiyou zài Zhōngguó yínháng gōngzuò guo.
   8. Tā māma yǒu méiyou zài Zhōngguó huàn guo qián?/Tā māma méiyou zài Zhōngguó huàn guo qián.
   9. Wáng Lǎoshī yǒu méiyou zài nà ge shāngdiàn mǎi guo dōngxi?/Wáng Lǎoshī méiyou zài nà ge shāngdiàn mǎi guo dōngxi.
   10. Nǐ dìdi yǒu méiyou zài Jiāzhōu zhù guo?/Wǒ dìdi méiyou zài Jiāzhōu zhù guo.

IV.
   1. Wǒ bú tài è.
   2. Běijīng kǎo yā hěn yǒumíng.
   3. Nán cèsuǒ zài èr lóu háishi sān lóu?
   4. Nǐ yào kāfēi háishi chá.
   5. Zhè jiā cānguǎn de cài hěn hǎochī.
   6. Nǐ qù guo Niǔ Yuē de Zhōngguóchéng ma?
   7. Nǐ hǎoxiàng hěn lèi.
   8. Zhè shì wǒ dìyí cì chī Rìběn cài. Wǒ huéde wèidào hěn hǎo.

9. Zhōngguó de cānguǎn bù shōu xiǎofèi.
10. Wǒmen qù kàn diànyǐng zěnmeyàng?

V.

1. Does your father work at a college or a middle school?
2. The green tea doesn't taste good, but the black tea does.
3. Is your girlfriend Chinese or American?
4. My husband has never seen a Chinese movie.
5. What dishes are famous in Guangzhou?
6. My older sister can't drink liquor, but she can drink a little wine.
7. I want neither rice or noodles. I want bread.
8. In his house, his wife cooks, but in my house, I cook.
9. Are you going to eat at home or in a restaurant tonight?
10. Chinese people sometimes only eat rice, not dishes, whereas Americans sometimes only eat dishes, not rice.

Lesson 9
II.

1. Nǐ zhīddao zěnme xiě zhè ge zì ma?
2. Nǐ bàba qù Xiāng Gǎng zuò shénme?
3. Tiānānmén lí wǒmende lǚguǎn hěn jìn. Zuò dìtiě zhǐyào shí fēnzhōng.
4. Míngtiān shì nǐ tàitai de shēngrì, nǐmen zěnme guò?
5. Qí zìxíngchē qù nǐde xuéxiào yào duōshao shíjiān?
6. Tā qù guo Fǎguó de shénme dìfang?
7. Hángzhōu hěn hǎo wán.
8. Wǒ qù guo Niǔ Yuē sān cì.
9. Cóng huǒchēzhàn qù Běijīng Dàxué yào zuò qìchē.
10. Nǐ zhīdao dìtiězhàn zai nǎr ma?

III.

1. Huáshèngdùn lǚguǎn hǎozhǎo bù hǎozhǎo?
2. Xī'ān lí Guǎngzhōu hěn yuǎn.
3. Cóng Běijīng zuò huǒchē dào Shànghǎi dàgài yào èrshí ge xiǎoshí.
4. Nánjīng yǒu méiyou dìtiě?
5. Hěn duō Zhōngguórén qí zìxíngchē shàngbān.
6. Nǐ cóng Xiāng Gǎng zěnme qù Guǎngzhōu?
7. Tā qù guo Rìběn wǔ cì.
8. Wǒ xiǎng míngnián qù Zhōngguó.
9. Wǒde péngyou bú zhù lǚguǎn. Tā zhù wǒ jiā.
10. Hěn duō Zhōngguórén xiànzài guò Shèngdànjié.

IV.

1. I'm going to the park with my wife this weekend.
2. My mother has been to England and France in Europe.

3. Train tickets are very cheap, but trains are very slow.
4. It is not easy to find a hotel now.
5. My house is very close to my company and I walk to work.
6. It takes 30 minutes to drive to my company from my house.
7. I think Suzhou is probably very fun.
8. Her father has been to many places in China. He likes Nanjing the best.
9. How do you go to the train station?
10. I sometimes eat lunch at home, sometimes in school.

Lesson 10

II.

1. Nǐ tàitai qù le shāngdiàn ma?/Nǐ tàitai yǒu méiyou qù shāngdiàn?
2. Nǐmende Zhōngwén lǎoshī lái le ma?/Nǐmende Zhōngwén lǎoshī yǒu méiyou lái?
3. Xià yǔ le ma?/Yǒu méiyou xià yǔ?
4. Niǔ Yuē jīnnián dōngtiān xià le hěn duō xuě ma?/Niǔ Yuē jīnnián dōngtiān yǒu méiyou xià hěn duō xuě?
5. Tāmen xiàbān le ma?/Tāmen yǒu méiyou xiàbān?

III.

1. Wǒ bàba māma zuótiān dōu méiyou lái.
2. Xīngqīliù wǎnshang wǒ méiyou kàn diànshì.
3. Yínháng méi yǒu guānmén.
4. Tā méiyou yòng wǒde qìchē.
5. Wǒ xiānsheng méiyou qǐchuáng.

V.

1. Wǒ zuótiān méiyou chī zǎofàn.
2. Tā māma jīntiān zǎoshàng zài jiā.
3. Nǐ shàng xīngqītiān yǒu méiyou qù jiàotáng? or Nǐ shàng xīngqītiān qù le jiàotáng ma?
4. Tāmen méiyou lái Zhōngguó.
5. Wǒ qùnián bú rènshi tā.

VI.

1. Shànghǎi qiūtiān de tiānqì zěnmeyàng?
2. Niǔ Yuē xiàtiān chángcháng xià yǔ ma?
3. Míngtiān shì qíngtiān.
4. Hángzhōu xià bu xià xuě? - Yǒushí xià, yǒushí bú xià.
5. Wǒmen zhèr dōngtiān fēng hěn dà.
6. Zuótiān duōshao dù? - Wǔshí sān dù.
7. Tīngshuō Fǎguó jīnnián dōngtiān xià le hěn duō xuě.
8. Guǎngzhōu chūntiān de tiānqì zuì hǎo.
9. Zuótiān de yǔ yǒu duō dà?
10. Nánjīng chūntiān yǒushí xià xuě.
11. Wǒ māma qù le shāngdiàn.

12. Tā jīntiān zǎoshang méiyǒu chī zǎofàn.
13. Nǐ yǒu méiyou kāi guo Zhōngguó chē?
14. Wǒ zuótiān wǎnshang xué le shí ge hànzì.
15. Tāmen jīntiān zài Zhōngguó yínháng huàn le wǔ bǎi Měiyuán.

VII.
1. It's cloudy today. It's cold and windy.
2. Was the snow heavy in New York this winter?
3. What do Chinese people like to do in the summer?
4. Many Americans like to go skiing in the winter.
5. It was not too cold last winter and not too hot last summer.
6. I don't like Beijing's spring. It's too windy.
7. Which was heavier, the rain yesterday or the rain today?
8. There are more students at Beijing University than at Nanjing University.
9. My house is farther away from the company than his house.
10. This book is three dollars cheaper than that book.

IX.
1. Jīntiān de xuě bǐ zuótiān de xuě dà.
2. Tāde Zhōngwén bǐ wǒde Zhōngwén hǎo.
3. Hóngjiǔ bǐ báijiǔ hǎohē.
4. Fēijī bǐ huǒchē kuài.
5. Běijīng bǐ Shànghǎi hǎowán.
6. Zhè běn shū bǐ nà běn shū guì shí kuài qián.
7. Wǒ bàba bǐ wǒ māma máng.
8. Niǔ Yuē de lǚguǎn bǐ Luòshānjī de lǚguǎn hǎo zhǎo.
9. Jīntiān bǐ zuótiān gāo shí dù.
10. Wǒmen xuéxiào bǐ tāmen xuéxiào duō èr bǎi ge xuésheng.

Pinyin Practice
b, p, m, f, d, t, n, l, z, c, s, zh, ch, sh, r, j, q, x, g, k, h

B	P
bā, bá, bǎ, bà	pā, pá, pǎ, pà
bō, bó, bǒ, bò	pō, pó, pǒ, pò
bī, bí, bǐ, bì	pī, pí, pǐ, pì
bū, bú, bǔ, bù	pū, pú, pǔ, pù
bāi, bái, bǎi, bài	pāi, pái, pǎi, pài
bāo, báo, bǎo, bào	pāo, páo, pǎo, pào
bān, bán, bǎn, bàn	pān, pán, pǎn, pàn
bāng, báng, bǎng, bàng	pāng, páng, pǎng, pàng
bēi, béi, běi, bèi	pēi, péi, pěi, pèi
bēn, bén, běn, bèn	pēn, pén, pěn, pèn
bēng, béng, běng, bèng	pēng, péng, pěng, pèng
biāo, biáo, biǎo, biào	piāo, piáo, piǎo, piào
biē, bié, biě, biè	piē, pié, piě, piè
biān, bián, biǎn, biàn	piān, pián, piǎn, piàn
bīn, bín, bǐn, bìn	pīn, pín, pǐn, pìn
bīng, bíng, bǐng, bìng	pīng, píng, pǐng, pìng

M

mā, má, mǎ, mà

mō, mó, mǒ, mò

mē, mé, mě, mè

mī, mí, mǐ, mì

mū, mú, mǔ, mù

māi, mái, mǎi, mài

māo, máo, mǎo, mào

mān, mán, mǎn, màn

māng, máng, mǎng, màng

mēi, méi, měi, mèi

mēn, mén, měn, mèn

mēng, méng, měng, mèng

miāo, miáo, miǎo, miào

miē, mié, miě, miè

miū, miú, miǔ, miù

miān, mián, miǎn, miàn

mīn, mín, mǐn, mìn

mīng, míng, mǐng, mìng

mōu, móu, mǒu, mòu

F

fā, fá, fǎ, fà

fō, fó, fǒ, fò

fū, fú, fǔ, fù

fān, fán, fǎn, fàn

fāng, fáng, fǎng, fàng

fēi, féi, fěi, fèi

fēn, fén, fěn, fèn

fēng, féng, fěng, fèng

fōu, fóu, fǒu, fòu

D

dā, dá, dǎ, dà

dē, dé, dě, dè

dī, dí, dǐ, dì

dū, dú, dǔ, dù

dāi, dái, dǎi, dài

dāo, dáo, dǎo, dào

dān, dán, dǎn, dàn

dāng, dáng, dǎng, dàng

dōng, dóng, dǒng, dòng

dēi, déi, děi, dèi

dēn, dén, děn, dèn

dēng, déng, děng, dèng

diāo, diáo, diǎo, diào

diē, dié, diě, diè

diān, dián, diǎn, diàn

dīng, díng, dǐng, dìng

diū, diú, diǔ, diù

duō, duó, duǒ, duò

duī, duí, duǐ, duì

duān, duán, duǎn, duàn

dūn, dún, dǔn, dùn

T

tā, tá, tǎ, tà

tē, té, tě, tè

tī, tí, tǐ, tì

tū, tú, tǔ, tù

tāi, tái, tǎi, tài

tāo, táo, tǎo, tào

tān, tán, tǎn, tàn

tāng, táng, tǎng, tàng

tōng, tóng, tǒng, tòng

tēng, téng, těng, tèng

tiāo, tiáo, tiǎo, tiào

tiē, tié, tiě, tiè

tiān, tián, tiǎn, tiàn

tīng, tíng, tǐng, tìng

tuō, tuó, tuǒ, tuò

tuī, tuí, tuǐ, tuì

tuān, tuán, tuǎn, tuàn

tūn, tún, tǔn, tùn

N

nā, ná, nǎ, nà

nē, né, ně, nè

nī, ní, nǐ, nì

nū, nú, nǔ, nù

nǖ, nǘ, nǚ, nǜ

nāi, nái, nǎi, nài

nāo, náo, nǎo, nào

nān, nán, nǎn, nàn

nāng, náng, nǎng, nàng

nōng, nóng, nǒng, nòng

nēi, néi, něi, nèi

nēn, nén, něn, nèn

nēng, néng, něng, nèng

niāo, niáo, niǎo, niào

niān, nián, niǎn, niàn

niāng, niáng, niǎng, niàng

niē, nié, niě, niè

nīn, nín, nǐn, nìn

nīng, níng, nǐng, nìng

niū, niú, niǔ, niù

nuō, nuó, nuǒ, nuò

nuān, nuán, nuǎn, nuàn

nüē, nüé, nüě, nüè

L

lā, lá, lǎ, là

lē, lé, lě, lè

lī, lí, lǐ, lì

lū, lú, lǔ, lù

lǖ, lǘ, lǚ, lǜ

lāi, lái, lǎi, lài

lāo, láo, lǎo, lào

lān, lán, lǎn, làn

lāng, láng, lǎng, làng

lōng, lóng, lǒng, lòng

lēi, léi, lěi, lèi

lēng, léng, lěng, lèng

liā, liá, liǎ, lià

liāo, liáo, liǎo, liào

liān, lián, liǎn, liàn

liāng, liáng, liǎng, liàng

liē, lié, liě, liè

līn, lín, lǐn, lìn

līng, líng, lǐng, lìng

liū, liú, liǔ, liù

luō, luó, luǒ, luò

lūn, lún, lǔn, lùn

luān, luán, luǎn, luàn

lüē, lüé, lüě, lüè

Z

zā, zá, zǎ, zà

zē, zé, zě, zè

zī, zí, zǐ, zì

zū, zú, zǔ, zù

zāi, zái, zǎi, zài

zāo, záo, zǎo, zào

zān, zán, zǎn, zàn

zāng, záng, zǎng, zàng

zōng, zóng, zǒng, zòng

zēi, zéi, zěi, zèi

zēn, zén, zěn, zèn

zēng, zéng, zěng, zèng

zuō, zuó, zuǒ, zuò

zuī, zuí, zuǐ, zuì

zūn, zún, zǔn, zùn

zuān, zuán, zuǎn, zuàn

C

cā, cá, cǎ, cà

cē, cé, cě, cè

cī, cí, cǐ, cì

cū, cú, cǔ, cù

cāi, cái, cǎi, cài

cāo, cáo, cǎo, cào

cān, cán, cǎn, càn

cāng, cáng, cǎng, càng

cōng, cóng, cǒng, còng

cēn, cén, cěn, cèn

cēng, céng, cěng, cèng

cuō, cuó, cuǒ, cuò

cuī, cuí, cuǐ, cuì

cūn, cún, cǔn, cùn

cuān, cuán, cuǎn, cuàn

S

sā, sá, sǎ, sà

sē, sé, sě, sè

sī, sí, sǐ, sì

sū, sú, sǔ, sù

sāi, sái, sǎi, sài

sāo, sáo, sǎo, sào

sān, sán, sǎn, sàn

sāng, sáng, sǎng, sàng

sōng, sóng, sǒng, sòng

sēn, sén, sěn, sèn

sēng, séng, sěng, sèng

suō, suó, suǒ, suò

suī, suí, suǐ, suì

sūn, sún, sǔn, sùn

suān, suán, suǎn, suàn

ZH

zhā, zhá, zhǎ, zhà

zhē, zhé, zhě, zhè

zhī, zhí, zhǐ, zhì

zhū, zhú, zhǔ, zhù

zhāi, zhái, zhǎi, zhài

zhāo, zháo, zhǎo, zhào

zhān, zhán, zhǎn, zhàn

zhāng, zháng, zhǎng, zhàng

zhōng, zhóng, zhǒng, zhòng

zhēi, zhéi, zhěi, zhèi

zhēn, zhén, zhěn, zhèn

zhēng, zhéng, zhěng, zhèng

zhuā, zhuá, zhuǎ, zhuà

zhuāi, zhuái, zhuǎi, zhuài

zhuāng, zhuáng, zhuǎng, zhuàng

zhuō, zhuó, zhuǒ, zhuò

zhuī, zhuí, zhuǐ, zhuì

zhūn, zhún, zhǔn, zhùn

zhuān, zhuán, zhuǎn, zhuàn

CH

chā, chá, chǎ, chà

chē, ché, chě, chè

chī, chí, chǐ, chì

chū, chú, chǔ, chù

chāi, chái, chǎi, chài

chāo, cháo, chǎo, chào

chān, chán, chǎn, chàn

chāng, cháng, chǎng, chàng

chōng, chóng, chǒng, chòng

chēn, chén, chěn, chèn

chēng, chéng, chěng, chèng

chuā, chuá, chuǎ, chuà

chuāi, chuái, chuǎi, chuài

chuāng, chuáng, chuǎng, chuàng

chuō, chuó, chuǒ, chuò

chuī, chuí, chuǐ, chuì

chūn, chún, chǔn, chùn

chuān, chuán, chuǎn, chuàn

SH

shā, shá, shǎ, shà

shē, shé, shě, shè

shī, shí, shǐ, shì

shū, shú, shǔ, shù

shāi, shái, shǎi, shài

shāo, sháo, shǎo, shào

shān, shán, shǎn, shàn

shāng, sháng, shǎng, shàng

shēi, shéi, shěi, shèi

shēn, shén, shěn, shèn

shēng, shéng, shěng, shèng

shuā, shuá, shuǎ, shuà

shuāi, shuái, shuǎi, shuài

shuāng, shuáng, shuǎng, shuàng

shuō, shuó, shuǒ, shuò

shuī, shuí, shuǐ, shuì

shūn, shún, shǔn, shùn

shuān, shuán, shuǎn, shuàn

R

rē, ré, rě, rè

rī, rí, rǐ, rì

rū, rú, rǔ, rù

rǎo, ráo, rǎo, rào

rān, rán, rǎn, ràn

rāng, ráng, rǎng, ràng

rōng, róng, rǒng, ròng

rōu, róu, rǒu, ròu

rēn, rén, rěn, rèn

rēng, réng, rěng, rèng

ruō, ruó, ruǒ, ruò

ruī, ruí, ruǐ, ruì

rūn, rún, rǔn, rùn

ruān, ruán, ruǎn, ruàn

J

jī, jí, jǐ, jì

jū, jú, jǔ, jù

jiā, jiá, jiǎ, jià

jiāo, jiáo, jiǎo, jiào

jiān, jián, jiǎn, jiàn

jiāng, jiáng, jiǎng, jiàng

jīn, jín, jǐn, jìn

jīng, jíng, jǐng, jìng

jiē, jié, jiě, jiè

jiū, jiú, jiǔ, jiù

jiōng, jióng, jiǒng, jiòng

juē, jué, juě, juè

juān, juán, juǎn, juàn

jūn, jún, jǔn, jùn

Q

qī, qí, qǐ, qì

qū, qú, qǔ, qù

qiā, qiá, qiǎ, qià

qiāo, qiáo, qiǎo, qiào

qiān, qián, qiǎn, qiàn

qiāng, qiáng, qiǎng, qiàng

qīn, qín, qǐn, qìn

qīng, qíng, qǐng, qìng

qiē, qié, qiě, qiè

qiū, qiú, qiǔ, qiù

qiōng, qióng, qiǒng, qiòng

quē, qué, quě, què

quān, quán, quǎn, quàn

qūn, qún, qǔn, qùn

X

xī, xí, xǐ, xì

xū, xú, xǔ, xù

xiā, xiá, xiǎ, xià

xiāo, xiáo, xiǎo, xiào

xiān, xián, xiǎn, xiàn

xiāng, xiáng, xiǎng, xiàng

xīn, xín, xǐn, xìn

xīng, xíng, xǐng, xìng

xiē, xié, xiě, xiè

xiū, xiú, xiǔ, xiù

xiōng, xióng, xiǒng, xiòng

xuē, xué, xuě, xuè

xuān, xuán, xuǎn, xuàn

xūn, xún, xǔn, xùn

G

gā, gá, gǎ, gà

gē, gé, gě, gè

gū, gú, gǔ, gù

gāi, gái, gǎi, gài

gāo, gáo, gǎo, gào

gān, gán, gǎn, gàn

gāng, gáng, gǎng, gàng

gōng, góng, gǒng, gòng

gēi, géi, gěi, gèi

gēn, gén, gěn, gèn

gēng, géng, gěng, gèng

guā, guá, guǎ, guà

guāi, guái, guǎi, guài

guān, guán, guǎn, guàn

guāng, guáng, guǎng, guàng

guō, guó, guǒ, guò

guī, guí, guǐ, guì

gūn, gún, gǔn, gùn

K

kā, ká, kǎ, kà

kē, ké, kě, kè

kū, kú, kǔ, kù

kāi, kái, kǎi, kài

kāo, káo, kǎo, kào

kān, kán, kǎn, kàn

kāng, káng, kǎng, kàng

kōng, kóng, kǒng, kòng

kēi, kéi, kěi, kèi

kēn, kén, kěn, kèn

kēng, kéng, kěng, kèng

kuā, kuá, kuǎ, kuà

kuāi, kuái, kuǎi, kuài

kuān, kuán, kuǎn, kuàn

kuāng, kuáng, kuǎng, kuàng

kuō, kuó, kuǒ, kuò

kuī, kuí, kuǐ, kuì

kūn, kún, kǔn, kùn

H

hā, há, hǎ, hà

hē, hé, hě, hè

hū, hú, hǔ, hù

hāi, hái, hǎi, hài

hāo, háo, hǎo, hào

hān, hán, hǎn, hàn

hāng, háng, hǎng, hàng

hōng, hóng, hǒng, hòng

hēi, héi, hěi, hèi

hēn, hén, hěn, hèn

hēng, héng, hěng, hèng

huā, huá, huǎ, huà

huāi, huái, huǎi, huài

huān, huán, huǎn, huàn

huāng, huáng, huǎng, huàng

huō, huó, huǒ, huò

huī, huí, huǐ, huì

hūn, hún, hǔn, hùn

Pinyin to Wade Giles: A Cross Reference

Pinyin	WG	Pinyin	WG	Pinyin	WG	Pinyin	WG	Pinyin	WG	Pinyin	WG
a	a	cou	ts'ou	gu	ku	kong	k'ung	mo	mo	qie	ch'ieh
ai	ai	cu	ts'u	gua	kua	kou	k'ou	mou	mou	qin	ch'in
an	an	cuan	ts'uan	guai	kuai	ku	k'u	mu	mu	qing	ch'ing
ang	ang	cui	ts'ui	guan	kuan	kua	k'ua			qiong	ch'iung
ao	ao	cun	ts'un	guang	kuang	kuai	k'uai	na	na	qiu	ch'iu
		cuo	ts'o	gui	kuei	kuan	k'uan	nai	nai	qu	ch'ü
ba	pa			gun	kun	kuang	k'uang	nan	nan	quan	ch'üan
bai	pai	da	ta	guo	kuo	kui	k'uei	nang	nang	que	ch'üeh
ban	pan	dai	tai			kun	k'un	nao	nao	qun	ch'ün
bang	pang	dan	tan	ha	ha	kuo	k'uo	nei	nei		
bao	pao	dang	tang	hai	hai			nen	nen	ran	jan
bei	pei	dao	tao	han	han	la	la	neng	neng	rang	jang
ben	pen	de	te	hang	hang	lai	lai	ni	ni	rao	jao
beng	peng	deng	teng	hao	hao	lan	lan	nian	nien	re	je
bi	pi	di	ti	he	ho	lang	lang	niang	niang	ren	jen
bian	pien	dian	tien	hei	hei	lao	lao	niao	niao	reng	jeng
biao	piao	diao	tiao	hen	hen	le	le	nie	nieh	ri	jih
bie	pieh	die	tieh	heng	heng	lei	lei	nin	nin	rong	jung
bin	pin	ding	ting	hong	hung	leng	leng	ning	ning	rou	jou
bing	ping	diu	tiu	hou	hou	li	li	niu	niu	ru	ju
bo	po	dong	tung	hu	hu	lia	lia	nong	nung	ruan	juan
bou	pou	dou	tou	hua	hua	lian	lien	nou	nou	rui	jui
bu	pu	du	tu	huai	huai	liang	liang	nu	nu	run	jun
		duan	tuan	huan	huan	liao	liao	nü	nü	ruo	jo
ca	ts'a	dui	tui	huang	huang	lie	lieh	nuan	nuan		
cai	ts'ai	dun	tun	hui	hui	lin	lin	nüe	nüeh	sa	sa
can	ts'an	duo	to	hun	hun	ling	ling	nuo	no	sai	sai
cang	ts'ang			huo	huo	liu	liu			san	san
cao	ts'ao	e	o			long	lung	ou	ou	sang	sang
ce	ts'e	en	en	ji	chi	lou	lou			sao	sao
cen	ts'en	er	erh	jia	chia	lu	lu	pa	p'a	se	se
ceng	ts'eng			jian	chien	lü	lü	pai	p'ai	sen	sen
cha	ch'a	fa	fa	jiang	chiang	luan	luan	pan	p'an	seng	seng
chai	ch'ai	fan	fan	jiao	chiao	lüan	lüan	pang	p'ang	sha	sha
chan	ch'an	fang	fang	jie	chieh	lüe	lüeh	pao	p'ao	shai	shai
chang	ch'ang	fei	fei	jin	chin	lun	lun	pei	p'ei	shan	shan
chao	ch'ao	fen	fen	jing	ching	luo	lo	pen	p'en	shang	shang
che	ch'e	feng	feng	jiong	chiung			peng	p'eng	shao	shao
chen	ch'en	fo	fo	jiu	chiu	ma	ma	pi	p'i	she	she
cheng	ch'eng	fou	fou	ju	chü	mai	mai	pian	p'ien	shen	shen
chi	ch'ih	fu	fu	juan	chüan	man	man	piao	p'iao	sheng	sheng
chong	ch'ung			jue	chüeh	mang	mang	pie	p'ieh	shi	shih
chou	ch'ou	ga	ka	jun	chün	mao	mao	pin	p'in	shou	shou
chu	ch'u	gai	kai			mei	mei	ping	p'ing	shu	shu
chua	ch'ua	gan	kan	ka	k'a	men	men	po	p'o	shua	shua
chuai	ch'uai	gang	kang	kai	k'ai	meng	meng	pou	p'ou	shuai	shuai
chuan	ch'uan	gao	kao	kan	k'an	mi	mi	pu	p'u	shuan	shuan
chuang	ch'uang	ge	ko	kang	k'ang	mian	mien			shuang	shuang
chui	ch'ui	gei	kei	kao	k'ao	miao	miao	qi	ch'i	shui	shui
chun	ch'un	gen	ken	ke	k'o	mie	mieh	qia	ch'ia	shun	shun
chuo	ch'o	geng	keng	kei	k'ei	min	min	qian	ch'ien	shuo	shuo
ci	tz'u	gong	kung	ken	k'en	ming	ming	qiang	ch'iang	si	ssu
cong	ts'ung	gou	kou	keng	k'eng	miu	miu	qiao	chi'ao	song	sung

Pinyin	WG	Pinyin	WG
sou	sou	yan	yen
su	su	yang	yang
suan	suan	yao	yao
sui	sui	ye	yeh
sun	sun	yi	i
suo	so	yin	yin
		ying	ying
ta	t'a	yong	yung
tai	t'ai	you	yu
tan	t'an	yu	yü
tang	t'ang	yuan	yüan
tao	t'ao	yue	yüeh
te	t'e	yun	yün
teng	t'eng		
ti	t'i	za	tsa
tian	t'ien	zai	tsai
tiao	t'iao	zan	tsan
tie	t'ieh	zang	tsang
ting	t'ing	zao	tsao
tong	t'ung	ze	tse
tou	t'ou	zei	tsei
tu	t'u	zen	tsen
tuan	t'uan	zeng	tseng
tui	t'ui	zha	cha
tun	t'un	zhai	chai
tuo	t'o	zhan	chan
		zhang	chang
wa	wa	zhao	chao
wai	wai	zhe	che
wan	wan	zhen	chen
wang	wang	zheng	cheng
wei	wei	zhi	chih
wen	wen	zhong	chung
weng	weng	zhou	chou
wo	wo	zhu	chu
wu	wu	zhua	chua
		zhuai	chuai
xi	hsi	zhuan	chuan
xia	hsia	zhuang	chuang
xian	hsien	zhui	chui
xiang	ksiang	zhun	chun
xiao	ksiao	zhuo	cho
xie	hsieh	zi	tzu
xin	hsin	zong	tsung
xing	ksing	zou	tsou
xiong	hsiung	zu	tsu
xiu	hsiu	zuan	tsuan
xu	hsu	zui	tsui
xuan	hsuan	zun	tsun
xue	hsueh	zuo	tso
xun	hsun		
ya	ya		
yai	yai		

Wade Giles to Pinyin: A Cross Reference

WG	Pinyin	WG	Pinyin	WG	Pinyin	WG	Pinyin	WG	Pinyin	WG	Pinyin
a	a	chuai	zhuai	hsüan	xuan	k'ua	kua	mieh	mie	p'i	pi
ai	ai	ch'uai	chuai	hsüeh	xue	kuai	guai	mien	mian	piao	biao
an	an	chuan	zhuan	hsün	xun	k'uai	kuai	min	min	p'iao	piao
ang	ang	ch'uan	chuan	hu	hu	kuan	guan	ming	ming	pieh	pie
ao	ao	chüan	juan	hua	hua	k'uan	kuan	miu	miu	p'ien	pian
		ch'üan	quan	huai	huai	kuang	guang	mo	mo	pien	bian
cha	zha	chuang	zhuang	huan	huan	k'uang	kuang	mou	mou	p'in	pin
ch'a	cha	ch'uang	chuang	huang	huang	kuei	gui	mu	mu	pin	bin
chai	zhai	chüeh	jue	hui	hui	k'uei	kui			ping	bing
ch'ai	chai	ch'üeh	que	hun	hun	kun	gun	na	na	p'ing	ping
chan	zhan	chui	zhui	hung	hong	k'un	kun	nai	nai	po	bo
ch'an	chan	ch'ui	chui	huo	huo	kung	gong	nan	nan	p'o	po
chang	zhang	chun	zhun			k'ung	kong	nang	nang	pou	bou
ch'ang	chang	ch'un	chun	i	yi	kuo	guo	nao	nao	p'ou	pou
ch'ao	chao	chün	jun			k'uo	kuo	nei	nei	pu	bu
che	zhe	ch'ün	qun	jan	ran			nen	nen	p'u	pu
ch'e	che	chung	zhong	jang	rang	la	la	neng	neng		
chen	zhen	ch'ung	chong	jao	rao	lai	lai	ni	ni	sa	sa
ch'en	chen			je	re	lan	lan	niang	niang	sai	sai
cheng	zheng	en	en	jen	ren	lang	lang	niao	niao	san	san
ch'eng	cheng	erh	er	jeng	reng	lao	lao	nieh	nie	sang	sang
chi	ji			jih	ri	le	le	nien	nian	sao	sao
ch'i	qi	fa	fa	jo	ruo	lei	lei	nin	nin	se	se
chia	jia	fan	fan	jou	rou	leng	leng	ning	ning	sen	sen
ch'ia	qia	fang	fang	ju	ru	li	li	niu	niu	seng	seng
chiang	jiang	fei	fei	juan	ruan	lia	lia	no	nuo	sha	sha
ch'iang	qiang	fen	fen	jui	rui	liang	liang	nou	nou	shai	shai
chiao	jiao	feng	feng	jun	run	liao	liao	nu	nu	shan	shan
ch'iao	qiao	fo	fo	jung	rong	lieh	lie	nü	nü	shang	shang
ch'ieh	jie	fou	fou			lien	lian	nuan	nuan	shao	shao
ch'ieh	qie	fu	fu	ka	ga	lin	lin	nüeh	nüe	she	she
chien	jian			k'a	ka	ling	ling	nung	nong	shen	shen
ch'ien	qian	ha	ha	kai	gai	liu	liu			sheng	sheng
chih	zhi	hai	hai	k'ai	kai	lo	luo	o	e	shih	shi
ch'ih	chi	han	han	kan	gan	lou	lou	ou	ou	shou	shou
chin	jin	hang	hang	k'an	kan	lu	lu			shu	shu
ch'in	qin	hao	hao	kang	gang	lü	lü	pa	ba	shua	shua
ching	jing	hei	hei	k'ang	kang	luan	luan	p'a	pa	shuai	shuai
ch'ing	qing	hen	hen	kao	gao	lüan	lüan	pai	bai	shuan	shuan
chiu	jiu	heng	heng	k'ao	kao	lüeh	lüe	p'ai	pai	shuang	shuang
ch'iu	qiu	ho	he	kei	gei	lun	lun	pan	ban	shui	shui
chiung	jiong	hou	hou	k'ei	kei	lung	long	p'an	pan	shun	shun
ch'iung	qiong	hsi	xi	ken	gen			pang	bang	shuo	shuo
cho	zhuo	hsia	xia	k'en	ken	ma	ma	p'ang	pang	so	suo
ch'o	chuo	hsiang	xiang	keng	geng	mai	mai	pao	bao	sou	sou
chou	zhou	hsiao	xiao	k'eng	keng	man	man	p'ao	pao	ssu	si
ch'ou	chou	hsieh	xie	ko	ge	mang	mang	pei	bei	su	su
chu	zhu	hsien	xian	k'o	ke	mao	mao	p'ei	pei	suan	suan
ch'u	chu	hsin	xin	kou	gou	mei	mei	pen	ben	sui	sui
chü	ju	hsing	xing	k'ou	kou	men	men	p'en	pen	sun	sun
ch'ü	qu	hsiu	xiu	ku	gu	meng	meng	peng	beng	sung	song
chua	zhua	hsiung	xiong	k'u	ku	mi	mi	p'eng	peng	ta	da
ch'ua	chua	hsü	xu	kua	gua	miao	miao	pi	bi		

WG	Pinyin	WG	Pinyin
t'a	ta	tsui	zui
tai	dai	ts'ui	cui
t'ai	tai	tsun	zun
tan	dan	ts'un	cun
t'an	tan	tsung	zong
tang	dang	ts'ung	cong
t'ang	tang	tu	du
tao	dao	t'u	tu
t'ao	tao	tuan	duan
te	de	t'uan	tuan
t'e	le	tui	dui
teng	deng	t'ui	tui
t'eng	teng	tun	dun
ti	di	t'un	tun
t'i	ti	tung	dong
tiao	diao	t'ung	tong
t'iao	tiao	tzu	zi
tieh	die	tz'u	ci
t'ieh	tie		
tien	dian	wa	wa
t'ien	tian	wai	wai
ting	ding	wan	wan
t'ing	ting	wang	wang
tiu	diu	wei	wei
to	duo	wen	wen
t'o	tuo	weng	weng
tou	dou	wo	wo
t'ou	tou	wu	wu
tsa	za		
ts'a	ca	ya	ya
tsai	zai	yai	yai
ts'ai	cai	yang	yang
tsan	zan	yao	yao
ts'an	can	yeh	ye
tsang	zang	yen	yan
ts'ang	cang	yin	yin
tsao	zao	ying	ying
ts'ao	cao	yu	you
tse	ze	yü	yu
tsei	zei	yüan	yuan
tsen	zen	yüeh	yue
ts'en	cen	yün	yun
tseng	zeng	yung	yong
ts'eng	ceng		
tso	zuo		
ts'o	cuo		
tsou	zou		
ts'ou	cou		
tsu	zu		
ts'u	cu		
tsuan	zuan		
ts'uan	cuan		

Resources for Students of Chinese

Bibliographic Resources

General
Barlow, Tani E., and Donald M. Lowe. 1985. *Chinese Reflections: Americans Teaching in the People's Republic.* New York: Praeger Publishers.

Clayre, Alasdair. 1985. *The Heart of the Dragon.* Boston: Houghton Mifflin Company.

Dernberger, Robert, etc. eds. 1991. *The Chinese: Adapting the Past, Facing the Future.* Center for Chinese Studies. Ann Arbor, MI: The University of Michigan.

Ebrey, Patricia Buckley. 1993. *Chinese Civilization: A Source Book.* New York: Free Press.

Fairbank, John King. 1992. *China: A New History.* Cambridge, Mass.: Belknap Press of Harvard University Press.

Hsu, Francis L.K. 1991. *Americans and Chinese: Passage to Differences.* Taipei: Bookman Books.

Hu, Wenzhong and Cornelius L. Grove. 1991. *Encountering the Chinese: A Guide for Americans.* Yarmouth, Maine: Intercultural Press, Inc.

Ho, Yong. 2000. *China: An Illustrated History.* New York: Hippocrene Books, Inc.

Morton, W. Scott. 1995. *China: Its History and Culture.* New York: McGraw-Hill.

Pye, Lucian W. and Mary W. Pye. 1991. *China: An Introduction.* New York, NY: Harper Collins.

Ross, Heidi A. 1993. *China Learn English: Language Teaching and Social Change in the People's Republic.* New Haven: Yale University Press.

Schneiter, Fred. 1992. *The Joy of Getting Along with the Chinese.* Heian International (available from China Books and Periodicals, Inc.).

Soled, Debra E. 1995. *China: A Nation in Trasition.* Washington, D.C.: Congressional Quarterly Inc.

Terrill, Ross. 1995. *China in Our Time.* Sydney: Hale and Iremonger.

Business
Becker, Gerhold K. 1996. *Ethics in Business and Society: Chinese and Western Perspectives.* Berlin, NY: Springer.

De Mente, Boye L. 1989. *Chinese Etiquette & Ethics in Business.* Lincolnwood, IL: NTC Business Books.

Genzberger, Christine and Edward Hinkleman, eds. 1994. *China Business: A Portable Encyclopedia for Doing Business in China.* World Trade Press.

Gibbons, Russell. 1996. *Joint Ventures in China.* Macmillan Education.

Huang, Quanyu, Richard S. Andrulis, & Tong Chen. 1994. *A Guide to Successful Business Relations with the Chinese: Opening the Great Wall's Gate.* New York: International Business Press.

Jan, George P. 1994. *How to do Business with China.* Toledo, OH: AIT Press.
Kenna, Peggy & Sondra Lacy. 1994. *Business China: A Practical Guide to Understanding Chinese Business Culture.* Lincolnwood, IL: NTC Business Books.
Macleod, Roderick. 1988. *China, Inc.: How to Do Business with the Chinese.* New York: Bantam Books.
Reuvid, Johanthan. 1994. *Doing Business with China.* London: Kogan Page.
Stross, Randall E. 1993. *Bulls in the China Shop and Other Sino-American Business Encounters.* Honolulu: University of Hawaii Press.
Tung, Shih-chung, Danian Zhang & Milton R. Larson. 1992. *Trade and Investment Opportunities in China: The Current Commercial and Legal Framework.* West Point, Conn.: Quorum Books.

Language

Beijing Language Institute: *Flashcards for Elementary Chinese.* San Francisco, Calif.: China Books and Periodicals, Inc.
Björksten, Johan. 1994. *Learn to Write Chinese Characters.* New Haven: Yale University Press.
Choy, Rita Mei-Wah. 1981. *Read and Write Chinese: A Simplified Guide to the Chinese Characters.* San Francisco, Calif.: China West Books.
Choy, Rita Mei-Wah. 1989. *Understanding Chinese: A Guide to the Usage of Chinese Characters.* San Francisco, Calif.: China Books and Periodicals, Inc.
De Francis, John. 1986. *The Chinese Language: Fact and Fantasy.* Honolulu: University of Hawaii Press.
Peng, Tan Huay. 1980-83. *Fun with Chinese Characters 1, 2, 3.* New York: Hippocrene Books.
Ho, Yong. 1993. *Aspects of Discourse Structure in Mandarin Chinese.* Lewiston, NY: Edwin Mellen.
Hu, Jerome P. and Stephen C. Lee. 1992. *Basic Chinese Vocabulary: A Handy Reference of Everyday Words Arranged by Topics.* Lincolnwood, ILL: Passport Books.
Kan, Qian. 1995. *Colloquial Chinese: A Complete Language Course.* London: Routledge, Kegan & Paul.
McCawley, James D. 1984. *The Eater's Guide to Chinese Characters.* Chicago: University of Chicago Press.
Norman, Jerry. 1988. *Chinese.* Cambridge: Cambridge University Press.
Ramsey, S. Robert. 1989. *The Languages of China.* Princeton: Princeton University Press.
Tung, P.C. and D. Polland. 1988. *Colloquial Chinese.* London: Routledge, Kegan & Paul.
Wang, Hongda. 1993. *The Origins of Chinese Characters.* Beijing: Sinolingua. (Available from Nan Hai Arts Center, 510 Broadway, Suite 300. Millbrae, CA 94030.)
Young, Linda Wai Ling. 1994. *Crosstalk and Culture in Sino-American Communication.* New York, NY: Cambridge University Press.

Dictionaries

Chinese-English Dictionary of the 500 Most Frequently Used Words: A Study Guide to Mandarin Chinese, by Yong Ho. Hippocrene Books, 2001.
Concise English-Chinese, Chinese-English Dictionary. Oxford University Press, 1987.
The English-Chinese Pocket Pinyin Dictionary. New World Press.
Oxford Advanced Learners English Chinese Dictionary. Oxford University Press. 1995.

The Pinyin Chinese-English Dictionary. Hong Kong Edition. Beijing Foreign Language Institute. 1984. (available from China Books and Periodicals, Inc.).

Major Publishers and Distributors of Chinese books and software in the U. S.
1. China Books & Periodicals, 2929 24th Street, San Francisco, CA 94110, Tel: 415-282-2994. Fax: 415-282-0994. E-mail: CHINABKS@sirius.com. Web site: http://www.chinabooks.com.
2. Cheng & Tsui Company, PO Box 576, Williston, VT 05495. Tel: 1-800-554-1964. Fax: 802-864-7626. Web site: http://www.cheng-tsui.com/
3. Nan Hai Arts Center, 516 Broadway, Suite 300, Millbrae, CA 94030, Tel: 415-259-2100. Fax: 415-259-2108. Web site: http://www.nanhai.com

Internet Resources

Guides, Indexes and Links
Chinese Language-Related Information
http://www.webcom.com/bamboo/Chinese/
A comprehensive subject guide to Chinese-language-related resources on the internet.

Chinese Language Study
http://www.nerdworld.com/nw1800.html
Large index of Chinese language study related internet resources.

Chinese Language Study Courses
http://www.webcom.com/bamboo/chinese/courses.html
Links to Web sites with information on Chinese language study courses offered by various institutions.

Chinese Software Web Sites
http://www.cd.ucdavis.edu/chinese/chinese.html
A list of Web sites for Chinese software and other Chinese-language topics.

Learning Chinese Online
http://philo.ucdavis.edu/CHINESE/online.htm
Xie Tianwei's Web links to various online Chinese learning sites.

Marjorie Chan's ChinaLinks
http://www.cohums.ohio-state.edu/deall/chan.9/c-links.htm
Annotated links to more than two hundred China and Chinese language and linguistics-related web sites.

Study Chinese in China
http://www.studyabroad.com/simplehtml/languages/chinese.html
http://www.fas.harvard.edu/~clp/China/abroad.htm
Lists of institutions offering Chinese language programs in China.

Teaching and Learning Chinese
http://topaz.kenyon.edu/projects/chinese/
A collection of resources for teaching and learning Chinese.

WWW Chinese Language Teaching Resources
http://www.ntnu.edu.tw/tcsl/Chinese/Resource/Wwwwccai.htm
Online language resources compiled by the National Taiwan Normal University.

Online Tutorials, Courses and Programs
Chinese Multimedia Tutorial
http://www.inform.umd.edu/EdRes/Topic/Humanities/.C-tut/C-tut.html
A tutorial on greetings, expressing thanks and food terms, including characters and sounds.

Conversational Mandarin Chinese Online
http://philo.ucdavis.edu/CHINESE/ccol.htm
A 15-unit course on everyday topics.

Cyber Chinese
http://www.nmc.csulb.edu/nmcpages/...e_Language_f/Chinese_Language.html
A series of interactive lessons covering the complete first-year curriculum, with video, sound and text.

Internet-based Chinese Teaching & Learning
http://chinese.bendigo.latrobe.edu.au/index.htm
La Trobe University's 8-level online Chinese language courses.

HyperChina
http://www.sinologic.com
A systematic and interactive CD courseware for learning Mandarin Chinese with all capabilities including recording your own voice and then compare it with the models.

Learn Chinese
http://pasture.ecn.purdue.edu/~agenhtml/agenmc/china/ctutor.html
An audio tutorial of survival Chinese.

Learn Chinese Online
http://www.khuang.com/chinese/
Mandarin classes with sound effects and information on useful software and books.

My Favorite Multimedia Inside Chinese Language Lab
http://peijean.ficnet.net.tw/
Page Lin's site for online pronounciation lessons using real-time sounds.

Practical Chinese Reader
http://www.nmc.csulb.edu/nmcpages/what/li.html
A series of interactive lessons using the popular textbook Practical Chinese Reader, *incorporating video, sound and text. This course covers the complete first-year Chinese curriculum.*

Wordprocessing Programs
Chinese Star
http://www.Suntendy.com/cstar/default.htm

NJStar
http://www.njstar.com

RichWin 4.2 Plus for Windows
http://www.richwinUSA.com

Rising Sun
http://www.accent.net/risingsun/

XLBR Chinese Wordprocessor for Mac
http://www.gy.com/ccd/acs/xlbre.htm

Twinbridge
http://www.twinbridge.com/

Aids, CD's, Tools, Videos and References
ABC Interactive Chinese
http://www.worldlanguage.com/chintut.htm
A learning program that includes speech recognition, character writing, animated articulation, dictionary, voice recording and comparison.

Animated Characters
http://www.ocrat.com/ocrat/chargif/
All the characters from Lesson 1-30 of the Practical Chinese Reader. *These animated characters show stroke by stroke how these characters are written.*

Bell Labs Mandarin Text-to-Speech Synthesis
http://www.bell-labs.com/project/tts/mandarin.html (traditional characters)
http://www.bell-labs.com/project/tts/mandarin-gb.html (simplified characters)
Type Chinese characters or pinyin, sound will be generated automatically.

China Bookshelf
http://www.gy.com/ccd/ccr/cbe2.htm
Besides providing cultural information on China, this CD program also includes an audio-visual Chinese-English dictionary. Chinese language learners listen to the pronounciation of each Chinese character and check Chinese writing styles and stroke orders.

Chinese & Characters
http://www.tradewatch.com:80/nite/main.htm
CD series that use animation to teach children and non-Chinese speaking people.

Chinese Books Cyberstore
http://www.chinesebooks.net
Internet Chinese bookstore.

Chinese Character Flashcards
http://www.erols.com/eepeter/flashcard.html
A Java application to assist in the learning of 1,000 most frequently used Chinese characters.

Chinese Character Genealogy
http://www.pitt.edu/~harbough/z/zipu.html
Online dictionary by Rick Harbough.

Chinese Character Genealogy
http://www.zhongwen.com
An etymological Chinese-English dictionary.

Chinese Character Pronounciations
http://www.webcom.com/ocrat/reaf/
A JavaScript application that shows how to pronounce Chinese characters.

Chinese Character Tutor
http://www.worldlanguage.com/chintut.htm
A Chinese dictionary and learning tool that includes 100 predefined lessons.

Chinese Character Tutor V4. 0
http://ourworld.compuserve.com/homepages/fergab/
An online dictionary and learning tool with audio and testing facility.

Chinese Dragon Writer
http://www.jics.com/LNGCHI.htm
A program that provides easy English to Chinese phrase translation input.

Chinese Express
http://www.china-guide.com/express.htm
CD series of Chinese language tutorial with 30 lessions and 2,000 characters.

Chinese Language Teaching & Learning Aids
http://www.wfu.edu/~moran/
Including Macintosh applications, printable flashcards for learning, printable calligraphy practice sheets, and links to other pages useful to teachers and students.

Chinese Language Video Lessons for Classroom Use
http://www.lll.hawaii.edu/nflrc
Fifteen lessons in Mandarin Chinese, comprising a books with instructions for the teacher and xeroxable student worksheets plus two accompanying video cassettes.

Chinese Multimedia Dictionary
http://www.china-guide.com/chinesedictionary.htm
CD interactive teaching and learning.

Chinese Pronounciation Guide
http://www.fas.harvard.edu/~clp/China/guide.htm
A tool that includes pinyin sheets and courses.

Chinese Radical Exam
http://execpc.com/~mbosley/
A study aid and test for beginners, covering 108 of the most common radicals that are also characters in thier own right.

Fascinating Chinese Characters
http://www.china-guide.com/characte.htm#Characters
CD program teaching how to write Chinese characters.

Flashcards
http://www.wfu.edu/~moran/flashcards.html
With a week by week schedule.

Harvard Chinese Language Program
http://www.fas.harvard.edu/~clp/China/harvard.htm
Teaching materials including essays, prose, novels, drama, and net resources.

HyperChina Interactive Chinese
http://www.sinologic.com/HyperChina.html
A complete CD courseware for learning Mandarin Chinese.

Ocrat Chinese Pages
http://www.ocrat.com/ocrat/
A collection of Chinese-related Web applications, a facility for Chinese character pronounciations which allows to input (copy-and-paste) any Chinese text and obtain the transliteration in Mandarin (pinyin) or Cantonese.

OK88 English-Chinese Dictionary
http://www.ok88.com/go/svc/ecdict.html
An OK88 Bilingual Internet Services product.

Online Chinese Tools
http://www.erols.com/eepeter/chtools.html
Erik Peterson's site with many online tools - Chinese character flashcards, online searchable Chinese-English, English-Chinese dictionaries.

Online Chinese-English, English-Chinese Dictionary
http://www.cit.gu.edu.au/~rwony/cdict/
Searchable two-way dictionary by Richard Wang.

Professional Interactive Chinese for Windows
http://www.china-guide.com/chinese.htm
CD program equivalent to two years of college courses using interactive dialog sessions. Students can practice and record their own voice for comparision with a native speaker.

Speech Wizard
http://www.catalog.com/inforg01/software.htm
English and Chinese text-to-speech system that allows you to listen to the reading of English and Chinese words, sentences or even an entire text through your multimedia speakers.

Tools for Learning Chinese
http://www.erols.com/eepeter/cintro.html
Chinese character flashcards, romanization converter and character dictionary.

TransPerfect
http://www.catalog.com/inforg01/trans.htm
Knowledge-based translation software running on PC to translate English text into Chinese.

Wenlin Software for Learning Chinese
http://www.wenlin.com/
CD-ROM software package with capacities of text editing, instant dictionary access and a flashcard system with automatic drill for memorizing characters.

Additional Chinese Learning Software
Chinese-English Dictionary
Contains nearly 5,000 of the most frequenetly used Chinese characters, plus over 100,000 phrases. Distributed by Cheng & Tsui.

Electronic Dragon
Software flashcard deck that enables students to listen to accurate pronounciations and record their voice for comparision. There is an animation box showing proper stroke order of chacters. For Mac only. Distributed by China Books and Periodicals, Inc.

Chinese Character Tutor for Windows Version 5.0.
Popular character tutorial, including powerful testing function with 100 lessons and a 5,000 word dictionary. Distributed by China Books and Periodicals, Inc.

Hanzi Assistant
CD-ROM Chinese study tool for the Mac. Animates the drawing of Chinese characters. Distributed by Cheng & Tsui.

Mao's Alphabet
Software for beginning character study with drills, tests and a 4,000-entry English index. Distributed by China Books and Periodicals, Inc.

Pinyin Master
Interactive program on CD-ROM for teaching and learning Pinyin pronounciation with video tutorial, sound table, listerning and recording for comparision, drills and exercises. For Mac only. Distributed by China Books and Periodicals, Inc.

Beginner's Chinese
CD Accompaniment Track List

DISC ONE

Lessons for Beginner's Chinese

1. Lesson One

2. Lesson Two

3. Lesson Three

4. Lesson Four

5. Lesson Five

6. Lesson Six

7. Lesson Seven

8. Lesson Eight

9. Lesson Nine

10. Lesson Ten

Beginner's Chinese
CD Accompaniment Track List

DISC TWO

Pinyin Practice (See pp. 151–160)

VOWELS

1. Simple Vowels
2. Vowel Compounds

CONSONANTS

3. Consonants
4. "B" syllables
5. "P" syllables
6. "M" syllables
7. "F" syllables
8. "D" syllables
9. "T" syllables
10. "N" syllables
11. "L" syllables
12. "Z" syllables
13. "C" syllables

14. "S" syllables
15. "ZH" syllables
16. "CH" syllables
17. "SH" syllables
18. "R" syllables
19. "J" syllables
20. "Q" syllables
21. "X" syllables
22. "G" syllables
23. "K" syllables
24. "H" syllables

INTERMEDIATE CHINESE
Now Available with Audio!

This continuation of *Beginner's Chinese with 2 Audio CDs* allows users with previous knowledge of Mandarin Chinese to expand their language abilities. Each lesson uses dialogues and new vocabulary to illustrate common grammatical patterns. At the end of each chapter, exercises such as text translation, sentence completion, and word matching test the user's newly acquired skills. Covered topics include duration and time markers, progressive actions, punctuation, and sentence formation in the conditional. The new audio feature, which comes in an enclosed CD, is especially helpful to learning and understanding the language as spoken. The glossary features the vocabulary lists from both this and the Beginner's volume.

320 pages · 5 3/8 x 8 1/2 · $21.95pb (CAN $30.50) · 0-7818-1096-5 · W · (193)
ISBN of Previous Edition: 0-7818-0992-4

Hippocrene Books
171 Madison Avenue
New York, NY 10016
www.hippocrenebooks.com
order by phone: (718) 454-2366

China: An Illustrated History

China is one of the world's oldest civilizations with a recorded history spanning almost 4,000 years. However, to much of the outside world, China remains a mystery. Today, with a quarter of the world's population and its imposing economy, the country is playing an increasingly important role on the world's stage.

This concise, illustrated volume offers readers a panoramic view of this remarkable land from antiquity to the present day. The topics explored include the sources of Chinese thought, the cornerstones of Chinese political, religious, and economic institutions, and, above all, the ties that have united the country for thousands of years.

142 pages • 50 illus & photos • 5 x 7 • 0-7818-0821-9 • $14.95hc • (542)

Chinese-English Frequency Dictionary
A Study Guide to Mandarin Chinese's 500 Most Frequently Used Words

This book, which functions as both a traditional dictionary and a study guide, offers the English-speaking student of Mandarin Chinese an essential source of vocabulary and a detailed reference to the world's most widely spoken language. Each entry includes the Chinese character for the word, the Pinyin romanized transliteration, the word's definition, explanations of usage with examples, and a selection of phrases that include the word. Indices list entries in alphabetical order and according to frequency of use.

500 entries • 240 pages • 5½ x 8½ • 0-7818-0842-1 • $16.95pb • (277)

Hippocrene's Children Illustrated Chinese (Mandarin) Dictionary
English-Chinese/Chinese-English

This book is designed to be the first foreign language dictionary for children ages 5-10. Each of the 500 entries consists of the English word and its Chinese equivalent, a full-color illustration, and common sense phonetic spelling to help with pronunciation. Entries include the people, animals, colors, numbers, and objects that children encounter every day.

500 entries • 94 pages • 8½ x 11 • color illus • 0-7818-0848-0 • $11.95pb • (662)

Treasury of Chinese Love Poems (*In Chinese and English)*
Translated and Edited by Qiu Xiaolong

This collection is the first translation of classic Chinese poems for contemporary English-speaking readers. The 74 poems include pieces by such authors as Li Bai, Guan Daoshen, Zhang Jiuling, and Li Shangyin. All poems are presented in the original Chinese opposite the English translation.
150 pages • 5 x 7 • b/w illus • 0-7818-0968-1 • $11.95hc • (515)

Dictionary of 1000 Chinese Idioms
Translated and Edited by Marjorie Lin and Schalk Leonard

Four-character idioms, known as chengyu are essential aspects of the Chinese language. This book collects 1,000 of the most frequently used idioms, listing them in alphabetical order with the original Chinese characters, Pinyin romanized transliteration, and the English translation.
168 pages • 6 x 9 • 0-7818-0820-0 • $14.95pb • (598)

Dictionary of 1000 Chinese Proverbs
Edited by Marjorie Lin and Schalk Leonard

This collection of the most common Chinese proverbs is designed for teachers, travelers, and students of both the language and culture. The proverbs are organized alphabetically by the key word and the sentence. They are arranged side-by-side with the English equivalent, which is marked as either a literal or free translation. The index is organized by the key words in English.
208 pages • 5½ x 8½ • 0-7818-0682-8 • $11.95pb • (773)

English-Chinese (Pinyin) Pocket Dictionary

Specially designed for English speakers studying Chinese, this dictionary contains nearly 10,000 entries including commonly used words, phrases, and expressions. Each entry consists of the appropriate Chinese characters, followed by the Pinyin romanized transliteration to facilitate pronunciation, with special definitions and examples demonstrating proper usage.
10,000 entries • 850 pages • 4 x 6 • 0-7818-0427-2 • $19.95pb • (509) • U.S. sales only

Emergency Chinese

This phrasebook is designed to give the user key Mandarin words and phrases when needed, from the most casual to the most urgent situations.
80 pages • 7½ x 4 • 0-7818-0975-4 • $5.95pb • (461) • **North American sales only**

The Best of Korean Cooking
Karen Hulene Bartell

Korean cuisine has its own distinctive flavors and cooking methods. While China's main meat is pork and Japan's mainstay is fish, beef is Korea's favorite entrée. Korean recipes also rely on grains such as barley and buckwheat in addition to rice. An interesting feature of Korean cuisine is the emphasis on wild roots, fiddlehead ferns, and wild mushrooms. However, ginger, chili pepper, garlic, green onions, sesame oil, soy sauce, and fermented bean paste are still the primary flavorings. With over 100 authentic recipes, this cookbook blends the rich diversity of Korean cuisine with the seasonal fare, holiday feasts, and auspicious foods suggested by the lunar calendar. Sample such delicacies as *Barbecued Beef Sirloin, Capon with Ginseng and Korea Dates, Azalea Pancakes,* and *Persimmon Punch.*
196 pages • 5½ x 8½ • b/w illustrations • $22.50hc • 0-7818-0929-0 • (55)

Japanese Home Cooking
Hans Kizawa and Rina Goto-Nance

This unique collection features recipes for "comfort foods" and meals eaten every day in typical Japanese households. With its emphasis on fresh seafood and vegetables, Japanese cuisine is very healthy and gaining popularity throughout North America. Among the 100 recipes included are all varieties of sushi and miso soup, along with other specialties like *Sukiyaki, Cold Somen with Ham and Vegetables, Tofu Steak with Mushroom,* and *Squid and Daikon.* Photographs illustrating techniques and sections on equipment, basic ingredients, and Japanese pronunciation ensure that even novice cooks can produce spectacular results. Full of little anecdotes and observations, this book will be a delightfull addition to any North American kitchen.
140 pages • 5½ x 8½ • b/w photographs • $19.95hc • 0-7818-0881-2 • (27)

A Vietnamese Kitchen: *Treasured Family Recipes*
Ha Roda

Americans are just beginning to discover the exotic culinary offerings of Vietnam. The country's history has resulted in strong Chinese, Indian, and French influences, which yield complex, delicate flavors. This collection of traditional recipes, modified for American kitchens, includes an introduction to Vietnamese culture, a glossary of Vietnamese culinary terms, and a chapter on meal planning.
175 pages • 6 x 9 • 2-Color • $24.95hc • 0-7818-1081-7 • (115)

Simple Laotian Cooking
Penn Hongthong

Located in between Thailand and Vietnam, Laos is a landlocked country covered by mountains and forests. Because vegetable oil used to be a costly commodity they had to import, Laotians used it sparsely, preferring to flavor their dishes with a profusion of herbs and spices. They also eat a cornucopia of fresh fruit and vegetables but very little meat, making their cuisine a healthful yet flavorful choice for home cooks. This cookbook offers 172 recipes, including a section on the traditional Lob, a beef dish also made with chicken, fish, as well as wild game, which is reserved for holidays and special occasions. Served with sticky rice and fresh vegetables, it is one of the few dishes served with wine. A glossary defines staple ingredients like bamboo shoots, cilantro, coconut milk, fresh ginger, kaffir lime leaves, and lemongrass. Western ingredients are incorporated into the dishes, easing preparation for North American cooks.
236 pages • 6 x 9 • b/w photographs • $24.95hc • 0-7818-0963-0 • (522)

Imperial Mongolian Cooking: *Recipes from the Kingdoms of Genghis Khan*
Marc Cramer

In the late 12th and early 13th centuries, Genghis Khan ruled one of history's largest land empires, dominating two dozen countries and stretching from the Black Sea in Russia and the South China Sea. *Imperial Mongolian Cooking* is the first book to explore the ancient cuisine of this empire, opening a window onto a fascinating culture and a diverse culinary tradition virtually unknown in the West. These 120 easy-to-follow recipes encompass a range of dishes-including Appetizers, Soups, and Salads, as well as Main Courses (Poultry & Game, Lamb, Beef, Fish & Seafood), Beverages, and Desserts. Among them are *Bean and Meatball Soup, Spicy Steamed Chicken Dumplings, Turkish Swordfish Kabobs,* and *Uzbek Walnut Fritters.* The recipes are taken from the four khanates, or kingdoms, of the empire which include such modern countries as Mongolia, Chinese-controlled Inner Mongolia, China, Bhutan, Tibet, Azerbaijan, Krygyzstan, Tajikistan, Turkmenistan, Uzbekistan, Kazakhstan, Georgia, Armenia, Russia, Poland, Ukraine, Hungary, Burma, Vietnam, Iran, Iraq, Afghanistan, Syria, and Turkey. The insightful introduction, glossary of spices and ingredients, and list of sample menus will assist the home chef in creating meals fit for an emperor!
228 pages • 5½ x 8½ • $24.95hc • 0-7818-0827-8 • (20)

The Best of Taiwanese Cuisine
Recipes and Menus for Holidays and Special Occasions
Karen Hulene Bartell

Hospitality and good eating are highly regarded in Taiwanese society. In fact, "Have you eaten?" is a common greeting. Taiwan is located in the Pacific Ocean about 100 miles from the southeastern coast of China. The island is midway between Korean and Japan to the north and the Philippines and Hong Kong to the south. Its unique geographical location and political past have contributed to the country's diverse cuisine. Dishes from the four corners of China are found in Taiwanese kitchens and restaurants. Because of Japanese influence, even suski and sashimi have their place on the table. Vegetarian dishes like *Five-Spice Tofu* and *Baby Corn Vegetable Medley* are also popular of Taiwan's Buddhist and Taoist legacies. This cookbook collects over 100 delicious Taiwanese recipes. It is divided into seasons and traditional celebrations such as the Lunar New Year, the Dragon Boat Festival, Chinese Valentine's Day, and the Mid-Autumn Moon Festival, with a complete menu for each one. Complementary and harmonious foods are organized in 18 carefully planned menus. The book also features various cultural tidbits, Chinese folk art paper cuttings, and a Chinese lunar zodiac calendar.

132 pages • 5½ x 8½ • b/w illus & photos • $24.95hc • 0-7818-0855-3 • (46)

The Best of Regional Thai Cuisine
Chat Mingkwan

This is the first cookbook to explore the specialties of each region of Thailand. The Thai people have taken the best of culinary influences from nearby countries such as China, India, Cambodia, Indonesia, Laos, Malaysia, Burma, and Vietnam. These have been adapted to produce such distinctly Thai creations as *Galangal Chicken*, *Green Curry Children*, and *Three-Flavor Prawns*. Chef Chat Mingkwan takes the reader-chef on a culinary tour of his home country, offering favorites from each of Thailand's four regions: the cool, mountainous North, where *Curried Egg Noodles* are the signature dish; the drier Northeast (Isan) where resourceful chefs rely on staples like glutinous rice and dried fish; the fertile Central region, which is home to Bangkok, abundant with seafood as well as fruits and vegetables; and the tropical South where locally grown coconut is a popular ingredient and where the majority of Thailand's Muslim population is concentrated, thus making seafood and chicken curries the classic dishes of the region. In addition to over 150 recipes, all adapted for the North American kitchen, Chat Mingkwan provides helpful sections on Thai spices and ingredients as well as cooking techniques.

236 pages • 6 x 9 • b/w photos and illus • $24.95hc • 0-7818-0880-4 • (26)

OTHER BOOKS OF REGIONAL INTEREST

Cambodian-English/English-Cambodian Standard Dictionary
15,000 entries • 355 pages • 5½ x 8½ • $18.95pb • 0-87052-818-1 • (143)

Japanese-English/English-Japanese Concise Dictionary
Romanized
8,000 entries · 235 pages · 4 x 6 · 0-7818-0162-1 · $11.95pb · W · (474)

Beginner's Japanese
290 pages • 5 x 8 • $11.95pb • 0-7818-0234-2 • (53)

Japanese-English/English-Japanese Dictionary & Phrasebook
2,300 entries • 231 pages • 3¾ x 7½ • $12.95pb • 0-7818-0814-6 • (205)

Japan: An Illustrated History
232 pages • 5 x 7 • $14.95pb • 0-7818-0989-4 • (469)

Korean-English/English-Korean Practical Dictionary
8,500 entries • 358 pages • 4¼ x 8¼ • $16.95pb • 0-87052-092-X • (399)

Korea: An Illustrated History
147 pages • 5 x 7 • 0-7818-0873-1 • $12.95pb • (354)

Lao-English/English-Lao Dictionary & Phrasebook
2,500 entries • 207 pages • 3¾ x 7 • $12.95pb • 0-7818-0858-8 • (470)

Mongolian-English/English-Mongolian Dictionary & Phrasebook
3,300 entries • 286 pages • 3¾ x 8½ • $12.95pb • 0-7818-0958 • (158)

Thai-English/English-Thai Dictionary & Phrasebook
1,800 entries • 200 pages • 3¾ x 7 • $12.95pb • 0-7818-0774-3 • (330)

Vietnamese-English/English-Vietnamese Dictionary & Phrasebook
3,000 entries • 248 pages • 3¾ x 7 • $11.95pb • 0-7818-0991-6 • (104)

Vietnamese-English/English-Vietnamese Standard Dictionary
12,000 entries • 506 pages • 5½ x 8 • $24.95 • 0-87052-924-2 • (529)

Beginner's Vietnamese
517 pages • 7 x 10 • $19.95pb • 0-7818-0411-6 • (253)

Vietnam: An Illustrated History
184 pages • 5 x 7 • $14.95 • 0-7818-0910-X • (302)

TO ORDER **HIPPOCRENE** TITLES, contact your local bookstore, call (718) 454-2366, visit our Web site at www.hippocrenebooks.com, or write to: 171 Madison Avenue, New York, NY 10016. Shipping costs are $5.00 for the first book and $0.50 for each additional title. Titles are shipped UPS. Please enclose check or money order with your order. All prices are subject to change without notice.